Praise for

White Tears/Bro.... ....

Short-listed for 2020 New South Wales Premier's
Literary Awards: Multicultural NSW Award

"With scholarly but highly engaging prose, Hamad details
white women's roles in oppression across continents, a much-
needed history lesson for those inclined to reduce racism to
individual behavior . . . For readers truly interested in dismantling white supremacy, this is a must-read. An extraordinary book."　　　　　　　　　*—Kirkus Reviews* (starred review)

"*White Tears/Brown Scars* is a must-read for all white feminists.
To develop the feminist coalitions that are so desperately
needed in these times, we need frank conversations between
feminists of color and white feminists, in which white women
take accountability instead of using tears to avoid it. Hamad's
book is an essential resource to help us do this."

　　　　　　　—ALISON PHIPPS, author of *Me, Not You*

"*White Tears/Brown Scars* belongs in twenty-first-century
feminist canon. It's grounded in deep historical context, yet
thoroughly of the present. It makes bold intellectual arguments, but is extremely readable and grounded in human
experience. If you are a white woman, it may make for uncomfortable reading: this book takes the most precise scalpel
to the way that white women leverage race and gender of
any book that I've read. If you are a woman of color, perhaps it will make you feel seen. If you are a man, read it for

your own education! Hamad has written a truly exceptional, agenda-setting work."

—RACHEL HILLS, author of *The Sex Myth*

"*White Tears/Brown Scars* is an essential guide for those who want to be truly intersectional in their feminism. Ruby Hamad skillfully distills history, academic research, and lived experiences of women of color to create an engaging inquiry into white supremacy and the role of white women within it."

—ZEBA TALKHANI, author of *My Past Is a Foreign Country*

"*White Tears/Brown Scars* is a powerful and scholarly critique of white-privileged 'innocence.' This is essential reading for anyone surprised that 52 percent of white women voters chose Trump. Hamad has written a devastating analysis of 'the white damsel' and the way her tears and dual status are routinely weaponised against much of the globe. If (racial) ignorance is bliss, then this book is a shattering of some supremely comfortable white illusions about race and gender, in Australia and beyond."

—MELISSA LUCASHENKO, author of *Too Much Lip*

"Reading *White Tears/Brown Scars* is not an easy experience, but it is a life-affecting one. Despite Ruby Hamad's remarkably concise but insightful review of racism, colonialism, and life in the modern West, this is a deep exploration of how our circumstances, behaviours, and unconscious attitudes shape power dynamics and our existence as humans on a planet we ravage daily. This is also, more specifically, a nuanced, multilayered portrait of the place of white women in the West, their role in upholding white supremacy as a norm, and how they relate to women of colour.

"As an Arab woman growing up in the West, I had come to accept, too often, the demeaning treatment I received from my white peers, without interrogating it. For me, and for many like me, it has been a case of quiet survival, never raising ourselves too high because when we do, we threaten not only the structures we co-inhabit, but the relationships that work as long as the power imbalance is maintained.

"It is not correct to say that Hamad's book is simply eye-opening or a revelation. It is an uncovering of so much we have hidden away, afraid to acknowledge even to ourselves. Reading this book, it occurred to me how deeply women of minorities internalize their experiences of mistreatment or discrimination. What you read in Hamad's book cannot be unread or overlooked or forgotten. But commendably, this book is not a self-pitying rant with no way forward. It prompts every reader to revisit their experiences through a revised lens, but not to remain in a state of anger or repose. This book asks us all how we can live together. It asks not just how we can do better, but how we can do right so that humans, no matter their class, their skin shade, or their cultural conditioning, can claim a place in society that is fair and just to all.

"This book is important not only for what it tells us but for what it asks of us."

—AMAL AWAD, author of *Beyond Veiled Clichés*

"A powerful testament, an act of witnessing, a work of depth and scholarship." —RASHIDA MURPHY, *ArtsHub*

"Ruby Hamad blows open inconvenient truths . . . in this powerful book." —*Marie Claire Australia*

"Hamad deconstructs the colonial narrative of 'white is right.' She challenges society to face the discrimination it has normalised, and to commit to a future where white women let go of their privilege and stand with women of colour." —*The Saturday Paper*

"Ruby Hamad should be applauded for writing this well researched and informative book . . . Hamad has not so much thrown a grenade into the arena, rather she has exposed an unexploded bomb set in the core foundations of western-settler societies." —*Independent Australia*

"[A] blistering take on feminism and race . . . Ruby Hamad takes readers on an eye-opening historical journey through the oppression and marginalisation of colonised and enslaved women . . . It's a book I couldn't recommend more highly." —JO CASE, *InDaily*

"An informative and compelling read. Ruby Hamad's work is absolutely essential reading for today—as it helps bring to the fore what was once only suspected." —*Indian Link*

"[An] often confronting and always challenging book . . . *White Tears/Brown Scars* is provocative and intelligent . . . Hamad has written a persuasive book which deserves to be read and thought about carefully." —*Queensland Reviewers Collective*

"Hamad is a writer of formidable talent and perceptiveness. *White Tears/Brown Scars* is one of the most important books of 2019, and I believe a copy should live on every single bookshelf in Australia." —*Kill Your Darlings*

"I loved Hamad's book for its unapologetic rigour and sharp threading of racial history . . . A powerful assessment of the institutional and cultural structures that have shaped the way we operate both as a society and individually." —JESSIE TU, *Women's Agenda*

"Hamad writes with a vigour and insight that is energising . . . At once academic and accessible, highly readable . . . *White Tears/Brown Scars* packs a powerful punch . . . A challenging, important read that will benefit all readers, regardless of gender or race." —ZOYA PATEL, *The Canberra Times*

"Hamad's work is meticulously researched, comprehensively catalogued and makes for a compelling critique of the ways in which the woman of colour is pilloried and crucified at the altar of white fragility . . . If a politics of solidarity is to have any meaning in a world torn apart by old wounds, let's join hands and celebrate Hamad's *White Tears/Brown Scars*." —DR. MRIDULA NATH CHAKRABORTY, *The Sydney Morning Herald*

WHITE TEARS

How White Feminism Betrays Women of Color

BROWN SCARS

RUBY HAMAD

CATAPULT  NEW YORK

ISBN: 978-1-948226-74-5

Cover design by Na Kim
Book design by Wah-Ming Chang

Library of Congress Control Number: 2020931161

Printed in the United States of America
7 9 10 8 6

for the forgotten ones

ضربني وبكى
وسبقني واشتكى

He hit me and wept . . .
Then he was first to protest.
—Arab proverb

Contents

Author's Note

Writing about race is a fraught business, as is writing about gender. Words and phrases you assume would be easily received exactly as you intended them are bafflingly interpreted as something else entirely. Concepts such as the meaning of racism itself, arrived at over generations of painstaking scholarship, research, and experience, are stubbornly brushed aside in favor of "the dictionary definition."

This note sets out the main terms and concepts I use throughout this book, both for the benefit of the reader and to safeguard as best I can against misrepresentations made in bad faith. My own experience as a media writer of twelve years' standing tells me that this will almost certainly occur regardless, but consider this my best attempt to ward off that regrettable inevitability.

I have opted to use "brown" in the title both as a poetic license indicating a catchall for all those people who don't qualify as "white," and to indicate where I place myself in the race scheme of things. However, "brown" (in which I include all nonblack people of color) will be differentiated from "black" throughout the book. It is important to understand that virtually all terms used when discussing race are imprecise because race is an imposition, not a biological reality. As such, who is white and who isn't is not as simple as it once was. While often used to denote the skin color of Europeans in relation to Native Americans and (enslaved) Africans, "white" is better understood as an indication of racial privilege: who is considered white is less about how pale they are and more about whether they are the right kind of pale. Many Arabs have fair skin, and my own is more olive than brown. This racial ambiguity affords me some degree of acceptance—until my ethnic background is inevitably brought to the foreground. Whiteness, then, is more than skin color. It is, as race scholar Paul Kivel describes, "a constantly shifting boundary separating those who are entitled to have certain privileges from those whose exploitation and vulnerability to violence [are] justified by their not being white."

Whiteness is the privileging of those racial, cultural, and religious identities that most resemble the typical characteristics associated with fair-skinned (Western) Europeans. Consequently, the terms "white" and "people of color" are not descriptive—they are political. When we talk about "white people," we are not really talking about skin color but about those who most benefit from whiteness. When we talk about "people of color," we talk about those who are excluded. I continue to have misgivings about the terms—due to the proximity of "people of color" to "colored" as well as the danger that it can collapse the needs and issues of certain marginalized racial groups into others—but the lack of better terms necessitates their use at times. Expressions such as "nonwhite" imply whiteness is a neutral default, and it can get cumbersome and redundant to list the various categories of "brown," "black," "Asian," "Arab," and so on individually. A content note: some of the out-of-use historical terms employed by colonizers to degrade women of color are reproduced in this book in order to discuss their meaning and usage. I have chosen, however, not to reproduce certain slurs that are still in widespread use and/or are particularly heinous, though I concede that this is a fine line and a subjective one at that.

Finally, a note on the featured interviews. I spoke with more than two dozen women from across the Western world during the course of writing *White Tears/Brown Scars*. Not all of them are directly quoted, but all of them informed the shape of this book. It has been quite the eye-opener to discover how similar the experiences of women of color who have never met can be. Some of these women I know personally and/or professionally, some I'd previously interacted with on social media, and others were either referred to me or contacted me directly asking to participate. Interviews took place in person, by telephone, via Skype, and in a few cases over email. Where an asterisk appears beside a name, the interviewee has chosen to remain completely anonymous, and where there is a first name only, that is her real first name.

PART ONE / THE SETUP

White Tears

*We talk about toxic masculinity but there is [also]
toxicity in wielding femininity in this way.*
— Luvvie Ajayi

I am so uncomfortable having this conversation," said Fox
News host Melissa Francis during a live broadcast of the
network's panel program *Outnumbered* on August 16, 2017.
The previous day, U.S. president Donald Trump held a press
conference denouncing the Charlottesville riots that ended
in tragedy when a white supremacist drove his car through
a group of people protesting a far-right rally, killing thirty-
two-year-old Heather Heyer. Trump had audaciously claimed
"both sides" were to blame for the violence—and that there
were "very fine people" on both sides. This sparked countless
debates across the country, much like the one Francis was
engaged in with her co-panelists Harris Faulkner, Juan Williams, and Marie Harf.

Defending Trump, Francis claimed he was being misrepresented and had never tried to apportion equal blame.
When her cohost attempted to correct her, she became visibly
emotional. "I know what is in my heart and I know that I

don't think anyone is different, better or worse, based on the color of their skin," her voice cracked. "But I feel like there is nothing any of us can say right now without being judged." No sooner had the word *judged* left her lips than the tears started. The panel fell into an awkward silence for a moment and it was left to cohost Faulkner, a black woman, to calmly step in and, without a trace of emotion in her voice or on her face, to respond. "You know, Melissa, there have been a lot of tears on our network and across the country and around the world," Faulkner began quietly but firmly while the other woman closed her eyes and shook her head as if in pain. "It's a difficult place where we are but it's not where we've been, it's where we are . . . and we can have this conversation. Oh, yes we can."

What should be remarkable about this clip is that it is the black woman who remains stoic and almost expressionless while the white woman is freely emotional and teary. Keep in mind, this is all in the midst of a conversation about race taking place in the same week that white supremacists had staged rallies waving Nazi and Confederate flags and shouting slogans such as "blood and soil" and "Jews will not replace us." I say it *should* be remarkable because, sadly, it is all too unremarkable. It has been so common for so long for people of color to tiptoe around the feelings of white people that until relatively recently it was barely ever commented on in the mainstream. Indeed, after Faulkner's comments, two of the other hosts, including Williams, who is a black man, quickly tried to soothe Francis, repeating how much they hated to see her cry.

How is it that we have been so conditioned to prioritize the emotional comfort of white people? Why does the sight of a white woman crying provoke such placatory responses, even in a context such as this where people of color have every reason to be scared, upset, and even angry? It was not until the following year that I finally began to understand just how crucial it is that we answer these questions.

Fast-forward to August 2018, and I almost missed the message in my Twitter inbox from a journalist in the United States asking to speak to me about an article I'd published in *Guardian Australia* three months earlier. That piece had proved to be very popular and very polarizing and had resulted in far more global attention than I was used to or felt comfortable with, and, still reeling from it all, I assumed she was messaging me to ask if she could interview me for a story. I cautiously agreed to supply my email but was unprepared for what came next.

Lisa Benson, an Emmy-winning African American television journalist in Kansas City, was writing to me not to request an interview, but to let me know that shortly after my piece was published in May, she had shared it to her private Facebook page, where two white female colleagues, Christa Dubill and Jessica McMaster, had seen it. The next day, Dubill and McMaster complained to management and Lisa was suspended immediately for "creating a hostile working environment based on race and gender." Shortly thereafter, she was terminated from her contract.

A little backstory: Lisa had already sued her television station employer for racial discrimination, alleging her race was used to determine which stories she was assigned. This included being sent on her own to interview a Ku Klux Klan member in his home, a situation that was both uncomfortable and possibly unsafe. A separate lawsuit was brought by another colleague of hers, a male African American sports anchor who claimed he was routinely passed over for promotions in favor of less qualified white men. Lisa was still working for the organization while awaiting her court date, and she told me she had shared the article in the hope that her colleagues would understand and empathize with her situation. Instead, it appears they used it as a handy justification for getting rid of a "problem" employee who'd inadvertently broke one of white Western society's unspoken but most binding rules: don't challenge or even acknowledge implicit racial bias—if you do, be prepared to suffer the consequences.

The article that apparently cost Lisa her contract and brought us into each other's orbit was titled "How White Women Use Strategic Tears to Silence Women of Colour." It was one of hundreds I've written over the past decade or so while I've been working in the media. This one, however, was a particularly painful and personal column to write, drawing on an emotional and psychological journey during which I had slowly (perhaps too slowly) and devastatingly come to realize that the way society saw me, the way people interpreted and responded to my behavior and my words, had very little to do with me as a person, my motivations, or the situation at hand, but everything to do with their ingrained perceptions of me based on my ethnicity. I highlighted what I had by then come to realize was a pattern so predictable it worked like a blueprint, predetermining how interpersonal conflict between women of color and white women plays out.

Brown and black women, I wrote, are deeply impacted, often without realizing it, by the grind of living in a society that does not recognize, let alone reward, their value. Overwhelmingly disbelieved when they try to shed light on their experiences of gendered racism, the lack of support they receive adds to the initial trauma, leaving them questioning reality as well as themselves. Most devastating is when this happens in interactions with white women, often women they consider friends or at least friend*ly*. Drawing on the concept of what author Luvvie Ajayi has referred to as the weaponizing of white women's tears, I outlined how, when challenged by a woman of color, a white woman will often lean into her racial privilege to turn the tables and accuse the other woman of hurting, attacking, or bullying her. This process almost always siphons the sympathy and support of any onlookers to the apparently distressed white woman, helping her avoid any accountability that may be due and leaving the woman of color out in the cold, often with no realistic option—particularly if it is a workplace interaction—but to accept blame and apologize.

At the time of writing the column, I was attempting to make sense of a number of conflicts I'd had that followed this unwritten script and left me wondering why, whenever I tried to approach a white female friend or colleague about something she had said or done that had had a negative impact on me, I somehow always ended up apologizing to her even though I was certain I was the one who had been wronged. With diminished confidence and second-guessing my own recollection and interpretation of events, I was left floundering, either angry and unheard or terrified I would lose a friend or a job if I didn't back down.

It was the work of black and brown women that helped me dissect what was happening. Women like Sister Outsider, who tweets under the handle @FeministGriote, who wrote a fantastic thread about the experiences of the many black

women who have "a story about a time in a professional setting where she attempted to have a talk with a WW [white
woman] about her behavior & it has ended with the WW
crying . . . The WW wasn't crying because she felt sorry and
was deeply remorseful. The WW was crying because she felt
'bullied' and/or that the BW [black woman] was being too
harsh with her." The end result, due to the potency of white
women's tears, is that the black woman is left with the op-
tions of either apologizing or risking being "blackballed" or
fired. The world doesn't stop for the tears of black women,
Sister Outsider concluded, and it is up to white women to
stop this destructive behavior.

I shared these tweets as well as Ajayi's piece on my public
Facebook page, asking brown and black women if they'd experienced anything similar. The response was so overwhelming that it was clear the phenomenon was not a bug in our
society but a feature of it. One Arab woman, Zeina, shared
her experiences of being "petted" by older white women
drawn to her thick, curly, waist-length brown hair. One at
her workplace "kept touching my hair, pulling my curls to
watch them bounce back. Rubbing the top. So when I told
her to stop and complained to HR [human resources] and
my supervisor, she complained that I wasn't a people person
or team member and I had to leave that position for being
'threatening' to a coworker."

What makes white women's tears so potent and renders
black and brown women so apparently "aggressive"? In her
blog post, Ajayi explains that what makes the distress of
white women so powerful is its association with femininity
and helplessness. "These tears are pouring out of the eyes
of the one chosen to be the prototype of womanhood; the

woman who has been painted as helpless against the whims of the world."

Ajayi's words hit me not so much as a revelation as an unveiling. They led me to look back over my life, forcing me to recognize with some degree of horror that what many people see when they look at me is a generic facsimile of an Arab, someone without their own inner world. "The manufactured reputation Arabs have for being threatening and aggressive follows us everywhere," I wrote. "In a society that routinely places 'wide-eyed, angry and Middle Eastern' people at the scenes of violent crimes they did not commit, having a legitimate grievance is no match for the strategic tears of a white damsel in distress whose innocence is taken for granted . . . Whether we are angry or calm, shouting or pleading we are always seen as the aggressors."

Was I nervous about writing all this? Yes. So nervous, in fact, that I considered withdrawing the piece. This was not because I don't stand by it—I do. Rather, it was because I knew there would be resistance to its contents and inconvenient truths. I knew I would be accused of dividing the sisterhood and of racism against white women. And I knew it would be another mark against my name in the suffocatingly white Australian media space that loves to extol the virtues of "diversity" but had already been slowly marginalizing my public presence year after year. Even knowing all this, I knew I couldn't withdraw it and that these kinds of things have to be said precisely because they make people uncomfortable, in the best way—the way that forces them to examine their own implicit biases and question their own relative power and privilege.

Even so, I was unprepared for the response. By the end

of the day, the piece had been picked up by *The Guardian* in the U.S. and the U.K. and all hell seemed to break loose. I was already bracing myself for those people I knew would be willing and able to misrepresent my ideas—not just to discredit the column as a piece of writing, but to discredit me as a person. I had, however, assumed the backlash would be contained to Australia and, within that, mostly to feminist circles already familiar with many of the concepts described, such as "white tears," which has gained currency across the internet and in activist spaces as a riff on "male tears." Neither of these concepts mocks legitimate distress: they refer to the fragility with which some individuals who belong to a dominant group respond when their dominance is questioned. Overwhelmed by the global backlash, I deactivated my Twitter account and sent a panicked midnight email to *Guardian Australia* begging them to take the piece down. But then it struck me that this was precisely the reaction the online mob wanted. More importantly, even if I did retract the article, it wouldn't be enough; they weren't acting out of genuine critique but from fury that I'd taken what was common knowledge among communities of color and lobbed it into one of the bastions of white liberal media. I also knew from watching the public humiliation of women of color before me that an apology would not placate them but would only validate their narcissistic injury. They would use it to attack me and discredit everything I said and did from that moment on. I fired off another email instructing my still blissfully sleeping editors to ignore the previous one, and I reactivated my Twitter account to cheekily let the world know that I definitely was *not* sorry by posting a link to the Tom Petty classic "I Won't Back Down."

That decision proved to be a profound one, as the abuse

gave way to global messages of support. White women told me they had seen this very thing happen too many times; some were ashamed to admit they were guilty of it. Men revealed that they either knew all too well what I was talking about, or that I had given them a framework through which to interpret behavior they had noticed but could not fully explain. But most importantly, there were the testimonials from women of color who shared their stories, their tragedies, their stolen years spent wondering why this kept happening to them, why they were "going crazy."

It's become a cliché for writers to note that online haters are far louder than lovers, that detractors can't wait to tell us exactly what they think of us (not much!) while those who value our work often opt to do it quietly. But this time, the positive response had shouted down the very loud and very numerous haters. It was at that point I realized this was bigger than me. Bigger than my piece. But what, exactly, is *this*?

The term "white fragility" was coined by sociologist Robin DiAngelo to describe the defensiveness into which many white people retreat in any discussion that reminds them of their race. DiAngelo, who is a white American, has worked as a diversity trainer in the United States, crisscrossing the country to run workshops for mostly white people on how they can contribute to a more racially inclusive workplace. In her book *White Fragility*, published in 2018, DiAngelo describes white fragility as a state of stress set off by the discomfort and anxiety white people feel when their internalized sense of racial superiority is challenged:

Socialized into a deeply internalized sense of superiority that we either are unaware of or can never admit to ourselves, we become highly fragile in conversations about race. We consider a challenge to our racial worldviews as a challenge to our very identities as good, moral people. Thus, we perceive any attempt to connect us to the system of racism as an unsettling and unfair moral offense. The smallest amount of racial stress is intolerable—the mere suggestion that being white has meaning often triggers a range of defensive responses. These include emotions such as anger, fear, and guilt and behaviors such as argumentation, silence, and withdrawal from the stress-inducing situation. These responses work to reinstate white equilibrium as they repel the challenge, return our racial comfort, and maintain our dominance within the racial hierarchy.

It is crucial to understand what we are talking about when we talk about "white tears." The kind of distress we are analyzing may well feel genuine, but it is neither legitimate nor innocent. Rather than denoting weakness, it signals power: "Though white fragility is triggered by discomfort and anxiety, it is born of superiority and entitlement. White fragility is not weakness . . . it is a powerful means of white racial control and the protection of white advantage." DiAngelo explores white fragility in explicitly race-based workplace interactions between women, but the issue goes further back in history and deeper into the present, and it is important to look at gendered racial dynamics beyond the professional context. These dynamics also shape and taint interactions between white women and women of color in social situations. The catalyst need not be explicitly about race: the act of being challenged or politely disagreed with or, heaven forbid, "called out" by a woman of color about almost anything at all is enough to raise the defenses and trigger a reaction based not on the immediate situation but on the mechanisms of white fragility.

More important still is the response from onlookers, for it is how they choose to interpret and respond to the conflict unfolding before them that determines the outcome and reinforces the respective behaviors, dooming them to be replayed again and again. When I began this book, my central question was: What happens when racism and sexism collide? My answer begins with the realization that the way people regard and treat us comes down to how well we match the stereotypical features associated with our perceived gender. Because women of color are always perceived as lesser women, then whatever the intersection—be it gender identity, sexuality, disability, or something else—every experience of marginalization is made more acute when race is thrown into the mix. And it impacts our lives in ways many of us may have never considered.

Women of color who attempt to address an issue that is detrimental to them in some way almost invariably come up against a wall of white fragility so immovable, so lacking in empathy, so utterly unrepentant, that the first few times it happens, you naturally assume you are imagining it, that you are the problem, that you should have gone about things differently and you will go about things differently from now on. So you do. You adjust your reactions, you try to play nice, you watch your tone. But it keeps happening—angry, sad, yelling, begging, it doesn't seem to matter—until at some point you, as a woman of color, realize in shock that regardless of the facts of the situation, the real problem isn't even about you. It is how white society regards you. It is how white society treats you. Because you, as a woman of color, do not measure up to their image of what a woman is and should be in order to be believed, supported, and defended.

Many white women reading this now will know exactly what I am talking about, because this very thing happens between men and women: the condescending dismissals, the exaggeratedly mystified claims of unprovoked hysteria and unhinged emotion, the gaslighting. What I and many women of color before me, and no doubt after me, are asking is that white women open their minds and hearts when women of color talk about the double whammy we are dealt. That even as we agitate against the sexism of a male-dominated society, because it is also a white-dominated society we are also assailed with racism, and often this comes from white women who turn their sanctioned victim status on us. White women can oscillate between their gender and their race, between being the oppressed and the oppressor. Women of color are never permitted to exist outside of these constraints: we are both women and people of color and we are always seen and treated as such.

As a black woman, Lisa Benson does not experience sexism in the same way white women do, nor does she experience racism in the same way as a black man. Rather, she is subjected to both racism and sexism at once, a compounded form of oppression now known as misogynoir. Similarly, because I am an Arab woman my work has made me a frequent target of online abuse, including epithets such as "whore for Hezbollah" and declarations that I "have clitoris envy as well as penis envy" (an allusion to female genital mutilation). The details and severity often differ, but what is common about the experiences of women of color is an unspoken assumption that we always lack a defining feature of womanhood that white women have by default.

When Lisa first reached out to me, I was overcome with intense guilt about what I had done to her, that she had lost her job because of me, that I should have known better. But this reaction is itself internalized racism, scolding people of color for whatever bad thing happens to us, telling us it's our own fault, keeping us in check by taking away our will to speak. Self-blame is a potent teacher: it can drain your self-belief, make you want to hide, compel you to beg for forgiveness even when you have done nothing to be forgiven for, all in the hope you can somehow undo the abuse, the scorn, the injustice, and go quietly back to where you were before.

Only . . . where were we before? Where was I before I wrote that article? Where was Lisa? We were unknown to each other on opposite sides of the world, both of us attempting to assert and defend ourselves, only to be branded "combative" and "bullies." Even before we speak, women of color are positioned as potential aggressors. Look closer at the interactions you see at work, on social media, at social functions. Make a note of just how often a woman of color who stands her ground, demands respect, or gives anything less than overwhelmingly positive affirmation to others is met with harsh rebuke and swift ostracism.

This nexus of race and gender, which can feel less like an intersection on a road being traveled and more like a permanent address to which we are chained, means that women of color are rarely given the benefit of the doubt, and even more rarely considered worthy of sympathy and support. If we are angry, it is because we are bullies. If we are crying, it is because we are indulging in the cult of victimhood. If we are poised, it is because we lack emotion. If we are emotional, it is because we are less rational human and more primitive animal. A white woman may well be punished for an emotional outburst when interacting with men, but if she is engaged in a terse interaction with a woman of color and she becomes emotional, by which I mean either angry or distraught, with or without actual tears, the deeply embedded notions of gender and femininity are triggered and it is the white woman who is likely to be vindicated.

How so? Because, as academic and author Richard Dyer writes, "White people set standards of humanity by which they are bound to succeed and others bound to fail." Over the course of centuries, as the proponents and beneficiaries of colonialism, whites have set the standards both for humanity as a whole, embodied in the white man, and for femininity that is designed to complement the white male and so is embodied in the white woman. In settler-colonial societies, and it is countries that began as settler colonies that are my greatest focus in this book, women were assigned dual roles and regarded as protected victims but also unsuitable for governing alongside white men or of living freely. When white women attempted to assert themselves, as the white suffragettes (themselves frequently openly racist) discovered for many a decade before they finally succeeded, they were treated with derision and accused of being unnatural. Married women were legally considered virtual property and rape within marriage impossible—the marriage contract was itself irrevocable consent. But when white women were perceived to be threatened by Indigenous or enslaved populations, and this was a manufactured threat to keep both the Natives and white women in their place, then they were jealously guarded as white men have always guarded what they consider to be their property, and the men of color who were alleged to have threatened or abused the white man's "property" were punished severely, disproportionately, and horrifically. It is impossible to say how many innocent black men in the colonies that became Rhodesia (now Zimbabwe), Australia, and the United States were jailed or killed on the pretext of having victimized a white woman.

This culture of fear has stayed with us. This weaponization of White Womanhood continues to be the centerpiece of an arsenal used to maintain the status quo and punish anyone who dares challenge it. Western society is built on a foundation of profound inequality that persists but that many people remain invested in denying, and though less attention has historically been paid to the role of gender in the construction of race and racial dynamics, as well as in the global interactions between the West and "the Rest," I want to address how women of color fit into this dynamic. Although strides in legal rights and some gains in "diversity" and representation have been made, what our society has yet to confront seriously is what I believe is the greatest obstacle to liberation and equity: the conscious and unconscious biases against women of color that we all carry and that are shaped and cemented by years of socialization into a system that is fundamentally racist and sexist.

In order to understand these biases and the damage they cause—as well as how they are so commonplace that they remain invisible to many—we need to study the stories that occur when race and gender collide in Western capitalist society. For it is here that the biases governing all our lives come into play, shaping and tainting interactions between women but also reflecting wider society in the process.

Lewd Jezebels, Exotic Orientals, Princess Pocahontas

HOW COLONIALISM RIGGED THE GAME AGAINST WOMEN OF COLOR

The oriental woman is no more than a machine: she makes no distinction between one man and another . . . What makes this woman, in a sense, so poetic, is that she relapses into the state of nature.

—Gustave Flaubert describing Egyptian women to Louise Colet, 1851

*I know the track from Spencer's Gulf and north
   of Cooper's Creek—
Where falls the half-caste to the strong, "black
   velvet" to the weak—
(From gold-top Flossie in the Strand to half-
   caste and the gin—*

If they had brains, poor animals! we'd teach
    them how to sin.)

—Henry Lawson,
Ballad of the Rouseabout, c. 1900

In March 2012 "Alana," a young fan of the hit dystopian fiction series The Hunger Games, logged on to Twitter under the now-defunct handle @sw4q to share her thoughts on the first film installment of the much-loved trilogy. The Hunger Games world is a post-apocalyptic future where people live permanently on the edge of starvation. As described by the author, Suzanne Collins, many of the main characters range from dark-skinned to, as in the case of protagonist Katniss Everdeen, olive-skinned. In the movie adaptations, Katniss is played by blond actor Jennifer Lawrence, who dyed her hair brown for the part. As Alana would demonstrate, the early debates over whether or not Lawrence was too white or too curvy to play the near-emaciated Katniss quickly gave way to something far more insidious.

One of the first book's most adored characters is Rue, a twelve-year-old innocent whose violent death is avenged by Katniss. Even before the film hit cinema screens, fan forums were rumbling with discontent—a rumbling that would rise to a roar within days of the film's release as more and more fans took to social media to vent their fury at the casting of young black actor Amandla Stenberg as Rue. In the novel, Katniss is instantly drawn to Rue, who seems to remind the older girl of her own younger—though fairer—sister, Prim: "And most hauntingly, a twelve-year-old girl from District 11.

She has dark brown skin and eyes, but other than that, she's very like Prim in size and demeanor." In keeping with the book's descriptions of the other characters, Rue's race isn't expressly stated or emphasized—a deliberate literary device meant to indicate many generations of race mixing. However, with dark skin and eyes, it's reasonable to assume she is at least likely to look black.

Well, not according to many of the book's fans—including Alana, who tweeted, "Awkward moment when Rue is some black girl and not the innocent blond girl you imagine." It was one of hundreds of negative comments posted across social media and fan forums that became so ubiquitous they were compiled into a Tumblr blog named Hunger Games Tweets. Many of the tweets were like Alana's, somewhat sheepish but frank about their prejudices, while others ranged from confusion: "Why is Rue a little black girl?" to outright hostility: "And for the record, I'm still pissed that Rue is black. Like you think she would have mention that?"

Of course, "she," meaning Collins, *did* mention that. What was most disturbing about these tweets, aside from their point-blank refusal to see "some black girl" as an innocent child, was the ease with which self-professed fans of the trilogy ignored the obvious cues placed by the author by defaulting Rue to white in their imaginations, and then reacted with fury when the film's producers followed the descriptions laid down in the book. The attachment to the ideal of blond female innocence was so strong that young white fans had turned Rue into an archetype the author had deliberately set out to subvert.

As if to prove this was no mere fluke, two years later a similar outcry greeted a 2014 remake of beloved Depression-era

musical *Annie* starring Quvenzhané Wallis. As the Hunger
Games furor was raging in the background, eleven-year-
old Wallis was wowing audiences and critics with her acting chops. At the ripe old age of nine, she had become the
youngest-ever Oscar nominee for Best Leading Actress for
her star-making turn in *Beasts of the Southern Wild*, a role she
performed at the age of six. This mattered not, however, to
many fans, for whom the notion of a cheeky imp like Annie
embodied in the figure of a black girl seemed impossible to
countenance. The resulting outrage inspired an exasperated
internet meme that quipped: "500 years of white Jesus and
one black Annie and you still mad?" It's true this case dif-
fers from Rue's in that the character of Annie was historically
written as "white"; however, she is not based on a real person.
In any case, given the fictional nature of both films as well
as the general lack of representation of women of color on-
screen, far more important is the sheer scale and venom that
greeted the casting of two preteen black actors. Clearly these
were characters that white people felt ownership of. This betrays a deep and ugly problem that goes right down to the
very foundations not only of American society, but Western
society in general—in particular, those societies that began as
European settler colonies.

The perceived incongruity of a Rue and an Annie who
are both black and innocent—and therefore lovable—was
not about respecting the source material, since the on-screen
Rue was as the book described her. It was a resurfacing of
the anxieties and entitlements of the white settler-colonial
identity, an identity that has long claimed innocence for itself and guilt for everyone else. More insidious still is the
association between female innocence and sexuality, which,

although unspoken by the outraged fans, is nonetheless the driving force behind the refusal to see black girls as innocent and lovable. From the very beginnings of settler colonialism, innocence was forcibly stripped from black girls and women through a pervasive and endemic process of hypersexualization and exploitation by white men that disregarded their personal autonomy, violated their bodies repeatedly, and then projected the responsibility for this fetishization and objectification back onto the women themselves.

Throughout the slavery era and peaking in the antebellum South, the dominant image of the black woman was that of the insatiable Jezebel. Black historian Deborah Gray White explains that the Jezebel archetype was constructed as the mirror opposite to the ideal Victorian-era lady of the house. Godless and promiscuous, "she did not lead men and children to God; piety was foreign to her. She saw no advantage in prudery, indeed domesticity paled in importance before matters of the flesh." The Jezebel was a sensual, animalistic creature governed by her physical sensations and carnal desires. Wildly promiscuous and perennially immoral, the word "no" was outside her vocabulary. Dissatisfied with black male sexual partners, she eagerly sought out white men to copulate with; she was always there for the taking. So driven by sexual urges was she that raping a black woman was considered impossible, both legally because of her status as property and morally because there was no way she could not have wanted it.

The rape and exploitation of enslaved black women was not just rampant, it was endemic. The writings of former

slaves such Harriet Jacobs, as well those of sympathetic white
women like abolitionist Sarah Grimké, paint a picture of
black girls in their early teens getting routinely bribed with
presents and "favors," such as promises of better treatment,
for agreeing to sex with white plantation workers or relatives
of the owner. Resistance was met with punishment by way
of a whipping. "When he make me follow him into de bush,
what use me to tell him no? He have strength to make me,"
one enslaved woman is quoted in the book *Intimate Matters:
A History of Sexuality in America*. Such testimony led the authors to conclude that the rape of female slaves was likely
the most common form of interracial sex. The dehumanization and hypersexualization of black women was so system-
atic it was woven into the very fabric of society: their optimal
breeding times were the topic of dinner conversations, and
they were sold at market in little to no clothing as potential
buyers prodded and poked their frequently pregnant bodies
to assess their "breeding" potential. Often forced to dress in
rags, with legs, arms, and sometimes chest showing, they provided a deliberately marked contrast to the fully and heavily
clothed white women, which, as bell hooks has noted, both
reinforced their supposed innate lack of chastity and morality and exposed them to yet more abuse: "the nakedness of
the female slave served as a constant reminder of her sexual
vulnerability."

We cannot put a number on how many black girls and
women were sexually abused, but we do know that such abuse
was the defining feature of their enslavement, prompting
Jacobs to proclaim, "Slavery is terrible for men, but it is far
more terrible for women." The abuse of black women served
at least three functions: it terrorized the black population in

order to reinforce white domination, it provided a source of continuous labor, and it was a sexual outlet that white men took advantage of in order to maintain the illusion of the moral superiority of white society in an era of supposed sexual chastity.

Were there willing encounters between white men and black women in this period? As many historians and critical theorists, including bell hooks, point out, any notion of consent has to be considered in the context of institutional slavery, where the power imbalance was distorted beyond what most of us can comprehend today. There were some long-term and possibly affectionate relationships, the most famous being that of Thomas Jefferson and Sally Hemings, who had six children together, all of whom, despite being so fair-skinned they could "pass" for white, inherited their mother's slave status. Though Jefferson never claimed them as his own, the six were all freed when they came of age at twenty-one. They were the only slaves he ever freed, and according to the history books, they were absorbed into white society.

Hemings's story demonstrates the paradox at the heart of white men's attitudes to black women. Breeding between blacks and whites was ostensibly regarded as an abomination, and sex with blacks as beneath the civilized white, but the evidence of rapes and liaisons was clearly present in the growing population of biracial slaves, who were disparagingly known as "mulattos," "coloreds," and "half-castes" ("caste" coming from the Spanish word for "pure race"). Biracial female slaves, known by such epithets as "fancy girls," were particular targets for the lascivious Jezebel trope, and were regarded as temptresses and competition by the plantation mistress for the affections of the master—and punished accordingly. They suffered both sexual abuse at the hands of the white man and physical and psychological abuse at the hands of the white woman. "The enslaved victim of lust and hate, Patsey had no comfort," wrote Solomon Northup in his famous memoirs *Twelve Years a Slave.*

This image of carnal, animalistic, purely sensation-driven creatures is not a footnote of history but the primary way in which white people in the nineteenth century distinguished themselves from other races and rationalized their right to subjugate them. With characteristic faux objectivity whites regarded themselves as the most highly evolved race, and by these self-serving standards of measurement they deduced that they were the only fully civilized society. The degradation of black women was taken as proof of the women's inherent lascivious nature, even though their sexualization was forced on them and was conveniently used as evidence of the superiority of the white race, whose morality was embodied in the figure of the virtuous, chaste Christian white woman. White women were not clueless as to what was going on around them, try as they sometimes did to act as though they were. One entry made in 1861 in the diary of Mary Boykin Miller Chesnut, a South Carolina plantation mistress, reveals: "Under slavery, we live surrounded by prostitutes . . . and the mulattos ones sees in every family partly resemble the white children. Any lady is ready to tell you who is the father of all mulatto children in everybody's household but her own. Those, she seems to think, drop from the clouds."

They say first impressions last, and this certainly seems to be the case when it came to first contact after Europeans landed in West Africa to muscle in on the slave trade. African clothing, appropriate as it was for the steamy tropical climate, was interpreted as lewd nudity; the cultural practices and dances as orgy-like displays of naked lust. In what seems a classic case of projection, the ostensibly sexually uptight and moralistic Europeans transferred their own anxieties about sex onto the bodies and minds of Africans. This projection would not only cement the image of the Lewd Jezebel in the minds of white society, but it continues to reverberate to this day as black women and girls continue to be regarded as less feminine, less innocent, less virtuous, and more promiscuous than white women.

Worst of all, this divestment from innocence begins from when black girls are as young as five. In 2017, Georgetown University researchers analyzed society's perception of black girls, surveying 325 Americans from a variety of backgrounds (though most were white and female). They found black girls were more likely to be viewed as behaving and coming across as older than their stated age: "participants perceived black girls as needing less protection and nurturing than white girls, and that black girls were perceived to know more about adult topics and are more knowledgeable about sex than their white peers."

And suddenly, it doesn't seem all that surprising that so many fans would react so viscerally to "some black girl" playing innocent little Rue: representation has real-world consequences. The Georgetown study found that in one school district black girls were at least twice as likely as white girls to be disciplined by teachers for minor misbehavior such as breaking the dress code or loitering in hallways, punished for disobedience, and cited for disruptive behavior. These perceptions, the researchers concluded, force black girls into adulthood before their time.

Black women are still paying the price of the Jezebel. The history of post-Columbus Western society, from North America to Australia to southern Africa, is one marked by the strict policing of racial boundaries that warned of the cataclysmic abomination of miscegenation but that white men were nonetheless free to transgress, which they did liberally. I believe that these actions and attitudes of white men and the accompanying silence of white women is the defining historical feature of Western settler-colonial society, and yet, despite the historical record, Western society is as reluctant as ever to discuss it, let alone atone for it.

Part of the national mythology of the Australian identity, for instance, is one of hearty frontier men and women of upstanding Christian morals and superior European stock battling and ultimately taming the harsh, inhospitable elements as well as subduing the "hostile natives." In "The Ballad of the Rouseabout" by iconic frontier-era Australian poet Henry Lawson, who himself worked as a rouseabout (an unskilled farm laborer), we get a glimpse of a vastly different social scape. Lawson devotes a stanza to the fetishization of Aboriginal women by white men, presenting illicit sex as a conquest in which "half-caste" women would surrender to the advances of the stronger-willed men while the dark-skinned "full blooded gins" went to the rest. Any sense of shame at this exploitation is quickly allayed with the punchline: "If they had brains, poor animals! we'd teach them how to sin."

That Aboriginal women were not regarded as fully human is obvious from the slew of crude names used to refer to them and their objectification, terms that seem tailor-made to assuage any feelings of guilt that may have arisen: black velvet, gins, lubras, pickaninnies. White men with a sexual fetish for Aboriginal women were known as "gin jockeys," while those who defied white norms and fell in love with them were outcast "combos" and were even presented with burnt corks as a representation of their charred character. In short, white male settlers masked their violation of Aboriginal women with dehumanizing language that positioned the women as inherently promiscuous, undesirable "prostitutes" too unintelligent to know right from wrong and incapable of being raped. The blame for their degradation was placed firmly on their own communities, who—unlike whites, of course—didn't respect "their" women enough to keep them chaste.

How might this have looked from the perspective of Aboriginal women? Historian Ann McGrath argues that some Aboriginal women were able to exercise a degree of agency and as elderly women shared fond memories of their relationships with white men. There were consensual relationships and transactions, though these were often not honored by the white men. "From the time white men invaded our shores, Indigenous women's sexuality was . . . represented as something to be exploited and mythologized," Aileen Moreton-Robinson writes in *Talkin' Up to the White Woman*. With Europeans unable to accept Aboriginal customs on their own terms, Indigenous sexuality was judged through the lens of sexual deviancy.

The sexual abuse of Aboriginal women by white men was an open secret during the frontier era, able to exist and persist as long as no one showed it for what it was in polite society. It was precisely this kind of attitude—do, but don't tell—that allowed it to continue for so long and eventually be given a "civilized" rationale through the policy of forced assimilation that came to be known as the Stolen Generations: the removal of light-skinned Aboriginal children from their families for the purposes of subsuming them into white society. The degrading language and characterizations of Aboriginal women as dirty, immoral, disease-ridden, and inferior allowed white men to rationalize flouting their own rules of racial separation. When the evidence—their own children—could be denied no longer, those children were taken and forced to adapt to white society in a crude and traumatic attempt to "breed the color out."

Like African women in what was to become the United States, Aboriginal women were blamed for their own victimization. However, whereas the children of the former were funneled into the slavery economy, those of the latter were first neglected and denied and then brought by force into white society. In both places, the labeling of black women as "easy" served a double purpose: as well as absolving white men of any shame or wrongdoing by positioning black women as less evolved, animalistic, and ruled by their own carnal desires, it differentiated black women from white women, thereby justifying the sexualization of the former and the sexual repression of the latter.

This created a false binary between white women and all other women. As I will explain throughout this book, not only is this binary still with us, if in a more muted form, it is the seed from which white supremacy was cultivated.

In her essay "Black Velvet," McGrath reveals the extent to which Aboriginal women were objectified and sexualized. Ostensibly a reference to the skin of Aboriginal women, "black velvet" is better understood as the entitlement white men felt to the women's bodies: some men refused work on remote farms unless sexual access to black women was part of the deal. Any Aboriginal woman who consented to sex with a white man was automatically considered a "prostitute," and the blame for her degradation was placed on her and Aboriginal men, who were regarded as having sold her. The archetype became so entrenched it functioned as a self-fulfilling prophecy, and Aboriginal women and girls in "respectable" employment, such as domestic servitude, were also expected to cater to the desires of the men of the house. Violence against Aboriginal women was not prosecuted: in a scenario that may sound all too familiar to many women today, one newspaper reported that the rape, torture, and murder of an Aboriginal woman in the late 1800s was not prosecuted because the effects would be too detrimental . . . to the lives of the four white men responsible.

Like the American plantation mistress, white settler women were aware of what was going on and frequently took out their frustrations by blaming the victim. "The black woman understands only sex, and that she understands fairly well," scoffed the journalist and travel writer Ernestine Hill. "She is easy for the taking." In "The Squatter's Wife," suffragist poet Louisa Lawson—mother of Henry—laments the ill treatment of white women on the frontier and alludes to black velvet as yet another one of the many transgressions white men made . . . against white women:

> *Bound to one who loves thee not,*
> *Drunken offspring of a sot;*
> *Even now at wayside inn*

Riots he in drink and sin,
Mating with an half-caste gin.

In the "new world" of European settler-colonies, the labeling of nonwhite women as promiscuous and animalistic was both the rationale for white supremacy and the key weapon in its arsenal, and it was there where it was applied most ruthlessly. It was not, however, where it was born.

In his classic critique of Western representations, *Orientalism*, the late Palestinian American academic Edward Said presents an illuminating account of how the West constructed an image of the Orient that positioned it as the antithesis of Europe: uncivilized, backward, barbaric, carnal, weak, and feminized. The Orient refers to all that which is not the Occident or West, though Said focuses predominantly on the Muslim and Arab-speaking world. The exotic presentation of a mysterious, inscrutable Orient, Said argues, helped Europe to define itself as everything the Orient was not: civilized, progressive, compassionate, chaste, strong, and masculine. This status as the most highly evolved race, the only race that truly saw and honored differences between the sexes by respecting the virtue of women, was all the justification Europeans seemed to need to export with much gusto and little mercy this view of animalistic, oversexed, non-sex-differentiated inferior races to wherever they decided to colonize—which was literally almost everywhere. The only countries to have entirely escaped some form of European control are Japan, Korea, Thailand, and Liberia.

It may be difficult to believe now, but Arab and Muslim

women were also sexually objectified in this manner. In his private letters, French author Gustave Flaubert described Egyptian women as machines who don't discriminate when it comes to sexual partners. Her life of immorality rendered the Arab woman little more than an animal in nature, unlike the superior white European woman to whom Flaubert's letters were addressed. As far back as the seventeenth century, European writers were producing work on the so-called Orient that imagined it as a land where the taboos of Europe did not apply, full of barbaric, unintelligent men and secluded but sensual harem-dwelling women. In 1696 Jean Dumont published *A New Voyage to the Levant*, in which Turkish women appeared to him as "charming creatures . . . made for love." Even the veil, which back then was a cultural rather than strictly religious garment, and was worn by Muslim and non-Muslim women alike across the region, was transformed into an accessory of seduction by the Western imagination. To the Italian writer Edmondo De Amicis, the veil was a toy Oriental women used "to display, to conceal, to promise," while the English aristocrat Lady Montagu described it as a tool that provided anonymity and could disguise love affairs. Rather than the symbol of oppression it is now frequently assumed to be, Montagu suggested the veil gave women the "entire liberty of following their inclinations without danger of discovery." She had a higher opinion of Islam and the Orient than her male contemporaries, claiming that Turkish women she met in the bathhouse were so horrified by the sight of her boned corset they described it as a box in the shape of a woman's body and felt that English men must be far worse husbands than their own for tying their wives up in such a thing.

The presentation of unrestrained Oriental sensuality was not benign. Such representations allowed Western men to project whatever erotic fantasies they had of the "exotic Orient" onto those women, serving as a means of simultaneously desiring and systematically devaluing the Oriental woman and her culture. As historian Hazel Simons puts it, "This domination over the native women was part and parcel of European man's power and control of her native land." Flaubert's Egyptian muse was the courtesan Kuchuk Hanem, whom he described as "a beautiful creature," albeit a "fleshy" one with "slit nostrils." As she snored in a Cairo bed beside him, he "thought of my nights in Paris brothels and I thought of her dance, of her voice as she sang songs that were for me without meaning and even without distinguishable words." To Flaubert, Kuchuk was a stand-in for all Near Eastern women, most of whom he would never even see, let alone get to know. In comparing her and them to the brothels of Paris he is essentially categorizing all Oriental women as "prostitutes," and I do want to stress here that I am not disparaging sex work but highlighting the negative perception of sex work and even sex itself as a hallmark feature of Western society in that time (and arguably still in ours). To look at Oriental women only as sex workers or in relation to sex while at the same time making references to the inscrutability of their dances and language is to again place them on a lesser rung of humanity, one that is close to nature and far from civilization.

Near Eastern women were perceived to live a life of both seclusion and sexual excess in their hidden-away harems, and this likeness was reproduced again and again in literature, drawings, posters, and even postcards destined for Western eyes and Western consumption.

Interestingly, nineteenth-century Iranian travel writers to Europe represented European women through a similarly distorted and highly sexualized lens, describing them as "generally pantsless and without a veil," making assertions such as "virgin women are rare" and claiming people can "commit fornication . . . in any place" without any consequence. Clearly these representations were not realistic depictions of nineteenth-century Europe but an indication that those Iranian writers, like the Orientalists, "see or imagine the relative sexual freedom of the other" and that wherever one seeks sex and adventure, one can find it. The key difference between them is power. The West had the power and resources to keep producing reductive representations and pseudo-knowledges of the "mysterious" East until those representations came to seem more real than the real.

This power-driven "knowledge" had disastrous consequences for all colonized women, and none more so than Native Americans. Unlike enslaved black women, Native women were not represented as lewd wantons, but they were nonetheless sexualized and stereotyped through the Princess Pocahontas myth. More than just a Disney princess, Pocahontas was a real woman in history whose story has been appropriated almost beyond all recognition.

As Disney and the popular Western imagination would have it, Pocahontas was a young, free-spirited maiden deeply attracted to the handsome explorer John Smith, whose life she saved by throwing herself between Smith's neck and her father's axe just as the Algonquian chief went to execute the

Englishman. As mediator between her people and the white man, the Disney Pocahontas cuts a dignified but magical figure. She is the quintessential noble savage who is so close to nature she can leap through waterfalls unscathed, talk to animals, and paint with the colors of the wind (whatever that means). She understands the inevitability of white civilization and begs her father to make peace as she falls in love with Smith, who she naturally chooses over the unappealing warrior that her father, Powhatan, has picked out for her. In the sequel, subtitled *Journey to a New World*, Pocahontas willingly volunteers to sail to England to represent her people before royalty, during which she falls in love with another white man: John Rolfe. After successful negotiations with the crown (of course), they sail into the sunset back to Virginia, presumably to live happily ever after.

Except not quite. The real Pocahontas was only ten years old when the middle-aged Smith landed in Jamestown, Virginia. The two never had a sexual relationship, and it's highly unlikely she ever saved his life given the only record of that incident is in Smith's own highly embellished writing, in which he presents himself as the object of many a Native maiden's affections and claims to have been saved in the same way more than once. Her real name was Matoaka, meaning "flower between two streams," likely a reference to her people's lands, and Pocahontas ("playful one") was her childhood nickname. She did go to England, marry Rolfe, and have a son with him, but only after she'd been kidnapped and held in captivity for a year. Converting to Christianity, she took the biblical name Rebecca and was hailed by white society as a successful "civilized native." Matoaka never saw her family again—although she and Rolfe did set sail for Virginia from

London, she fell ill and died before the ship had so much as sailed out of the Thames. She was twenty-one years old. Her body was not returned home but buried in England, her grave subsequently forever lost following a churchyard fire.

The Princess Pocahontas myth represents a passive sex symbol, the "Good Indian" who unites the white man and the Native, the civilized and the savage, the past and the future. But—and this is a big but—through her attraction to white men she also affirms the superiority of white society over her own, and so functions as tacit permission for whites to conquer, assimilate, and destroy Native culture. Even her "princess" status was a fabrication (it is not a role that exists in Native cultures) that imbues the Pocahontas legend with gravity and weight, making her enthusiasm for white society all the more meaningful. As the young, sexy, virginal, and animal-like mediator, Pocahontas represents the feminized and inferior Native's willingness to be dominated, penetrated (quite literally), and civilized by the superior masculine white society, as though agreeing to her own erasure and demise.

This imposed legacy of passive submission to erasure continues to haunt Native women today. Angel is a Cherokee and Lakota woman in her early forties with Irish ancestry on her father's side. Communicating online, I asked her what she thought was the main stereotype holding back Native women. Without hesitation, she replied it was the Princess Pocahontas myth, which, she says, reduces Native women to either sex symbols or mystical creatures who can talk to animals, or even to animals themselves. "I mean, she is a cartoon, we are real people, we don't fucking talk to raccoons and trees!" Angel joked, exasperated.

What's no joke, however, are the real consequences this

archetype has had. The sexualizing and animalizing of Native women through the perpetuation of the Princess Pocahontas myth is occurring in a context where violence against Native women is increasing. According to the Indian Law Resource Center (ILRC), violence against Native women is so rife that they are up to ten times more likely to be murdered than non-Native women. Four in five Native women in the continental United States experience violence and one in two experience sexual violence. Ninety-six percent of reported sexual violence against Native women is committed by non-Natives. Incredibly, until 2016 Native Indians on tribal lands were not permitted to prosecute non-Natives despite the fact that the Census Bureau reports that non-Native people now comprise 76 percent of the population on tribal lands and 68 percent of the population in Alaskan Native villages. Such prosecutions remain a challenge in practice and, as the ILRC states on its website, "it is unacceptable that a non-Indian who chooses to marry a Native woman, live on her reservation, and commit acts of domestic violence against her, cannot be criminally prosecuted by an Indian nation and more often than not will never be prosecuted by any government." Add to that data from seventy-one U.S. cities that found 506 murdered or missing Native women and girls as of November 2018, and it's easy to see that what is happening to Native women and girls in North America is nothing short of catastrophic. We just pretend it isn't happening, because ignoring Native Americans has long been the preferred method of dealing with their deliberate and violent erasure.

The lingering legacy of Princess Pocahontas—the willing exotic princess who chooses intrepid and strapping white suitors and white society over her static, dying culture and community with its unattractive, war-minded men—is a false construction that conveniently gives consent for the eradication of her people. A clear line can be traced from this to the deafening silence around the modern violence against Native women and girls.

The Native princess myth has taken slightly different forms through the years, falling in and out of favor depending on the needs of the white majority. In *Broken Arrow* (1950), she is embodied in the character of Sonseeahray ("Morning Star"), a teenage Apache "maiden" played by white actor Debra Paget. Sonseeahray meets the almost middle-aged Tom Jeffords, played by James Stewart, while she is undergoing a tribal custom in which she becomes the "Painted Lady," providing wise counsel beyond her tender years and even able to cure ailments: pulling his injured hand to her heart, she says it "will never hurt again." A few days later, she is again a normal Native teenager and their courtship begins. Like Pocahontas, she rejects the Apache warrior chosen for her and marries Jeffords. Tragically, but entirely predictably, she is shot by a white settler who breaks the fragile peace treaty Jeffords has brokered with his "blood brother," Chief Cochise. Her death was the seal needed so that peace would hold. Sonseeahray was the sacrifice the Natives had to make, dying in order that white society might live without guilt or consequence.

Such passive sexualization in the form of preference and sacrifice for the sake of white men—and therefore civilization itself—also dominates the historical representation of East Asian women. The quintessential China Doll is submissive, eager to please, obedient, and permanently pleasant, and lives for no reason other than to make her white lover happy.

Nowhere has she been embodied quite so roundly as in the most-performed opera in the United States today, Puccini's classic *Madama Butterfly*, based on a one-act play that was in turn based on an 1887 smash-hit semiautobiographical French novel, *Madame Chrysanthème*, by Pierre Loti. Butterfly's love for the U.S. naval officer Pinkerton is both her saving grace and her undoing. The fifteen-year-old concubine is merely a brief infatuation for him. She is a tantalizing creature he wants to possess, knowing full well that embracing her will "crush her delicate wings," but he is also aware that she is ultimately a toy, something with which to pass the time until he marries a proper American woman. Setting Butterfly up in a house overlooking Nagasaki, Pinkerton leaves for the United States promising to return come springtime when the robins build their nests. She spends years pining for him, during which those around her try to convince her he won't be coming back. Eventually he does, but with his American wife Kate in tow and only to pick up the son that Kate has agreed to raise. Through the white gaze, becoming a white man's concubine both humanizes Butterfly, compelling her to convert to Christianity and designating her as worthy of temporary love, and renders her worthless without him. She must sacrifice herself, and this she does with her grandfather's hara-kiri knife—but not before placing a small American flag between the fingers of her young, blond son.

It's not subtle. The China Doll renders Asian women—and Asia itself—submissive, primitive, carnal, adoring of white society, and, like Princess Pocahontas, preferring white men over those of her own people. Her life is given meaning by the affections of the white man, and this love requires total submission. It's the victory of West over East, told in such a way as to make total surrender appear not only inevitable but desirable. "I am following my destiny," says Butterfly, "and, full of humility, bow to Mr. Pinkerton's God."

More than three quarters of a century after Butterfly made her debut, she was updated in the stage musical *Miss Saigon*, and more than one hundred years after Pierre Loti's novel, she was again fetishized in the cult-hit album *Pinkerton* by American indie band Weezer. The album chronicles lead singer and songwriter Rivers Cuomo's infatuation with Japanese women and culture, and though it is outright cringeworthy in parts, such as when Cuomo adopts a broken, presumably Japanese inflection, there is also an element of self-awareness. In the final song, the metaphorical "Butterfly," a plaintive Cuomo sings of catching a beautiful butterfly as a young boy, trapping it in a mason jar, and leaving it to die of neglect. As Pinkerton, Cuomo then does something no Pinkerton has done before him: he apologizes. Borrowing lyrics from Puccini's opera, Cuomo admits he lied when he promised Butterfly he'd return in the spring when the robin builds his nest. *I'm sorry*, he repeats, leaving the door to redemption slightly ajar. *I'm sorry, I'm sorry.* Unfortunately, this regret is tempered by the song's self-pitying tone with its chorus lamenting our hero's inability to hold on to what he wants as it slips away. "Slips away," of course, being a euphemism for death. Weezer's Pinkerton is sad, but it is Butterfly who actually suffered. And how is that for an analogy for the West's relationship to the Rest?

Nonwhite women as the object of the white male power fantasy, it seems, are simply expected to sacrifice themselves. This sexually available, eager-to-please, and infantilized sex object can be traced back to Britain's opium wars with China in the mid-nineteenth century. The conflicts got their name because the Brits trafficked opium into China with the intention of creating mass addiction. It worked: more than twelve million Chinese became addicted, and entire cities along the coast were decimated. As Europe widened its territory and indulged its sexual fantasies, it cemented the archetype.

The China Doll lives on in the mystique that Southeast Asia holds for white men. In particular, the twentieth-century encounters between American military men during the Vietnam War were—unsurprisingly considering the circumstances—centered around sex work, giving the Americans, much like Flaubert and his Egyptian courtesan before them, a skewed perception of all Asian women. And they took that perception home with them. This image has so dominated Western views of Southeast Asian women that it became a key driver of Thailand's sex industry. Sex tours of Southeast Asia remain hugely popular among white men, which ensures that the distorted image of Asian women persists.

"This is what they expect me to be," Billie*, a thirty-one-year-old community services worker in Sydney, tells me, the strain showing on her face. Increasingly ostracized at work by male colleagues who expect her to be unfailingly polite, smiling, and immediately responsive to their workplace needs, she says that if she fails to comply, they quickly become hostile, leaving her feeling "as though it's my job to make them comfortable." As a result, Billie, who is Filipina and Anglo-Australian, has started limiting her range of expressions and emotions. The unofficial role of helper she was silently assigned without her consent is one in which anger, dissatisfaction, or even simple withdrawal is not tolerated. If her coworkers feel she is not smiling enough at them, or is not talkative enough, or she walks to her desk without saying hello to them, she is accused of being aggressive and unfriendly. Billie did not know she was echoing the horror of those long-dead Turkish women at Lady Montagu's corsetry when she described her work life as akin to being "kept inside a box"; the roles, of course, are flipped. If she tries to escape the box by not acting sufficiently chirpy while deferring to her male coworkers, she goes "from being the helper to the aggressor." In other words, if she won't play the watered-down version of the China Doll, she becomes something far worse: the dreaded Angry Brown Woman.

This is how colonialism rigged the game against women of color. For centuries, the West has regurgitated representations of colonized women that came to be accepted as more real than the real. Jezebels. Black velvet. Harem girls. China Dolls. Princess Pocahontas. All of these reduced complex human beings to cardboard cutout sexual objects without agency and whose surrendered sexuality was de facto justification for white supremacy. Colonialism rigged the game against all colonized women by reducing them to caricatures that were at once desirable and disgusting, conveniently allowing white men to both sexually abuse them and render them beneath sexual abuse.

This degradation served as both metaphor and rationale for the inevitable march of Western civilization. "They express unlimited sensuality," wrote Said. "They are more or less stupid, and above all they are willing." In all cases this surrender was an indictment of colonized men, who were presented as barbaric but weak, unable to control their women and even willing to sell them into prostitution. Whereas the white man honored white women as paragons of virtue, colonized men showed "their" women no respect, making it all the easier for white men to help themselves to them. Even films such as *Broken Arrow* that claimed to give a positive depiction of Native Americans took backhanded digs at the perceived lack of masculinity of Native men. When Stewart catches his doomed future wife gawking at him as he shaves by the river, he laughs kindly at her confusion, explaining this is what white men have to do—unlike Indian men, who didn't grow facial hair.

The history of white society as shaped by the ventures of colonialism is a history of white men objectifying, exploiting, and abusing colonized women while simultaneously denying it was happening and blaming it on colonized men when it did. But it doesn't end there. Most devastatingly for women of color today, when it was no longer enough to rely on the archetypes of oversexed, submissive, and wanton harlots, the colonizers created binary archetypes into which racialized women were and still are forced to fit. These binaries, as we shall see, have evolved over the years to fit the changing needs of white supremacy, ensuring it is women of color and not the descendants of the corset-wearing white women who remain trapped inside that box.

Angry Sapphires, Bad Arabs, Dragon Ladies

BOXED IN BY THE BINARY

We are the easiest to get discredited. It's a well-known fact. So he went back, attacking the two women of color, in the hopes that he could discredit us.

—Salma Hayek on Harvey Weinstein

Alexandria Ocasio-Cortez is something like a phenomenon. In the 2018 U.S. midterm elections, the then twenty-eight-year-old bartender, who had never before run for office, took on longtime incumbent and Democrat Caucus chair Joe Crowley to pull off the biggest upset in the primaries. She went on to win the seat for the Fourteenth Congressional District of New York City and become the youngest-ever woman in the United States Congress.

AOC, as she soon became known, is a quintessential millennial in that she is savvy and prolific on social media. Amassing well over two million followers within two months of taking office, her Twitter timeline is replete with witty rejoinders and bold challenges to the status quo. When a reporter from a conservative magazine described her shock victory as a perfect example of the importance of the Electoral College, tagging her in a tweet warning that without it, "the people who voted for her would make decisions for [all] of us," Ocasio-Cortez tweeted back: "Ah yes, God forbid a diverse working-class district . . . actually have equal say in our democracy as your weird uncle with questionable racial beliefs who shares fake conspiracy memes on Facebook."

It's unsurprising, given not only her lightning-quick rise to stardom but her unapologetic democratic socialist stance, that AOC has become a favored target of the Republican right. They have attacked her for everything from her college-era video reenacting a dance scene from *The Breakfast Club* to her inability to afford to rent in Washington, D.C., when she first moved there. Her prolific online presence and penchant for clapping back on social media when attacked in the traditional media have led to a litany of highly questionable charges leveled against her, including being called a "leftist Donald Trump." The supposed evidence for this assertion includes being a "media scold" because she criticized the CBS network for failing to hire a black journalist as part of its hyped 2020 election coverage team.

Attacks from the right are sadly routine in this era of unbridled culture wars. More unexpected was the revelation in a *Politico* report in early 2019 that members of the Democratic Party were "living in fear that AOC will send a mean tweet about them." It's an extraordinary piece of reporting not least because some of those apparently terrified of the then twenty-nine-year-old freshman congressional representative actually put their names to it. Warning Ocasio-Cortez that she is in for a lonely and unproductive time in Congress if she continues to "attack her own people," Rep. Emanuel Cleaver (D-MO) reprimanded her, "We just don't need sniping in our Democratic Caucus," and Rep. Grace Meng (D-NY) ventured, "It's not unreasonable for people to wonder whether she will come after them." *Politico* calls Ocasio-Cortez an "enigma" who is "very friendly in person, chatting up fellow lawmakers and security workers in the Capitol as she's tailed by admirers and reporters," but whose Twitter persona "frequently snaps at critics and occasionally at fellow Democrats." This, said the reporter on her Twitter account, @rachaelmbade, has made some Democrats "afraid of AOC & her massive Twitter following." Two compared her Twitter use to Trump's and one told the reporter that he likes AOC and "wants to give her advice but he's worried she will mean-tweet him."

What is fascinating here is how little Ocasio-Cortez had to do to get likened to Trump, who, apart from being the *president*, has a notorious Twitter output that includes everything from threatening nuclear war to calling journalist Harry Hurt a "dummy dope" and Republican senator Rand Paul a "truly weird . . . spoiled brat without a functional brain." AOC's tweets have bite, and though they are often critical, the attempts to equate her with the deliberately outrageous and elaborately offensive Trump betray an effort to paint a picture of her as the quintessential Angry Brown Woman.

The younger cousin of the Angry Black Woman, the Angry Brown Woman is not critical: she is vitriolic. She does not disagree: she attacks. She is not confident: she is aggressive. She is not assertive: she is scary. She is, by sheer virtue of her inherent nature, permanently, well, angry—not because of anything that has been done to her, mind you, but simply because that is what she is.

There is a cruel logic to the stereotype of the Angry Brown Woman. As Billie discovered in Chapter 1, it is a trap that neuters the capacity of a brown or black woman to get emotional or frustrated about anything that happens to her. If she does, she is proving all her detractors correct. Her anger naturally invalidates whatever she is saying or is upset about, since "anger" is just her normal and irrational state. The Angry Brown Woman and Angry Black Woman are dehumanizing, self-fulfilling prophecies that keep brown and black women boxed into the narrowest range of human experiences. If a brown woman should happen to snap, it is gleefully held as "proof" of her "mean" character, ensuring that both she and her arguments are summarily dismissed. When Harvey Weinstein issued a statement denying the sexual assault allegations made against him by Salma Hayek and Lupita Nyong'o, even though he'd ignored earlier accusations made by white actresses, Hayek suggested he knew women of color would be easiest to discredit: "It is a well-known fact. So he went back, attacking the two women of color, in hopes (that) he could discredit us."

The Angry Brown Woman is the binary opposite of the hyper-sexual colonized woman. Her existence is a testament to the endless capacity racism seems to have to shape-shift, adapt, and reinvent itself with changing circumstances. Whereas the archetypes of lascivious Jezebels, exotic Orientals, submissive

China Dolls, and Princess Pocahontas emerged as colonization was taking hold and served as a means of rationalizing
the subjugation of women of color along with their lands, the
Angry Black Woman trope emerged in the wake of Abolition, when white supremacy became seriously threatened
for the first time. With blacks legally free and rape of black
women now technically a crime, the Jezebel was no longer
sufficient to keep black women in their place. But, as bell
hooks explains, because slavery had so thoroughly devalued
black womanhood through the Jezebel, it simply paved the
way for further archetypes that continue to inhibit black
women today. A new means of limiting the ambitions of
the black population emerged in the form of the Jim Crow
segregation laws in the South, which saw a proliferation of
minstrel shows featuring caricatures of black women as either
self-sacrificing "Mammy" figures, later symbolized by Hattie
McDaniel in the movie *Gone With the Wind*, or emasculating
"Sapphires."

The Mammy is asexual, always puts the needs of her
white bosses and their children first, and, most importantly,
never gets angry. The Sapphire, by contrast, is irrational, sar-
castic, cruel, and angry toward white people and the black
men in her life. The Mammy was a means of neutralizing
black women, presenting them as lacking agency, obedient,
and grateful. Meanwhile, the grotesque minstrel caricatures
ridiculed black men as bumbling buffoons and black women
as grotesquely masculine. Large of body, loud of mouth, and
bitter of tongue, they were depicted with exaggerated red lips
and rough, wild hair. Although these representations emerged
immediately after the Civil War, the Sapphire gets her name
from the 1920s radio program *Amos 'n' Andy*, where Aunt

Sapphire provided such a perfect embodiment that the archetype was named after her. Directing most of her frequent ire at her hapless husband, Sapphire was a double whammy that took aim at both black women who were masculinized and black men who, emasculated by their angry wives, were feminized. Once again, the racialized notion of sex difference (or lack of it) was employed, this time to reassert the white dominance that had been threatened by Abolition.

The Mammy/Sapphire binary gave black women a choice: be the good black woman who knows her place (Sassy Black Sidekick, anyone?) or be the bad Sapphire, who must inevitably be punished. The Angry Black Woman stereotype is both prophecy and prison. Anger is a normal and healthy response to sustained mistreatment. By characterizing all black women as inherently angry, the stereotype denies them the majority of human emotional experiences and ensures that when they do get angry, it is not interpreted as a response to aggression or provocation but as an act of aggression in itself, an act that is intrinsic to black women.

The Angry Black Woman and Angry Brown Woman are tools of gaslighting. The very existence of these tropes should serve as a warning sign that women of color are living their entire lives on the wrong end of a lopsided, controlling relationship with whiteness. "I'm incredibly afraid to be by myself in work spaces [because] I'm constantly trying not to fall into stereotypes," Danai*, a thirtysomething Zimbabwean immigrant to Australia, tells me. As with Billie, traumatic experiences at work led Danai to diminish herself lest she draw further attention and ire. Despite regular mistreatment, she rarely complained, not even when she saw "people I had trained given promotions ahead of me." When she borrowed a pen from a colleague and forgot to return it, he snapped that this was exactly what the African woman before her had done: "Is this something you do in your culture—take people's things without returning?" Danai says she was routinely compared to other black women, and for two years was called by the name of an African former employee, ostensibly because both were "very loud." But, she protests, "I'm soft-spoken and quiet."

"No one has so had their identity socialized out of existence as have black women," bell hooks writes in *Ain't I a Woman*. While hooks refers to black women in America, Danai's story also supports this assertion. She treads on eggshells, constantly aware of her dark skin when she interacts with white people—which, since she has lived in Australia for two decades, is almost every day. She exercises such "extreme caution around whiteness" that she is finding it easier to avoid attempting friendships with white women altogether: "The most I do is just [say] hi and smile. That's it. My friends would describe me as someone who used to be super friendly, always smiling and trying to find good in white people, but that's changed now." After taking maternity leave, Danai kept delaying going back to work because "it would destroy me emotionally." She eventually chose to resign rather than return. She has yet to seek other employment "because of the racism I fear is waiting for me." She refuses to apply for unemployment benefits, preferring to survive on her husband's salary because she fears perpetuating the stereotype of black people on welfare.

"Happiness is limited when racism is in your face every day," she sums up. Danai has learned to mitigate this trauma by reading the work of activists and writers who, she says, validate her experiences and help her stop second-guessing herself. Validation is a need almost all humans share. When broader society refuses to validate women of color, it becomes vital for us to share our experiences with each other as a means of coping with these damaging stereotypes and archetypes, and to help us recognize the gaslighting techniques and stereotypes that keep us in a subordinate position.

Serving more or less the same function as the Sapphire but with a hypersexual twist is the Dragon Lady, the anti–China Doll. Unlike the Sapphire, the Dragon Lady is sexual and feminine but deceptive, cunning, and malicious: she uses her sexuality to get what she wants only to callously discard her prey when she is done. First personified in the female villain in the popular 1930s *Terry and the Pirates* comic strips, the Dragon Lady spun out of the "yellow peril" fear that swept much of the Western world in the late nineteenth and early twentieth centuries. Victorian-era anxieties about sex merged with the xenophobic belief that the West would become, as Australian senator Pauline Hanson infamously warned a century later, "swamped by Asians." The term "yellow peril" was coined by Germany's Kaiser Wilhelm II in the 1880s following a nightmare in which he saw the Buddha riding atop a fire-breathing dragon that was threatening to invade the great cities of Europe.

As well as inspiring dozens of films over the decades, cementing her as a reality in the minds of anxious Westerners seemingly always on the lookout for the next great racial threat, the Dragon Lady epithet is frequently applied to Asian women in positions of political power. When Soong Mei-ling, the wife of ruler Chiang Kai-shek, died in 2003, an article marking her passing in *The Guardian*, titled "The Sorceress," described her as "the beautiful and extremely powerful Dragon Lady wife of China's autocratic ruler." According to the author, Jonathan Fenby, Soong was not content with merely ruling China with her husband: she dreamt of ruling the world. Naturally, she sought to do this by using her uncanny ability to seduce Western men, "even . . . a would-be American president." Fenby describes Soong in typical Dragon Lady style as "one of the most beautiful, intelligent and sexy women" any man was likely to meet, recounting one incident where she allegedly scratched her long, painted fingernails down a hapless man's cheeks so deeply "the marks remained for a week."

Recent hit offerings such as *Crazy Rich Asians* indicate some improvements in the screen representation of Asian women, as Sandra Oh noted at the 2018 Golden Globe Awards. However, shades of the Dragon Lady can still be seen, both in female characters that explicitly use sex to attain political power and in characters that appear inordinately obsessed with their careers. The latter includes—ironically—a pivotal scene in medical melodrama *Grey's Anatomy* where Dr. Cristina Yang, played by Oh, is desperate not to lose her mentor, who also happens to be in love with Oh's white boyfriend. Cristina looks almost as surprised as the other (white) woman when she literally offers to give him away: "Fine! Done! Take him!" Overall, the character of Cristina does seem to buck both the Dragon Lady and China Doll archetypes, unlike Lucy Liu's character, Ling Woo, in the late 1990s/early 2000s show *Ally McBeal.* Ling Woo uses her beauty and sexuality to get ahead in her law career and is stereotypically cold and ruthless. Nonetheless, that *Grey's Anatomy* scene links the Dragon Lady to East Asian women in competitive and high-stress professions. In doing so, it betrays an unspoken implication that they don't really belong there, they don't play fair, and everything they've achieved can be explained by their lack of emotional attachment and their willingness to use, abuse, and discard white Western men—an absurdly inverse relationship to the historical reality.

"There seem to be only three choices for East Asian women," says Sharyn Holmes, a forty-one-year-old Asian and Anglo-Australian who works as an anti-racism coach and consultant in Queensland. "We can be the submissive girlfriend (China Doll), the evil girlfriend (Dragon Lady), or a literal animal." With the latter, Sharyn is referring to the character of Nagini from the Harry Potter universe. In the original series, Nagini is the embodiment of evil: a giant, sinister snake who is eventually slain by the unlikely white warrior Neville Longbottom, leading to the defeat of her master and companion, Lord Voldemort. In *Fantastic Beasts 2*, released in late 2018, Nagini is revealed to have been a human woman placed under a blood curse. She is played by South Korean actor Kim Soo-hyun (also known as Claudia Kim). East Asian actors are not exactly prolific on our screens, so when one of them turns into a giant reptile before our eyes, the links to the Dragon Lady are glaring whether or not they were consciously intended by author J. K. Rowling. "Is this really all I could have hoped to be in my life?" says Sharyn, who doesn't expect or wait for an answer from me. "We can never play the role of the maiden; we can only hope for the small roles. It really inhibits us from getting into these fields. It's a real headfuck." Are things looking up for the younger generation? Maybe. Lara Jean, the Asian American heroine in the thoroughly enjoyable Netflix teen rom-com *To All the Boys I've Loved Before* is ultra-romantic and eminently likable. She has a doting white father and a Korean mother . . . whose acquaintance the audience never gets to make, as she is already dead. The storyline involves a love triangle with two white boys, one of whom is the ex-boyfriend of Lara Jean's older sister Margot, who "threw [him] away" when she left for college because he was "no longer useful." Hmmm.

The sexuality of women of color is either amplified or negated depending on its usefulness to whiteness. AOC is Puerto Rican and her congresswoman status saw her quickly cast as an Angry Brown Woman rather than the most common archetype associated with Hispanic and Latina women: the Spicy Sexpot. You've all seen her. She is loud and passionate, with a quick, fiery temper that is softened by her sex appeal. With her curvy body, glossy dark mane, and gleaming olive skin (Afro-Latinas have no place in this derivative image of what a typical Latina looks like), her sensuality turns what would otherwise be regarded as unpalatable anger into manageable zest. And that's the point: there's no need to take a woman, her opinions, or her legitimate concerns seriously when they can be dismissed with an "Oh, you're so cute when you're mad" wave of the hand.

The Spicy Sexpot trope is not merely about sex appeal; it is part and parcel of the legacy of violence that has been enacted on Mexicans and other Latin Americans from at least the time of the Mexican-American War. The Treaty of Guadalupe Hidalgo ended the war in 1848, but not without first conceding the entirety of Alta California to the Americans. What was once Alta California is now comprised of California, Nevada, Utah, and parts of Arizona, Wyoming, Colorado, and New Mexico. Racial violence occurred before the ink was barely dry. Between 1848 and 1928, white mobs anxious about economic competition lynched at least 597 Mexicans in the Southwest, mostly in territory that had recently been Mexican. One of them was Josefa Segovia, the only woman ever to be lynched in California. She had killed a white man who was part of a group who'd broken into her home and attempted to rape her. Given the emphasis on women's virtue, the successful defense of her honor by a married woman should have resulted in praise. But Segovia was Mexican and this sealed her fate: condemned as the criminal aggressor, she was hanged in 1851.

Crimes of this magnitude reverberate in traumatized communities for generations. "It's always there . . . It's an injustice. It never leaves you. It's inherited loss," describes Norma Longoria Rodríguez, an author, poet, and descendent of Antonio Longoria and Jesús Bazán, two men who were shot and killed in 1915. In *The Injustice Never Leaves You: Anti-Mexican Violence in Texas*, academic Monica Muñoz Martinez notes that these killings have been largely omitted from official documents, leaving it to the victims' families to keep this history alive. Muñoz Martinez estimates at least 232 Mexicans were lynched by vigilantes between 1848 and 1928 in Texas alone, with anywhere from 300 to a few thousand murdered by state-sanctioned forces, including the famed Texas

Rangers, between 1910 and 1920. Such killings were justified on the basis the Rangers were protecting the innocent white landowners from the criminal Mexican "bandits." Incredibly, even though far fewer Mexicans were lynched than blacks would be during the Segregation era, their smaller population meant they were even more likely to be targets of vigilante mob violence. The lynching of Mexicans was driven by the philosophy of manifest destiny: the belief that U.S. settlers were ordained by God to expand across the entire North American continent. To aid this expansion, Mexicans were depicted in newspapers and films as all-around uncouth people. The men were criminals, dim-witted, dirty, and untrustworthy, and the women were singled out—in shades of the Dragon Lady—as sexually manipulative, cunning, promiscuous, and without morals. The 1920s star Lupe Vélez, for example, was described in the American press as a "Mexican Spitfire" and "Just a wild Mexican kitten." Her response: "I'm not wild! I am just Lupe."

By 1922, the Mexican government had so tired of this degradation they issued an embargo on Hollywood films that contained the crude depictions. That the Mexican government went to the extent of banning U.S. cultural products reveals that the old adage "It's just a film!" belies the serious impact that media representation has. People may know they are watching a fictional story, but the way in which "otherized" groups are portrayed comes to be seen as very real. How people are represented matters because it is in popular media that our social world is both constructed and reflected back at us. Popular culture, wrote the late, great Jamaican British cultural theorist Stuart Hall, is "one of the sites where this struggle for and against a culture of the powerful is engaged:

it is the stake to be won or lost in that struggle. It is the arena of consent and resistance. It is partly where hegemony arises, and where it is secured."

To see this hegemony in action, consider that ten years after the Mexican embargo, keen to soothe tensions as part of his New Deal, President Franklin D. Roosevelt ushered in a new era of diplomatic relations and representation with the 1933 Good Neighbor Policy. Suddenly, Mexicans, and Latin Americans more broadly, were no longer dour and cunning criminals but jovial, colorful, and—in a sly nod to the fruit trade that was so important to the U.S. economy that the government agreed to cease military interventions in exchange for trade benefits—overwhelmingly tropical. Enter Carmen Miranda, stage and screen star known as "the Lady in the Tutti Frutti Hat." The "Brazilian Bombshell" danced and sang her way into American hearts with stage and screen performances in which she crooned about everything from heartbreak in Rio to hot nights in Havana. By the mid 1940s, Miranda and her trademark plastic fruit headgear were a key weapon in the U.S. government's trade wars. So much so, she inspired the Chiquita Banana Lady, one of American advertising's more recognizable brand mascots. Unsurprisingly, Miranda came to be resented by her fellow Brazilians, who felt she ridiculed and misrepresented their culture, almost as much as she was loved by American audiences, who delighted in her caricature that reassured them their southern neighbors were silly and harmless.

The Spicy Sexpot is still a fixture on our screens. From Gabrielle (played by Eva Longoria) in *Desperate Housewives* to Gloria (Sofía Vergara) in *Modern Family*, she provides an alternative to the ubiquitous Latina maid, although the two tropes appear to come together in the more recent *Devious Maids*, the title of which probably says it all. This is no shade on those actresses: they are who they are. The problem is when their appearance is used to reduce millions of women of the various races and ethnicities that populate the twenty-one countries that make up Latin America into one hot-blooded sex symbol. Not only does this erase the racial complexity of the region, it leaves real-life Latinas anxious about their looks and their behavior as they struggle to either confound or conform to this archetype. "Men I have gone on dates with expected me to display maximum cleavage from the start . . . and complimented my curves at every turn," writes Irina Gonzalez on the website Hip Latina. "It felt as if my anger and passion were taken as a joke because it's simply an expected part of my personality to be 'passionate' like Sofia Vergara [and] 'angry' like Michelle Rodriguez in *The Fast and the Furious* . . . Why can't I just be a human who happens to be curvy and is passionate, sometimes angry, occasionally loud, and rarely sexy?"

The answer is because stereotypes dissolve any requirement to take certain people seriously or to empathize with them. As Richard Dyer said, when it comes to the matter of representation, the way people treat us depends on how they see us. Images gleaned from the news media, movie screens, books, magazines, postcards, advertisements, and anywhere else images can be found combine to give us the false illusion that we can know almost everything there is to know about certain people just by looking at them. This illusion is magnified when these certain people are rare enough to come across in real life that our assumptions and biases are never seriously challenged.

Stereotypes account—at least partly—for the huge discrepancy between the way white audiences tend to view portrayals of minorities and how members of those minorities view the portrayals. In her analysis of audience responses to the depiction of Native Americans in the popular 1990s television program *Dr. Quinn, Medicine Woman*, anthropologist S. Elizabeth Bird found that, whereas white audiences felt the Cheyenne characters were positive and authentic, Native audiences saw them, in the words of one respondent, as "caricatures . . . not human beings with their own language, their own thoughts, their own feelings."

Indeed, although Native women often held positions of prestige and influence within their traditional communities, the hallmark of their depiction on-screen is an abject lack of complexity. When they weren't Princess Pocahontas, they were the Dumpy Squ*w. Usually nameless and unimportant—in 1980, Lakota/Dakota actress Lois Red Elk revealed that she'd never played a role that actually had a name—the squ*w was a drudge: a sexless, unattractive workhorse who was relegated to the kind of manual work that white women were considered too highly prized for. Native Americans regard the term as a slur and have been lobbying for years to have place names that include it renamed. The word "squ*w," explained Mohawk woman and Native rights activist Suzan Harjo on *The Oprah Winfrey Show* back in 1992, comes from the Algonquin word for "vagina," and "that'll give you an idea of what the French and British fur trappers were calling all Indian women."

If Princess Pocahontas was the noble savage who desired and succumbed to the white man and his ways, the squ*w was the enslaved drudge whose joyless and thankless life was the reassurance that white society was doing Natives a favor by "saving" them from their own dying and degraded culture. If any resisted, it was only because they didn't know what was best for them. "They can't see that our system has any advantages over their own, and they have fought stubbornly against the innovation," complained the U.S. Department of the Interior in 1897.

As of 2015, there remain at least one thousand places in the United States with the word squ*w in the name. Mountains, creeks, meadows, even large rocks are testament to the disdain held by white settlers for the original inhabitants of the land. Despite the law being on their side, Native activists have found it exceedingly difficult to get the names changed. "I really didn't think it would be this hard," Teara Farrow Ferman, from the Confederated Tribes of the Umatilla Indian Reservation, told *The New York Times* in 2015. "I didn't think that we would still be disputing this after so much time." Twenty years earlier, Jonathan Buffalo of the Mesquakie Settlement in Idaho was similarly incredulous: "It degrades our females. We've been degraded for 500 years and to the general public they're walking around thinking that they did something great by naming a creek or a river Squ*w. It stings a little . . . We're not angry, we know what it means. But we have to educate the general public."

When it comes to educating the public on representation, also having our work cut out for us are Arab and West Asian women. Change for all racial minorities is slow, but in an era some insist on defining as a clash of civilizations between Islam and the West, for the "Middle East" this change has been almost nonexistent.

As the uptight, performative morals of the Victorian era gave way to the Roaring Twenties and the sexual revolution of the 1960s, Western women shed their restrictive clothes and inhibitions. The representation and perception of the "Arab world" also changed dramatically, as the cultural revolution sweeping the West corresponded with the rise of religious fundamentalism and a "return to Islam" in the Arabic-speaking world. The first half of the twentieth century saw Egyptian women and those throughout the Levant begin to shed their traditional dress to the point where it looked to be dying out altogether. Indeed, by her own childhood in the 1940s, writes renowned Egyptian American academic Leila Ahmed, unveiling was common among both devout and secular Egyptian women, and not wearing the hijab was "part of the normal assumptions and self-evident truths of the day." Rather than signal a lack of faith or secularism, it was "simply the 'modern' and 'advanced' way of being Muslim." This changed rapidly in the late 1960s following the humiliating Six-Day War with Israel, which prompted Arabs to lose faith in the Arab nationalist project spearheaded by Egyptian President Gamal Abdel Nasser. Despairing of Arab nationalism's potential to throw off the yoke of Western colonialism, the second half of the century saw the adoption of an Islam and a veil that were far more conservative than ever before. As Ahmed notes in her book *A Quiet Revolution: The Veil's Resurgence from the Middle East to America*, this new veil, like the new Islamism championed by the Muslim Brotherhood, was more restrictive than the one Arab, Turkish, and

West Asian women in general had traditionally worn and had begun to discard in the first few decades of the twentieth century. Rather extraordinarily, in the white Western imaginary, the positions of Arab women and white women were effectively switched as Arab women ceased being represented as sexually insatiable harem dwellers whose veils doubled as tools of seduction. Rather than the slovenly opposite of the chaste, white Victorian European woman, Arab women came to be seen as they are largely seen today: sexually repressed, frigid, virginal, burdened by virtue, shame, and family honor, and more or less silenced—ironically, pretty much the things that supposedly made white women so special for so long.

This audacious switcheroo by no means indicated a change in the inferior status of the Arab world. Since the underlying logic of Orientalism is to position the Orient as the eternal binary opposite to the West, now that the West approved of sexual liberation the Arab world had to be condemned for not being sexually liberated enough. As Robin DiAngelo quipped during her talk on white fragility in Sydney in 2018, "Racism doesn't have to be rational; it just has to work." Boy, has it worked.

My family hails from the Levant region of what is geographically West Asia but was once known to Europeans as the Near East and has since been subsumed into the so-called Middle East. That the name *Middle East*—which literally identifies a region of many diverse languages, cultures, religions, and nations only insofar as it is positioned relative to Europe—is still in common usage indicates not only how Eurocentric but how anti-Arab our social world remains. There is no longer a *Near East*, and the term *Far East* has dropped out of favor, but the Middle East remains, forever trapped in a kind of nonexistence, suspended in time and space and only coming into view and relevance when the West deigns to pay it some attention, with usually disastrous consequences. To Arabs, it's *al-Sham* or Greater Syria: literally, "the land to the north." Though my father's side of the family is Lebanese and my mother's is Syrian, these are different nations today only because France and Britain joined forces in 1916 to divvy up the spoils of the defeated Ottoman Empire in what became known as the Sykes–Picot Agreement. Just like that, a heterogeneous province in which people had been living relatively (and I do stress *relatively*) peaceably with each other for centuries was literally drawn into the modern world of the nation-state, in which hastily conceived national identities were superimposed over cultural and lingual ties, and nationalism battled with religion for loyalty. It's never had a moment's peace since.

The Near East, so geographically close to Europe, has long occupied an outsized position in the Western imagination. Centuries before Sykes–Picot, it was regarded as both a formidable foe and an inferior land of heretics. As Edward Said brought to light, over the centuries, the West fashioned an image of the so-called Middle East that existed more in the imagination of Orientalists than it did in the Orient, and constructed its own flattering self-image in the process. Whatever the East was, the West was not. Through the works of Western travel writers, colonialists, artists, diplomats, and "experts" who positioned Arab and other Eastern cultures as barbaric, backward, violent, animalistic, lewd, and oppressive of women, by default the West became advanced, merciful, civilized, moral, and respectful of women.

Here is where it all comes together. For all its assigned savagery, the East was also feminized in the Western imagination—meaning, naturally, that the West was masculine. This is not as contradictory as it may appear. The peculiar logic of Eurocentrism was fueled by the rise of scientific racism in the nineteenth century, which regarded true differentiation of the sexes as a status that had only been achieved by the more highly evolved white Europeans. Although brown and black bodies were designated female and male, the science promoted by the American School of Evolution regarded sex difference as a racial characteristic and argued that only white European-derived people had evolved to the point of having distinctly separate male and female brains and dispositions. According to Kyla Schuller, associate professor of race, gender, and science studies at Rutgers University, the prevailing scientific thought at the time regarded this crucial sex difference between men and women to be behind the development of rationality and reason, which to the scientists was a hallmark feature of (Western) civilization.

Racialized people, in other words, lacked the proper differentiation between men and women required in order to be rational and, therefore, civilized. In her stunning analysis of nineteenth-century race, sex, and science, *The Biopolitics of Feeling*, Schuller outlines the ways in which binary sex was regarded as both cause and effect of reason—which only white people had—making binary sex itself a function of race. To the leading evolutionary scientists of the era, the supremacy of Western civilization lay firmly in "its ability to restrain animalistic impulses and maintain sexual differentiation of the civilized."

Binary sex is both function and feature of white supremacy.

That is not to say that other cultures did not have their own ideas about gender and what constitutes a man or a woman. Nor is it to deny these may have been oppressive in their own right. It *is* to say that the West imposed its own definitions as a uniform measure, and, unsurprisingly, everyone else came up short. This is why Western representations of Arab and Asian men over the centuries have seemed to contain baffling contradictions—simultaneously depicting them as monstrous and violent *and* emasculated and androgynous. Their alleged inferior evolution justified the so-called white man's burden, the self-assigned responsibility to civilize the uncivilized races of the world. Whether or not this was fair was regarded as a nonissue since, as Edward Said grimly summarized, by sheer virtue of belonging to a subject race their fate was to be subjected.

African women like Sara Baartman, the so-called Hottentot Venus, were exhibited across Europe as an example of the defective, oversexed, and under-civilized black woman. Baartman's body was regarded as a physical manifestation of her inferior culture. This "inferiority" was then rationalized to justify colonization. This self-appointed responsibility to save racialized women by bringing them true civilization muffled the incredible violence imposed on their bodies. It was also a complete fabrication in more ways than the obvious: white Europeans colonized the world on the presumption they were "civilizing" it, but by strictly policing both race and sex, they did everything in their formidable power to ensure nonwhites were never able to penetrate the inner sanctum of white society even if they wanted to.

White people set the standard for humanity by which they, and only they, could succeed. And this standard meant a strict hierarchy that placed white men at the top with white women just below them, followed by men of color, and then women of color occupying the lowest rung. I do not mean to say here that what all women of color experience is exactly the same or that there is not a discrepancy in privilege among them; only that whatever their race or ethnicity, women of color are always considered below both white people and men of color. White women were the beneficiaries of a status higher than that of people of color but subordinate to white men, and it is this very status that enabled colonialism to succeed. The American School of Evolution, explains academic Kyla Schuller, acknowledged that both thinking and feeling—sentiment—were crucial to evolution and civilization; however, too much sentiment led to sentimentality, which could hinder objective thought. To solve this dilemma, evolutionary race scientists effectively split the civilized, a.k.a. white, body in two. To the male half went the higher intellectual faculties of reason, logic, and objectivity, and to the female went excessive sentimental responses and the accompanying tendency to irrationality and impulsivity. Women would take on the role of feeling, of sympathizing, of "letting emotions override the facts," leaving men to carry on the important work of intellectual endeavors and empire-building. In this way, Western civilization would be secured and stabilized.

This race–sex hierarchy is demonstrated in the attitudes of Lord Cromer, the nineteenth-century British imperialist who oversaw the occupation of Egypt and who was a scathing critic of the status of Arab women. Cromer had ambitions to restructure Egyptian society and politics along European lines—that is to say, he wanted to save Arab women from Arab men. Do not mistake him for a feminist: not only did he fiercely oppose the education of Egyptian women, he was a vociferous opponent of suffrage for white women. Indeed, he was a founding member of the British Men's League for Opposing Woman Suffrage, and served as president. Cromer scoffed that Islam "degraded" women by secluding them behind veils whereas Christianity "elevated" them, but he nonetheless fear-mongered about calamities that would strike if suffrage were to "dethrone woman from that position of gentle yet commanding influence she now occupies . . . and substitute in her place the unsexed woman at the polling booth." To Cromer, a woman who votes is no longer a woman. This battle of the sexes—his words—would create confusion and discord in every British family, leading to a breakdown of the sex binary. Any inversion of the natural separation of the sexes, he warned, would echo across the empire. Cromer opposed veiling not out of sympathy for the women who wore it, but because it had a corrupting effect on Arab men: it was a "fatal obstacle" that prevented Arab men from achieving rationality and civilization as European men had done. If we apply Schuller's argument, we can see that in Cromer's imagination, Arab women and Arab men had not attained the evolutionary ability to adhere to their proper gender roles. This made them uncivilized.

Schuller argues—and I agree—that this is the foundation of our modern notions not only of race but of gender. The sex binary is not purely about biology—it is about assigning character traits according to sex and using these, in turn, to rationalize racism. White women were regarded as more emotional and closer to nature (and therefore closer to people of color), relieving white men from the burden of emotions in order to pursue reason and rationality. This is why Cromer both claimed to want to "free" Arab women *and* denied them education. To him a free woman was nonetheless subordinate to a man, but she was subordinate in the right—white—way. Even for Western women, higher education (as well as suffrage) was so vehemently opposed by so many white men for so long because any attempts to transgress the man/woman binary was considered not only a threat to white patriarchy but to Western civilization. The binary permitted white men to ruthlessly abuse women of color with no consequence: as civilized men, they were spared any burden of guilt or remorse since it was literally regarded as their rightful role not to feel sympathetic or sentimental. The refrains of "facts, not feelings" and "civility" that dominate our contemporary public discourse are rooted in this racialized and gendered enforcement of white supremacy. These refrains are not designed to facilitate robust and good-faith debate but to avert it, so that white society can continue to separate emotion from intellect to its own benefit and to the detriment of everyone else.

The Western perception of Arab women remains overwhelmingly negative. A Lebanese friend of mine recently posted a Twitter poll asking whether her followers thought Arab women were liked or disliked by the public. She was careful to emphasize that the question wasn't whether they themselves personally disliked Arab women but how they felt others perceived us. Out of 188 anonymous votes made over a twenty-four-hour period, 86 percent responded that Arab women were disliked by the public. It wasn't a scientific poll by any means, but it certainly painted a bleak picture. It is also supported by more stringent research into the representation of Arabs in Western media, the most famous being the late Lebanese American professor Jack Shaheen's 2003 study, *Reel Bad Arabs*, which was later made into a documentary.

Readers are likely familiar with many of the Islamophobic tropes that have dominated Western perceptions of Muslims since the attacks of September 11, 2001. Regarding Muslims as natural-born terrorists, the tropes regurgitate images of them as irrational, dirty, bloodthirsty, stupid, emotional, immature, violent, fanatical, subjugated, oppressed, and manipulative. What readers may not know, however, is that all of these derive from already-existing perceptions of Arabs. When he analyzed more than one thousand depictions of fictional Arab screen characters, the results were so overwhelmingly negative—only twelve portrayed Arabs in a positive light—that Shaheen subtitled his study *How Hollywood Vilifies a People*. Arabs, he found, were routinely portrayed as "heartless, brutal, uncivilized, religious fanatics through common depictions of Arabs kidnapping or raping a fair maiden; expressing hatred . . . and demonstrating a love for wealth and power." Only 5 percent of Arab film roles depicted Arabs as "normal, human characters."

Not enough has changed since *Reel Bad Arabs*. In its 2018 analysis of small screen representation, the U.S.-based MENA Advocacy Arts Coalition found that out of 2,052 series regulars, only 1 percent were from a MENA (Middle East and North Africa) background. Of this 1 percent, 78 percent were presented as threats. Only 8 percent of shows have regular characters from a MENA background, and more than three quarters of those are terrorists, tyrants, or secret agents, trapping Middle Easterners in a binary of either friend or foe of the West. British Iranian actress Nazanin Boniadi has trouble bucking this typecasting: her biggest roles to date are as a security analyst on *Homeland* and a sleeper agent on *Counterpart.*

When actors from Arab backgrounds make it to our cinema and television screens in non-stereotypical roles, their ethnicity is almost always whitewashed: How many people are aware that Catherine Keener, Salma Hayek, and Wendy Malick have some Arab ancestry? Apart from *Bohemian Rhapsody*'s Rami Malek and *Aladdin*'s Mena Massoud, there is a dearth of openly Arab/Middle Eastern actors in the public eye. Alia Shawkat has an Iraqi Arab father; however, her signature role is that of rebellious daughter Maeby Fünke in *Arrested Development.* For the most part, it seems that to be successful as an Arab in the entertainment industry requires passing for white: *American Pie* star Shannon Elizabeth's career took off after she dropped her Lebanese surname, Fadal. Speaking of *Aladdin*, the 2018 Broadway production of the musical theater version of the film boasted a very diverse cast, but none was from an Arab or Iranian or other Middle East background. It was *1001 Arabian Nights* without the Arabians. Two of my favorite TV shows of recent years, *Crazy Ex-Girlfriend* and *The Good Place*, both featured an effortlessly diverse cast where black, white, Jewish, South Asian, Southeast Asian, and Latin American characters all mingle as they do in real life. No Middle Easterners, though. Egyptian American stand-up comic Ramy Youssef is bucking the trend with his Golden Globe–winning eponymous hit show that debuted in 2019. His visibility and refusal to mask his Arab heritage both on- and off-screen is admirable and promising, but the show's reported problem with female writing staff is sadly evident in the first season's shallow portrayal of Arab women that relegated them to the virgin/whore dichotomy.

It's no real surprise then that many Americans and white people in general regard Arabs as violent and threatening. There seems no lower limit to how disparagingly Arabs can be discussed in the news media. *New York Times* columnist Thomas Friedman amused himself by using the popularity of the film *Crazy Rich Asians* as a hook to take a swing in a column titled "Crazy Poor Middle Easterners." In it, he blamed all of the region's problems on its refusal to "leave the past behind," as if endless foreign intervention had nothing at all to do with the ongoing conflicts in the region. Meanwhile, studies have found that negative depictions of Arabs and Muslims (the two are routinely conflated, making it both necessary and impossible to try to separate them) have been steadily increasing. This duality—Arab villainy offset only by absence—creates a very lopsided caricature of what it means to be an Arab. Either we are terrible people or we just don't exist.

This has created a highly skewed perception of Arab women that relegates us to what I call "Pets or Threats": we are positioned as helpless, repressed victims without agency or a voice worth listening to, desperately in need of a white savior to rescue us from the clutches of our Bad Arab kin; or we are Bad Arabs ourselves, threats that must be contained and kept in our place. If we are not one, we must be the other. There is no room for complicated human experiences when it comes to the lives of Arab women. In *Beyond Veiled Clichés*, Palestinian Australian author Amal Awad interviewed dozens of Arab women in the Middle East and Australia, unmooring them from the stereotypes that dominate how the West views them. Taking particular aim at the assumption that Arab is synonymous with Muslim, as well as at the perception of Arab women as uniformly frigid, conservative, and fundamentally at odds with all things considered Western and modern, she writes: "It's not 'Western' to want love or physical connection." Two years down the track, Awad tells me she still encounters much resistance to Arab women telling their own stories. Even though self-representation is increasingly seen as vital, Middle Eastern women continue to be largely excluded from this forward momentum.

In such a climate, any woman of color who manages to achieve a measure of success and influence in her life without succumbing to whiteness herself is a testament not to the acceptance of this society, but to her own talent and determination to keep going in a society that will do anything it can to stop her. Through a series of distorted and self-serving representations and repetitions, the West created a series of binaries that came to be seen as immutable laws of nature—if they are even seen by many at all. Man/woman. East/West. Civilized/savage. Binary oppositions, oversimplified as they are, leave no room for individual distinctions and complexity. The existence of a binary means that one pole in the structure is almost always going to dominate. It is better to be a man than it is to be a woman, and if one must be a woman then it is far better to be a virgin than a whore. It is better to be from the West than the East and white is better than black, but if you can't be white then it is better to be as close to white as you can.

By marking out and then exaggerating these differences through science, art, literature, and politics, racial meanings were created and rigidly policed. The dichotomy separating white women from all other women was initially and ruthlessly enforced through the imposition of hypersexualized and submissive archetypes on brown and black women. Over time, as Western society changed and the colonized began resisting white supremacy, additional archetypes were created and imposed with the same zeal and ruthlessness. The coldhearted Dragon Lady uses her sexuality to deceive and destroy. The Spicy Sexpot's curves and broken English take the smoke out of her fire. The Bad Arab is judged by the sex she supposedly doesn't have and the sensuality she is cut off from feeling. Awad recalled to me how the attitude of one boss in her old newsroom workplace changed toward her once she stopped wearing the hijab: he became harsher in his criticisms of her work and more inappropriate in his verbal interactions, such that during one disagreement he told her to "Get fucked" before smirking and adding, "Oh, that's right, *you can't.*"

Likewise, the emergence of the Sapphire did not transform the way black women were seen: it merely added another unfair dimension that continues to reverberate as black women and girls are still regarded as less feminine, less innocent, and more promiscuous than white women. One of my professional regrets is a column from 2014 in which I included Beyoncé in a roundup of pop stars who use sexual objectification to sell their music. But I was viewing Beyoncé through the white feminist gaze, which filters out the centuries of degradation of black women's bodies and cannot see the revolutionary power of black women owning sexualities after centuries of being exploited by others.

The bodies of black women are still being used as props.

There seems no shortage of white pop singers who are keen to ditch their "good girl" image for an edgy one and who use the culture and bodies of black women to do so, only to revert to their original demure persona when that phase has run its course. Women of color are not free to cross racial boundaries in this way; their position is fixed. While white women such as Miley Cyrus and Ariana Grande can flirt with hypersexualized images derived from the Jezebel, the option is always there for them to return to proper white society, and they almost always do. The "hooker with a heart of gold" film character, for instance, is invariably a pretty white woman who finds respectability again through the love of a white man.

White women's whiteness can always help them find their way back to respectability; that option is not there for women of color. But there is room for optimism. The emergence of the Sapphire and Angry Brown Woman is itself a telltale sign of resistance on the part of colonized peoples. The frankly absurd attempts to position AOC as the left-wing Donald Trump are a testament both to how well the game against women of color has been rigged and to the fear that smart, gritty, talented, and assertive women of color strike in the hearts of the white establishment. Describing AOC as "scary" and "mean" is not random. Rather, these word choices tap into the centuries-in-the-making tropes of women of color as inherently outside the realms of womanhood and respectability, negating any need to take AOC seriously. Indeed, almost a year after their initial report, *Politico* followed up with an article that implied her endorsement of Democrat presidential hopeful Bernie Sanders at his hospital bedside was an underhanded attempt to set the foundations for a future presidential bid of her own. AOC was only thirty years of age at the time and the minimum age for a U.S. president is thirty-five. This means that less than one year out from the 2020 election, journalists and pundits were already speculating on and tacitly condemning something that AOC *might* do in 2028.

Although a warning that Ocasio-Cortez's fledgling career can be sabotaged at any time since women of color are so easy to discredit, these attacks also signal a sliver of hope that more women like her will find a way to rise above the mere scraps our society expects brown women to survive on. AOC didn't come through the ranks of the white establishment of politics: she went directly to the people of the Bronx, New York, and it is they who elevated her, and it is they who, by the time most of you read this, will have decided whether or not to reelect her come November 2020.

Yes, it is true women of color have been the targets of a setup of monumental proportions, something that amounts to nothing short of a covert war against us. But it is also true that these attacks are their own proof of just how serious a threat to the status quo all women of color really are. So serious, in fact, that the very concept of the innocent white woman was constructed to keep us firmly in our place.

Only White Damsels Can Be in Distress

I tell you that if there is any class of people who need to be lifted out of their airy nothings and selfishness, it is the white women of America.
—Frances Ellen Watkins Harper,
National Women's Rights Convention, 1866

The lady of the house was in a right pickle. Life on the frontier in Southern Rhodesia was monotonous, and with her husband away much of the time, as was the lot for most of those few white women who'd somehow been enticed to settle in the small and rather backward colonial outpost, it was also lonely. To fill the long nights, Mrs. Cromer (no relation to Lord Cromer) had taken one of her black house servants as a lover, but the morning her affair was no longer a secret meant that both she and her lover, Alukuleta, were in grave danger.

By 1910 in Southern Rhodesia, domestic servitude, though far easier physically than the low-paying and backbreaking jobs in the mines and on farms, was nonetheless on its way to being one of the riskiest occupations a black man could have. African women were not permitted to work in white households as part of the relentless efforts to maintain racial "purity" through segregation. The white population, who couldn't entertain the thought of not having servants since this would indicate a loss of prestige, hired black men instead. At the same time, anxieties about black male sexuality led to the introduction in 1903 of the death sentence for rape and attempted rape, a law that would be selectively and liberally applied to black men in the absence of logic and evidence.

What Mrs. Cromer did next would not only seal the fate of her lover and that of hundreds of men after him, it would help to cement the construction of the white settler-colonial identity as one of white male ownership of property—which included white women. It also galvanized the white aversion to black male sexuality that shaped the form of political dominance across the imperial world.

Mrs. Cromer knew she was in a compromising position. As the significant number of mixed-race children in the colony attested, white men frequently lived with black women as their "concubines" and had them as casual sex partners with no repercussions. Their white female counterparts were afforded no such liberties. In the colonies as well as in Europe, white women were, as the late Australian historian Jock McCulloch notes in *Black Peril, White Virtue*, "the subordinate members of a dominant race." In Rhodesia this meant that a white woman who engaged in sexual relations with a black man was subject to a prison sentence and certain ostracism from the white community—an unthinkable consequence for most white women in an already remote landscape. To save herself, Mrs. Cromer used the only get-out-of-jail-free card available to her: she accused her black lover of rape.

With roughly thirty black locals to every white settler, Southern Rhodesia was one of the smallest and most isolated British colonies. In the first few decades of the twentieth century, it would be gripped by a series of moral panics known as Black Peril. Convinced that African men were driven wild with uncontrollable desire for white women and were attempting to rape them en masse, the white population, under the guise of "protecting" (white) women, executed at least twenty black men and sentenced hundreds more to years of hard labor. The overwhelming majority of the men were almost certainly innocent. The fear of Black Peril—the name whites gave to the specter of black male sexual desire for white women—was so wildly disproportionate to the actual threat that historians now regard it as a kind of psychopathology.

While in Mrs. Cromer's case there had been (consensual) sexual activity, the white anxiety ran at such a fever pitch that one of the Black Peril trials included an unfortunate man named Kuchi who had clipped the rear wheel of a white woman's bicycle with his own. She was knocked to the ground and he, understandably terrified at the repercussions, fled. In his haste he didn't realize he'd taken the woman's bike by mistake. So deep was the white fear of Black Peril that the woman merely imagining that Kuchi must have wanted to rape her was enough to condemn him to a decade of hard labor.

Then there was the case of Miss Janette Falconer, a shop assistant who, in 1908, was walking to her lodgings after her late-evening meal at a nearby hotel when she was alarmed to see an African man suddenly materialize beside her. She was pushed to the ground. "My dress was a good deal torn. I was bruised considerably," she later recounted. "While I was screaming and struggling a gentleman came up. My assailant ran away." The "gentleman" who came to the rescue of this damsel in distress did not catch sight of her attacker, and it was left to Miss Falconer, a highly regarded single woman whose "perceived asexuality" placed in her good stead with the jury, to identify him. She pointed out a black man, Singana (part of the policing of racial boundaries was to refer to black individuals by a singular name), who had happened to be in the police station at the time she was making her report. Despite the inconsistencies in her evidence and doubts over her ability to recall any identifying features of her attacker, Singana was found guilty of attempted rape and initially given the death sentence due to, in the words of the court, "the seriousness of the attack." But that wasn't the end of it. An inquiry into the case was launched by a skeptical official and it was eventually revealed that Miss Falconer had indeed been knocked to the ground that night—by an escaped baboon. The black man she saw just before the animal shoved her over and jumped on her was its caretaker, Shikube. In a rare occurrence, albeit only after two trials and an inquiry, Singana's conviction was overturned.

What brought this situation about? Why the obsession with "protecting" white women from the threat of rape by black men, given that such threats were almost nonexistent? Not only that: in Southern Rhodesia, as elsewhere in the British Empire, white women rarely reported rape at the hands of white men, and when they did they were dismissed as either lying or "asking for it."

A clue can be found in the treatment of those white women who were not deemed worthy victims of Black Peril. While the jury was so excessively sympathetic to the distress of the apparently virginal Miss Falconer that they forgave her inability to tell a baboon from a human man, according to McCulloch other allegations of attempted rape and rape made by white women against African men were met with contempt. These include the case of Miss Andrie Darvel in 1909, a single Frenchwoman who ran a coffee house in an area known for its brothels. Darvel claimed she'd successfully fought off her attacker. Unlike Miss Falconer, Darvel was cross-examined, during which she admitted to having been a little drunk at the time of the assault. These three factors—that she was single, ran a café in an undesirable area, and admitted to drinking alcohol—combined in the eyes of the court to make her a prostitute unworthy of protection. The following year, Miss Mary Simm was raped in public in broad daylight; her body wore the signs of the forceful attack. Nonetheless, her status as an unmarried single mother led to an acquittal after the investigating doctor emphasized that he couldn't prove whether penetration had occurred since she was not a virgin. Finally, in 1913, Mrs. Elizabeth Applebee, a middle-aged white widow who'd successfully taken over the farm of her late husband and chosen to remain single and live alone, saw her case collapse after her character was seemingly put on trial—again, a rare occurrence in a court system enthusiastic to convict black men.

All three of these women were humiliated by a court that disapproved of the way they lived their lives: free from white male authority. That financially independent and sexually active single women were excluded from the "protected" class indicates that Black Peril was about controlling white women as well as subduing the black population. The relatively few white women who existed outside these parameters of virtue found themselves shunned by white society and disregarded by the law. The Black Peril moral panic was ostensibly geared at protecting white women's virtue and innocence, and these depended entirely on her chastity, sexual morality, and—most importantly—financial dependence on white men. There were no such concerns for the virtue of black women, so attempting to rape them was not even considered a crime, let alone one punishable by death. In the settler-colonial context, class, sexuality, gender, and race were becoming firmly enmeshed.

When news of Mrs. Cromer's infidelity reached the authorities, they declined to commute Alukuleta's sentence. He received ten years rather than the noose, the court rationalizing that the audacity that had led him to sleep with a white woman was reason enough to punish him. This was not, however, to protect the wayward wife but to avoid the scandal that the news of an affair between a white woman and a black man would inevitably bring. Black Peril positioned consensual sex between white women and black men outside the realms of reason and probability. That an innocent man received an intolerably harsh sentence remained of little consequence to powerful men who were more invested in maintaining white authority and the illusion of a pure white race than justice.

Southern Rhodesia was not the only or even the first colony of the British Empire to outlaw sexual relations between white women and black men. In North America, laws banning such liaisons date back to at least the late seventeenth century. The first anti-miscegenation law, passed in Virginia in 1691, subjected a white woman who had a "bastard child" by a black or "mulatto" father to either a hefty fine or five years of indentured servitude. Again, this law revealed a glaring double standard, since no such law existed against white men regarding black women. In truth, sexual access to enslaved black women was a key way of producing more slave labor for personal use and for profit.

Think about how dehumanized black people were in the minds of whites for this to happen. White men kept their own children as slaves or sold them to be enslaved by others, but were freed of any moral responsibility because the children's blackness automatically excluded them from white society. Children, it was expected, would remain with their mothers, regardless of the race of the father. This freed up white men to pursue and assault nonwhite women while doing everything in their formidable power to prevent black men from getting intimate with white women.

The slavery-era United States was similarly obsessed with the idea of uncontrollable black male desire for white women, to the point of paranoia. At one time, the punishment for attempted sexual assault of a white woman by a black man included castration, and by the nineteenth century the antebellum South had imposed the death sentence for a black man who was convicted of raping a white woman, a crime for which white men received a short prison sentence—unless of course they were married to their victim, in which case it wasn't a crime at all. The rape of black women went unpunished because the lascivious black Jezebel archetype rendered black women inherently unrapeable.

Slave owners anxious about the sexual desires of black men, however, were no more concerned about the welfare of white women than their Rhodesian counterparts. Their rage was fueled not by anger at the violation of a woman's body but by violation of their property: they believed they owned the sexuality of white women as surely as they owned the bodies of black people. As historian Peter Bardaglio wrote in *The Journal of Southern History*, "protecting this property was a key to preserving their position in society." As in Rhodesia, there was skepticism for any claims made by white women who lacked a "respectable" sexual history. The Arkansas appellate court of 1855 gravely pronounced that the only type of white woman who would willingly have sex with a black man was one who had already "sunk to the lowest degree of prostitution." Sex work, if it has not yet been made abundantly clear, was reviled not so much because it implied dubious ethical character as because it allowed white women a degree of independence that most could not access. White male settlers, it seems, hated the very idea of a white woman who had no need of them, and so they set about constructing a society that made it almost impossible for her to be so. As an anonymous letter to the editor of South Carolina's *The Rosebud* put it in 1832, "If a female possesses beauty, wealth, and, in short, all the accomplishments which wealth can purchase . . . without VIRTUE, she is 'nothing worth.' Her accomplishments may be admired by some for a little while, it is true; but she will never be truly esteemed." There was literally nothing, *not a thing*, that a white woman could ever have that was worth more than her sexual virtue, and this obligated mandatory chasteness and sexual vulnerability. At the same time, black women were considered fair game; and this created an unbridgeable and lingering binary distinction between women. If the most important thing a woman has is virtue, and only white women can have virtue, then by definition only white women can be women.

Undoubtedly, this binary, which essentially justified the brutalization of black women through the corresponding overprotection of white women, placed white women on a pedestal. It was a lonely pedestal that could easily double as a prison. Since their sexual innocence was the most valuable asset they had, white women were treated as though they required constant supervision, ostensibly for their own protection. Once the northern states had abolished slavery in the early 1800s, the cotton-fueled agrarian economy of the South rose so astronomically that by the time of the Civil War, had the South been a separate country its economy would have been the fourth largest in the world. During this antebellum period, racial boundaries in the southern states were strictly policed and higher-class white women were (theoretically, at least) not permitted to travel without an older male chaperone. The burden of representing the inherent superiority of white civilization fell not on the shoulders of white women, but firmly between their legs. As long as upper-class white women performed their ordained role of the "angel in the house," were impeccably chaste, and were vulnerable to the mythologized sexual whims of the uncivilized black population, then they had to be defended, protected, and shielded from view by white men. This placed them in a fundamentally and inherently inferior position; like children, they were subordinated through their dependency on their masculine protectors. Also like children, they were expected to be obedient: spousal physical abuse was an acceptable means for a white husband to rein in a recalcitrant wife.

For all these white fears and anxieties, sexual assault by

black men was not a common occurrence either before or after Abolition. Because slavery ensured white supremacy, and black men were a source of free labor, white fear had not yet resulted in the kind of moral panic seen in Rhodesia or the lynching of Mexicans following the end of the Mexican-American War. This all changed after Abolition. With black men theoretically enfranchised and no longer legal property, the perceived threat to the status and power held by white men grew as they became obsessed with miscegenation and its potential to erode their status. These fears of being "replaced" manifested in the increased persecution of black men, and shockingly brutal attacks on them skyrocketed. Lynching was driven partly by the fear of interracial relationships between white women and black men and the impact mixed-race offspring would have on white supremacy. Once again, the rampage was wildly disproportionate to any actual threat.

White women were integral to this spectacle of violence. Apparently not in need of protection from witnessing torture and murder, they were encouraged to attend lynchings, which often had the atmosphere of family picnics. Women can be seen smiling in many of the postcards that were fashioned from the gruesome scenes and sold for a dime a dozen in corner stores. The images show mangled black bodies burned alive or hanging from trees while white people swarm around mugging for the camera. How could they be enjoying this? The answer is, I believe, that the white women were smiling because they knew it was occurring on their behalf. The extent to which white men were prepared to go to protect *their* bodies and *their* virtue gave them a vested interest in maintaining themselves as a protected class. It was a source of power, albeit one with inherent limitations.

As for the smiling white men in the pictures, the self-satisfaction was simple: the more black men they eliminated in ever-more-horrific displays of sadism, the less likely surviving black men were to consider liaisons with white women or to challenge white men in general. The violence went virtually unabated and unchallenged because any white person who opposed it was quickly silenced by accusations of failing to protect white women.

Not that fear was a reasonable excuse for such silence. The most important contemporary work on lynching comes from the pioneering black female journalist Ida B. Wells, whose investigative reporting was integral to documenting and spreading word of what was happening in the southern states. Wells was justifiably scathing toward those "men and women in the South who disapprove of lynching and remain silent on the perpetration of such outrages," denouncing them as criminal participants, accomplices, and "accessories before and after the fact, equally guilty with the actual law breakers who would not persist if they did not know that neither the law nor militia would be employed against them."

Between 1877 and 1950, at least 4,075 black people were lynched; about 200 of these were women. Wells proved herself to be well ahead of her contemporaries by arguing that lynching and rape were first and foremost a means of terrorizing the black population into submission in order to reassert the control over the bodies of black men and women that emancipation had taken from white men. There was much resistance to the documentation Wells provided. She was fired from her teaching position only to use her extra spare time to write more articles, and *The New York Times*, which finally gave her a belated obituary in 2018, described her at the time as "a slanderous and dirty-minded mulatress." From our vantage point in the present it should be as clear to us now as it was to her then that lynching was motivated primarily by the desire to undo the rights Abolition had ostensibly granted black people.

The simultaneous "protection" and subordination of white women was central to the professed logic of lynching. Black women were raped without consequence by white men because their blackness placed them outside the construction of womanhood. Black men were killed with impunity because of perceived transgressions against the virtuous bodies of white women, which white men still regarded as their property. In this way, lynching and rape reinforced the racial and gender hierarchies of the Jim Crow era—the state and local laws that enforced racial segregation from the late nineteenth century until 1965—that had been constructed during slavery. As pioneering black feminist academic Hazel V. Carby puts it, "White men used their ownership of the white female as a terrain on which to lynch the black male." As in other European colonies, only white men were free to cross boundaries with impunity. As white men, they decided they could have sexual access to the bodies of both white and black women and reserved the right to guard this access by terrorizing the black population, all the while projecting their own sexual violence onto their victims. The concept of white women's virtue is a corollary of white men's sin: by keeping this false image of impeccable White Womanhood alive, white masculinity was absolved of its terrible crimes and black sexuality could be demonized and mythologized.

❖

Such was the absurd imagination of the white man, wrote the psychiatrist and cultural theorist Frantz Fanon in 1952, that "no longer do we see a black man; we see a penis: the black man has been occulted. He has been turned into a penis: he *is* a penis." This reveals the underlying anxiety and cause of the violence and hatred directed at black men by white men: white men feared that white women would willingly enter into sexual relationships with black men, and that their mixed-race children would threaten the economic and social dominance of white men.

To understand race in the settler-colonial context, we must understand the centrality of sex. It all came down to sex: who was allowed to have it, when, and with whom. It was through sex work that some white women were able to assert financial and social independence. It was through rape that slavery was enforced and reinforced. And it was through procreation that whiteness and white male authority could be both bolstered and undermined. Segregation, lynching, and Black Peril all occurred for the same reasons: to keep white men on top. White society, then, hinged on the myth of "protecting" white women from rape, but in reality, what they were really "protected" from was their own liberation and any capacity to form meaningful relationships with people of color.

Miscegenation was reviled not because it was unnatural or against God's will, as claimed, or because white people really thought black people were dirty; it was feared because it threatened white male domination and white supremacy, which hinged on maintaining a fictional notion of racial purity as a mask for economic and political power.

This fiction of a white race unravels as soon as we consider that "white" is the only racial category where any mixing automatically excludes one from the racial group. Indeed, for a long time the South's "one drop" rule meant that just one drop of black blood, even going back several generations, could, and often did, leave even the fairest-looking white ostracized from white society. Any white-appearing person who socialized with black people was viewed with suspicion and suspected of attempting to "pass" as white in order to access white entitlements and privileges. A popular genre of romantic fiction in the Jim Crow South revolved around the "tragedy" of a white Southern belle or gentleman who discovers on the eve of their wedding day that one of them is "black"; the wedding, naturally, has to be called off. As sociologist Abby L. Ferber explains, "The frequency with which these revelations occurred immediately before the individual was to be wed highlights anxiety over ensuring racially pure reproduction."

The situation was similar in other settler colonies. Historian Ann Stoler has written extensively on the construction of race, gender, and white society in European colonies in Southeast Asia and Africa. What they all had in common, she argues, was the double standard that allowed white men to have sex with and rape colonized women while white women were not only expected to remain sexually virtuous but were charged with policing the overall sexual morality of their community. White women had little to no contact with the local colonized populations, and as such their perceptions of brown and black sexuality likely had even less relationship with reality than those of white men. As in the cases of Miss Falconer with the baboon and poor Kuchi with the wrong bicycle, some of those white women who accused colonized men of attempted rape in the most absurd of circumstances probably genuinely believed they were telling the truth.

Unsurprisingly, similar anxieties arose in all the colonies regarding the "safety" of white women. These concerns intensified whenever the white population perceived their control to be threatened, regardless of whether the threat was coming from within their own white community or from the restless native population. In Papua, now a province of Indonesia but which was under Australian administration at the time, paternalism and racism blended into a toxic stew culminating in the Black Peril–like White Women's Protection Ordinance of 1926–34. White women were often blamed by their own community for enticing the colonized men, and, as in Southern Rhodesia, the "solution" for their lax ways was to infringe on their freedom as well as on that of colonized men. The ordinance made the attempted rape of a white woman punishable by death even as the movements of white women were increasingly surveilled and restricted under the guise of chivalry. When colonized men from Papua to Algeria to South Africa began to agitate for their civil rights, the number of rape charges (conveniently) increased. These "attempted rapes" include a Papuan man who happened to be not far from a white residence, a Fijian man who had the misfortune of entering the hospital room of a female European patient, and an African servant who paused outside the door of his sleeping white mistress. If merely being in the same vicinity as a white woman rendered colonized men vulnerable to accusations of attempted rape, writes Stoler, then this effectively means that "all colonized men of color were potential aggressors." And, naturally, all white women were potential victims who had to be closely guarded, their movements restricted, their innocence protected, their distress alleviated.

And so "white damsel" as an archetype was one of racial purity, Christian morality, sexual innocence, demureness, and financial dependence on men all rolled into one. A privilege, yes, but a perilous one, for to step off this pedestal meant no longer being regarded as a "woman."

One of the earliest critiques of this model of White Womanhood comes from one of the most deliberately underrated figures of the suffragette era. Frances Ellen Watkins Harper was a poet, journalist, and fiction writer, as well as a formidable presence on the abolitionist speakers' circuit. In 1866 she gave a farsighted speech at the Eleventh National Women's Rights Convention in New York City before a crowd that included key suffragist figures Elizabeth Cady Stanton and Susan B. Anthony. "We are all bound up in one great bundle of humanity," she declared, "and society can't trample on the weakest and feeblest among its members without receiving the curse in its own soul." Harper compared the white man's treatment of the black man to white women's treatment of black women. "You white women speak of rights. I speak of wrongs," she asserted. "I do not believe that giving white women the ballot is immediately going to cure all the ills of society. I do not believe that white women are dew-drops just exhaled from the skies." She argued that the condition of the poor white men of the South was a direct consequence of the law favoring rich slave owners: in oppressing enslaved black men, white men also paralyzed the moral strength of the nation and the rights of lower-class whites. Likewise, in the North, white women were turning away when black women, including Harper herself, tried to hail streetcars in great cities such as Philadelphia only to find that the conductor refused to let them ride. "Have women nothing to do with this?" She answered her own question by recounting the story of a conductor who instructed all his passengers to exit the tram when a black woman hopped on. They all—including the white women—complied and the car was sent back to the station. "While there exists this brutal element in society which tramples upon the feeble and treads down the weak, I tell you that if there is any class of people who need to be lifted out of their airy nothings and selfishness, it is the white women of America."

In other words, the suffragists, even as they were agitating for their own rights, were still complicit in the oppression of those with less power and status than them, including black women. The key, then, to white women's liberation lay in whether or not they considered black women to be women like themselves, and in using this recognition as the first step in building a fairer society. Sadly, those white women didn't, and arguably many still don't. Think of how many feminists still mistake movement for progress, insisting that more female CEOs or a female president will automatically translate into positive change for everyone. Rather than rejecting the image of white women as virtuous "dew-drops" inherently equipped to right all the wrongs of their white male counterparts, white women have largely chosen to navigate and bolster the existing system to gain some advantages, which necessarily have had to come at the expense of people of color. And this has meant adopting the persona of the damsel in distress.

Perhaps no story encapsulates this more clearly and

tragically than that of Emmett Till. The fourteen-year-old from Chicago was visiting family in 1955 Mississippi when he was accused of whistling at a white woman, Carolyn Bryant, in a convenience store. Abducted by a group of white men who included Bryant's husband, Till was beaten to death and dumped in the Tallahassee River. His killers were acquitted by an all-white jury. This is the power of the white damsel in distress.

It is a power that is not in the past. We see this modern-day dynamic of white women's innocence and virtue used as a justification for the oppression of brown and black bodies in the rhetoric of our politicians. U.S. president Donald Trump invoked the protection of women as a rationale for demonizing the so-called "migrant caravan"—the dehumanizing name given to the thousands of people who in 2018 attempted to make their way from Central America to the U.S. border on foot in the vain hope of finding safety and security. He conjured up the image of the white damsel, declaring, "Women want security. Women don't want that caravan," echoing the messages of slavery, segregation, Black Peril, and more recent white supremacist literature.

In *White Man Falling*, her 1998 discourse analysis of newsletters and magazines printed by white supremacist groups, sociologist Abby L. Ferber deconstructs a preoccupation with "saving" Western civilization and restoring the reputation of the white Western male. Like the colonial policies of old, this obsession manifests in policing the bodies of white women and the borders of "white" countries. "America is being invaded by a deluge of legal and illegal non-White intruders: swarms of Mexican, Puerto Rican, Negro, Oriental and Jewish scum who are thronging across our wide-open borders," thundered one publication. This "unarmed invasion" threatened the white race because of the possibility of white women "crossbreeding with inferior specimens," which would lead to the end of the white race through the contamination of white blood with "inferior blood." The logic of policing racial boundaries, while rarely stated so explicitly these days, is not new. It is the foundation that all settler colonies were built on.

The white damsel has enjoyed an online resurgence in this era of viral memes. The past few years have seen a proliferation of white women caught on camera calling the police on black people for simply existing, either oblivious to or unbothered by the potential consequences for black people. "Permit Patty" achieved viral status after calling the police on a young black girl selling water outside a busy sports stadium. Another damsel in distress was "Cornerstore Caroline," who, reminiscent of Carolyn Bryant and Emmett Till, wrongly claimed a twelve-year-old black boy had sexually assaulted her in a New York grocery store. Security footage revealed that his backpack had lightly brushed her when he strolled past, oblivious to her presence.

White women in apparent distress have called the police on black people for everything from sleeping in the student lounge of their own college dorms to waiting in line for the restroom at Starbucks. But perhaps no meme exposes the dangerous fiction that lies at the heart of the white damsel in distress trope than "BBQ Becky," the viral meme that achieved something of a symbiotic relationship with my *Guardian* article on white women's tears. The day after my piece was published, a slew of followers on Twitter tagged and linked me to the footage, which at forty minutes was surprisingly lengthy for a viral video, swearing that it demonstrated my piece in action. In it, the middle-aged white woman who would quickly come to be dubbed "BBQ Becky" can be seen on her mobile phone angrily requesting police to show up to eject a black family barbecuing in a park in Oakland on a Sunday; she allegedly said they were using the wrong kind of barbecue for the area. After many words of consternation between Becky and the white woman who is filming her, a defiant Becky physically refuses to return a business card belonging to the other woman and storms off. The camera follows her, and the transformation in Becky's demeanor is remarkable to witness. In a matter of minutes, she goes from assertive to combative to aggressive to defiant, and finally, when she spots and rushes toward a bewildered-looking white male police officer, becomes the white damsel in distress. Bursting into tears when she reaches her apparent rescuer, she manages to heave out a few words between gulping sobs: "I am being harassed."

This incident that so clearly demonstrated my thesis—that white women are not only aware of their privileged status in society but use it to surreptitiously manipulate and dominate people of color, only to resort to the damsel in distress archetype of white female innocence and victimhood when challenged—was a timely coincidence. It led many people to read my article who may not have otherwise come across it, and vice versa. One person messaged me to say they had been skeptical of what I had written until they saw it play out literally before their very eyes in the form of BBQ Becky.

✸

The original damsel in distress trope was a way for white women to exercise some limited power. I say *limited* not because it didn't have far-reaching effects—just ask Emmett Till's mother, who was courageous enough to request an open casket at her son's funeral—but because it required white women to adhere to strict rules to be accepted. The damsel is an infantilized woman whose purity and innocence are both inherent and sanctified, leading to her perceived reliance on men and to the obsession with virginity that persists even in a Western world that is supposedly sexually liberated. The damsel ensured that white women were at least considered human, even though it came at the cost of relegating them to subordinate status.

But it did so by ruthlessly excluding nonwhite women from the construction of womanhood. It is not just that nonwhite women were considered inferior specimens to white women: it's that they were not considered to be women at all. The damsel could only be white. Only white women were considered worthy of protecting, because only white women could ensure the continuation of a "pure white race." Black women, Indigenous women, Native women, brown women—all colonized women were regarded as lacking in innocence because their bodies were already freely, openly, and liberally transgressed by white men. White women could achieve acceptance by behaving in certain ways—or at least pretending to. Racialized women, however, as the case of Josefa Segovia demonstrates in Chapter 2, were doomed no matter what they said or did.

When white women invoke the damsel, they resurrect this bloody history. This is what makes white women's tears so damaging and, yes, so violent when they are turned against people of color, and especially, as is increasingly often the case these days, against women of color.

White women's tears have little effect on white men—just ask Christine Blasey Ford, whose emotional testimony was not enough to prevent her alleged abuser from being confirmed to the U.S. Supreme Court—because the damsel was never intended to implicate white men. This is why sexual violence by white men was rarely punished historically and why to this day so many white people still react so blithely to sexual assault and domestic violence perpetrated by white men, even when the victims are white women. This is why a self-confessed "pussy grabber" can be elected president of the United States. To be a white man in this white supremacist construction of society is to have the right to sexual access to all women, while at the same time sequestering the bodies of white women to prevent men of color from ingratiating themselves into white society.

A white man raping a white woman is not a threat to white male power, and if it destroys or threatens to destroy the woman's life, then so be it. And this, I believe, is why, despite all our claims, our society still does not take violence against women seriously. When perpetrated by white men, frequently either such violence is ignored or the blame is heaped onto the victim. It is only when white women are violated or even imagined to be violated by nonwhite men that white society suddenly seems to find its moral compass.

This is not to say that men of color never assault white women—they do—but the scale of the white fear of brown and black men raping innocent white women with no repercussions is a gross perversion of the historical reality, whereby it was white men who raped brown and black women with impunity. White fear betrays deep-seated anxieties about white men being "replaced" at the top of the racial and gender hierarchy and white society collapsing. I don't mean to suggest they fear the total destruction of society here—merely it no longer being solely in the control of white men and women. White people as a collective still fear sharing power and status. They fear no longer being the special race. The Enlightened race. The civilized and civilizing race. This is likely obvious to anyone watching the trajectory of right-wing "populism," the alt-right, and the resurgence of the neo-Nazi movement. Perhaps, as many of us racialized folk half-joke, white people fear being treated the way they have long treated the minorities they have subordinated. At the very least, there appears to be a complete denial that the only thing that has made white people "superior" is their own insistence that they are.

The damsel in distress reveals that from the beginnings of settler-colonial societies, race was gendered and gender was raced. Only white men were Man and only white women were Woman. For hundreds of years, excluding women of color from womanhood has been key to maintaining this racial hierarchy, and white women have been both privileged and subordinated by it. It seems clear to me that this is why it is women of color who remain most marginalized and most at risk of violence and discrimination. There are other intersections, such as sexual orientation, gender identity, disability, and, of course, class, that each deserve their own extended treatment of how they intersect with whiteness—and it is my hope that *White Tears/Brown Scars* inspires more books of that nature—but add race into the mix and every single one of them becomes exponentially more prohibitive and dangerous.

Looking back over the history of race and gender, it is startling to see how it all came down to sex—or, more specifically, to the regulation of sex in order to sustain structural power. White supremacy is economic and political domination through the policing of racial purity. For it to succeed and appear natural at the same time necessitated the manipulation of the image of virtuous white women to represent the white race as one of impeccable morals, far superior to the sex-crazed and animalistic inferior races, and therefore the peak of civilization. At the same time, the damsel's true purpose was to prevent the races from mixing and procreating freely, equally, and happily. The damsel in distress is always white because in order to justify white men's self-granted right of access to the body of any woman they chose, regardless of how she felt about it, only white women were considered capable of being in distress: of being raped.

Think about this for a moment. Rather than consider respecting the bodies of brown and black women, white men and their female accomplices removed them from the concept of womanhood and humanity altogether. Chivalry, "protecting" white women by restricting their movements and suppressing their sexuality, imprisoning brown men, lynching and executing black men, raping colonized women; all of this bolstered white male and, by extension, female power while conveniently absolving white people of any wrongdoing by permitting them to project their own sexual violence onto black and brown men. And then to punish them ruthlessly.

When I think of this history, I think of Oscar Wilde's *The Picture of Dorian Gray*. The handsome but hedonistic antihero sells his soul to the devil and, rewarded with everlasting youth and beauty, embarks on a decades-long rampage knowing his portrait hidden in the attic will bear the scars and sin of his cruel and criminal behavior. As the years pass, Dorian stays young and beautiful while his pictorial likeness becomes withered and grotesque as every irredeemable act he commits, from callously breaking a lover's heart to murder, is recorded on its passive body. Eventually, faced with the true horror of his crimes and the knowledge he has been damned to hell, Dorian attempts to destroy the painting, only to fatally stab his own heart.

The crimes of white supremacy have not gone unrecorded. They are etched into the bodies of brown and black people the world over. Our scars, past and present, physical and emotional, bear witness to the violence white men and women insisted they were not inflicting. White society marked the bodies of women of color as a receptacle for its sins so that it may claim innocence for itself, and, as the chosen symbol of the innocent perfection of whiteness, the white damsel with her tears of distress functions as both denial of and absolution for this violence. From Mrs. Cromer to Carolyn Bryant to BBQ Becky, the white damsel in distress has never shied from damning people of color to bolster her own status and help white society prosper at our expense.

But absolution is not for the perpetrator to grant, and white people will eventually have to reckon with the true horror of their own brutal history. Frances Harper's challenge rings as clear in its truth now as ever, whether white women are ready to face it or not. For women of color to be free of racism and for white women to be rid of patriarchy, it is the damsel who must be damned.

PART TWO / THE PAYOFF

When Tears Become Weapons

WHITE WOMANHOOD'S SILENT WAR ON WOMEN OF COLOR

Being victimized when you're seen as "strong" is really difficult, because no one believes you.

—Nadine Chemali, community organizer

Mary Beard is no stranger to social media storms. The Cambridge professor, a.k.a. "Britain's best-known classicist," has said she regards a prolific online presence as part of her responsibility as an academic. This means she has frequently drawn the ire of Twitter's troll patrols.

In 2017, the historian who counts ancient Rome among her specialties responded to alt-right figure Paul Joseph Watson, who had mocked a BBC cartoon depicting a family in Roman Britain with skin tones ranging from pale to black by tweeting, "Thank God the BBC is portraying Roman Britain as ethnically diverse. I mean, who cares about historical accuracy, right?" Watson was undeservedly assured in his mockery. Ancient Europe was far more diverse in its history than our current concepts of identity assume. Beard let him know about Quintus Lollius Urbicus, a governor of Britain who'd been born in what is now Algeria. This unleashed a barrage of abuse against Beard, whose qualifications were somehow deemed irrelevant. Twitter users who knew better dismissed her perspective as political correctness gone mad and accused her of trying to rewrite history, treating her to a torrent of aggressive insults "on everything from my historical competence and elitist ivory tower viewpoint to my age, shape and gender."

But on February 17, 2018, Beard posted a tweet that ignited a different kind of storm, one in which she played a different role—though perhaps her past experience with trolls did not lead her to see it this way. In response to the unfolding scandal involving Oxfam aid staff abusing sex workers in the aftermath of the 2010 Haiti earthquake, Beard tweeted, "Of course one can't condone the (alleged) behavior of Oxfam staff in Haiti and elsewhere. But I do wonder how hard it must be to sustain 'civilized' values in a disaster zone. And overall I still respect those who go in to help out, where most of us wd [would] not tread."

It's a particularly disappointing tweet coming from a history professor. The backlash was immediate, this time from people of color. One of these critics was fellow Cambridge scholar Priyamvada Gopal, who took exception to Beard's apparent minimization of the brutality of colonization. Gopal wrote a Medium post outlining to Beard why her tweet was being criticized, calling it an example of a "genteel patrician racist manner" that is pervasive in academia while noting that "this is the more progressive end of the spectrum."

Twitter pile-ons can be so over the top that separating the wheat of legitimate critique from the chaff of abusive trolling can sometimes feel like an exercise in futility, so I have no doubt that much of the criticism leveled at Beard got unnecessarily nasty. Nonetheless, there are attacks and there is constructive criticism, and Beard seemed to make no differentiation between the two. Apologizing not for the content or implications of her tweet but for attempting to inject "nuance" into the discussion, she posted a teary selfie of herself, pleading, "I'm really not the nasty colonialist you think I am . . . If you must know I am sitting here crying."

This is where things took what is a now-familiar turn. Writer and academic Flavia Dzodan marveled at Beard's "white feminist tears" and commented on "the extent of sentimentality people will go through, debasing themselves if necessary in order to sustain their ignorance, bigotry or both," and Anaïs Duong-Pedica described Beard's tearful display as "a typical white woman's move to innocence." Others quickly came to the defense of Beard, namely white feminist journalists such as Helen Lewis, who claimed Beard wasn't playing the victim but just being "honest," and Hadley Freeman, who dismissed the criticism of Beard as "the textbook definition of bullying: mocking someone for showing weakness."

These defenders really, *really* didn't get it. In this context, Beard's tears were not a sign of weakness: they were a reminder of her relative power. It is significant that of all the times Beard has been dragged on Twitter, usually by sexist, racist trolls, this is the first and only time—when her critics were women of color—that she responded by publicly crying.

Most disappointing is that Beard clearly is intimately knowledgeable with how women's voices as a whole have been marginalized from power. In fact, she literally wrote a manifesto on it: *Women and Power*, published in 2017. And yet, when it came to criticism even from fellow academics and feminist writers who warned her she was contributing to the silencing of nonwhite women by dismissing their concerns, she was unable to see past her own innocence and victimhood. Her tears made Gopal and other women of color critiquing her seem all the nastier and more irrational; Gopal in particular became the target of vicious attacks. The entire incident demonstrates how easily white women can slip between their "one up" and "one down" identities.

When I first wrote about it, I did not know that this had been a subject of academic study for much longer than the topics of white women's tears and white feminism have been in the public eye. In 2007, researcher Mamta Motwani Accapadi, then a postdoctoral fellow at the University of Houston, wrote a paper called "When White Women Cry: How White Women's Tears Oppress Women of Color," in which she argues that white women's experience of gender is not racially neutral. Rather, just as black and brown women are caricaturized by the negative images governing society's perception of their racial communities, so too are white women's experiences "shaped by internal expectations and external perceptions of what it means to be a woman" in a white-dominated society.

White women's racial privilege is predicated on their acceptance of their role of virtue and goodness, which is, ultimately, powerlessness. It is this powerlessness—or, I would argue, this *appearance* of powerlessness—that governs the nature of White Womanhood. As Accapadi notes, womanhood in general has been subordinated in patriarchal societies, but whiteness has positioned White Womanhood above other women. This leaves women of color "defined by two layers of oppression." To put it simply, women of color are both too racialized and too gendered to be taken seriously and treated with respect. The history of the white damsel has entrenched the notion of white women's innocence, and it is this that sees onlookers flocking to soothe white women's emotional distress. At the same time, the historical debasement of women of color positions them as the guilty party.

By posting a close-up of herself literally crying, or at least appearing to be, Beard pivoted from her one down identity—woman—to her one up identity—white—from her usual public role of feminist agitator to the "powerless" role of the damsel in distress. Not only did she perpetuate the derogatory rhetoric about "uncivilized" non-Western countries, but the moment she began crying the entire tone of the incident necessarily shifted. It was no longer about what she said or why it upset many people of color: it was about her feelings. Her innocence. Her victimhood. Her strategic White Womanhood.

It is presented as helplessness and sentimentality, but it is a power move. The power of the damsel is that she provokes the protective urge. Whoever is making her cry must be the one at fault (unless it is a white man, but more on that in the next chapter). At the same time, the reductive archetypes governing the representation of women of color also kick into play. Angry. Scary. Cold. Aggressive.

This doesn't mean the tears aren't always genuine, even

if they are strategic. I have no doubt many white women genuinely feel they are being attacked simply by virtue of a woman of color disagreeing with them. "White people are so rarely ever outside of our racial comfort zones and we've been warned all our lives not to go outside of our racial comfort zone and we come to feel entitled to racial comfort," Robin DiAngelo explained to me when I interviewed her during her U.S. book tour in the summer of 2018. "So if you challenge any of that . . . we can't handle it, our capacity to handle that is basically zero. And I will lash out and do whatever I need to do to get you to stop challenging me. And so if that's cry, I'll cry. I might not even be consciously thinking about that but that's how it works."

In other words, those tears may well be genuine, but that does not make them innocent and harmless: the opposite, in fact. "As soon as I cry all of the resources are going to go back to me, and you [the person of color] are going to be bad. And that's why I think it's a form of bullying," DiAngelo continues. "I bet you put up with way more racism from white people every single day than you bother talking to us about. And why don't you bother? Because you're probably going to get punished worse. And so it's just a beautiful form of white racial control. You stay in your place, and I stay in mine, then I get to claim you as my friend, you're my coworker, see how I'm not racist? But [only] as long as you don't challenge my identity and my position."

DiAngelo is right, of course: I do put up with a lot more racism than I bother to point out—and I am someone who writes about racism for a living. In fact, I would say there is barely a woman of color alive today who hasn't been on the wrong end of a white woman's tears multiple times in

her life and with far worse consequences than those faced by
Professor Gopal in her challenge to Mary Beard. Gopal's status as a high-profile academic, as well as her self-admittedly
privileged upper-caste background in India, mean she isn't
subject to the same consequences as women with less status,
although racism does make her job more strenuous than it
would be otherwise. It has only been in the process of writing
this book that I have begun to gain an understanding of how
pervasive this experience is for the majority of women of color
living in the West—how much it shapes, limits, and mars
their lives and, most frustratingly, how little recourse they
have to seek accountability from those who do it to them.

Perhaps few conflicts are more ubiquitous and contentious
for women of color than the one that arises due to the insistence of white women on playing with their hair. Zeina, the
thirtysomething Palestinian Canadian we met in the introduction, has lived in Australia for about five years. She claims
to have had the same hairstyle—long, thick, curly brown hair
to her waist—since her late teens, and a common occurrence
for her is for white women to touch and play with it. "Only
white people touch my hair," she told me over the phone.
"Only middle-aged white women touch my hair. I have never,
ever had a black woman or an Aboriginal woman come up
to me, or a Chinese person. Even in Canada, you know we
have a lot of Japanese tourists, and they take pictures with
everyone, they're like, 'Can I take a picture with you, please?
You look so exotic,' but if you say no, they won't. They're very
polite. But these [white women] just walk up to me and just
put their hands on my hair and I'm like, 'What the fuck are
you doing?'" She laughs, but it's out of frustration rather than
amusement. "They say, 'Can I touch your hair?' and they

touch. It's not a question, because they're not pausing, it's in the process of them already touching me . . . it's not like they are asking, it isn't actually a question. It isn't asking permission whatsoever . . . they just do what they want anyway."

The fascination with curly hair is not harmless. It is performing playfulness while sending a loud message. One recent scenario took place in a tourist shop in which an older, white-haired woman approached Zeina and said animatedly that while people with curly hair "hate" it when she touches it, she can't help herself and has to do it anyway. "And this woman . . . she said to me, 'Can I pet you?' while she was touching my hair." Zeina pauses. "She said 'pet.'" At that point I remark that it sounds a lot like a display of power and domination, as if they are showing her who's the boss. "Who's boss, exactly!" she exclaims. "I feel like they're trying to show me who's boss because I've already said no, and they just do it anyway and they pet me—like, they actually pet me like you pet a puppy . . . if I turned around and pet her head, she would not accept it. She would swipe at my hand, or step back, or she would have a reaction . . . they are taking charge of the situation. It doesn't really matter if I say yes or if I say no, it's just not part of the discussion. She wants to do this, she'll do this."

So what happens when "she wants to do this" at work? Zeina describes her interaction with that coworker at an old job of hers in Canada when they were both in the bathroom. "She came out of the stalls and touched my hair before she washed her hands, and I'm going to throw up. Like, I feel disgusted. So I complained, and she turned it into some kind of reverse racism thing. She was saying to the supervisor that I'm making it an uncomfortable working environment, I'm making it a toxic or hostile work environment because I'm not being friendly. That I should have manners, and I should be more open to being kind with my coworkers."

When Zeina made her complaint, she claims her supervisor asked her to "let this go," and HR responded by asking whether or not the coworker had punched her or sexually harassed her. When Zeina said no but that the touching was still uninvited and inappropriate, "they said I was acting aggressive, and that I wasn't a team player . . . Somehow, I was the guilty party in this." She ended up losing that job after bringing up the incident again at a staff meeting. "I'm like, please, we need to talk about boundaries and personal space, and what's sexual harassment and what's racism." The management agreed to undertake sensitivity training, during which a video was played featuring a woman with dreadlocks instructing colleagues not to touch each other's hair. "She burst into tears," Zeina says of her coworker, "and said we were obviously shaming her and targeting her in front of the rest of the department . . . She complained to HR about it, HR decided I owed her an apology, and they said I had to apologize in front of everybody in a meeting, the same way I 'humiliated' her in front of everybody. I refused . . . I said no, and then I gave my resignation."

Not only did her workplace not try to change her mind about resigning, Zeina says they were pleased to let her go. Her manager thanked her for the resignation. "Have a great last two weeks, bye." Zeina believes this was because "they were so shocked that I stood up for myself that they were just relieved I was going to go. Nobody had ever called them out on their soft racism before . . . they were just so happy to see me go."

Perhaps the most startling aspect of Zeina's experience is where this all occurred: she was an immigration officer for the Canadian Ministry of Immigration and had worked there for seven years. If this seems surprising (it certainly did to me), perhaps it shouldn't be given that even in areas servicing brown and black people, the overwhelming majority of positions are held by white people. Zeina's workplace was no exception. "It was around 80 percent white people," she says of her time at the ministry. "We had one Sikh guy, there was me—I was the token Arab—and one Asian person, but it wasn't very diverse . . . I mean, the department had fifty-one people and we had five people who were nonwhite."

If there is any field where you'd logically expect this kind of thing not to take place, it would be in the aid and not-for-profit sector. However, in early 2019 the sector was rocked by allegations of a "toxic working culture" at Amnesty International, one of the most recognized nongovernment organizations (NGOs) in the world. A report that had been commissioned following the suicide of two of Amnesty's U.K. staff members found routine bullying, harassment, and discrimination against racial minorities and LGBTIQ workers as well as favoritism and nepotism in the hiring and promotional process.

"The nonprofit and philanthropy sector is really based on privilege, and that implies white privilege a lot of the time," Kristina Delgado tells me. The twenty-seven-year-old recently started her own coaching and consulting business, Hearts on Fleek, aimed specifically at the aid and nonprofit sector, after she grew disenchanted with its racism and favoritism. She sums up her experience of bringing up race issues as a "narrative of taking victimhood" away from people of color to undermine their allegations: "It positions us not as a target of racism but as an agent of racism. So whenever I bring up something to do with racism, I'm always targeted as the person being divisive and making something up, and I am the one with the problem. Even though there's a lot of training that teaches that reverse racism isn't a thing, it's still culturally and socially reinforced whenever you bring it up."

Kristina, who lives in Germany, is from the Bronx, New York. Her mother is Indigenous El Salvadorian and her father is from Puerto Rico and has Palestinian Arab heritage. Though she identifies as Latina, she describes herself as ethnically ambiguous looking, which, she says leads to objectification and tokenization. "I was working at a humanitarian NGO in Turkey working to serve Syrian and Palestinian refugees," she recalls. "The founder of the organization was a white woman who had the money to fund such work but no previous experience. I have a background in Arabic language, international development, and public health and that's why she took me on; she tokenized me often to get legitimacy with the community, although I don't identify as Arab."

Kristina told me that the organization sought to dictate the needs of the community by the founder's "white, privileged standards" rather than to "empower them and see them as true partners to develop and sustain programs geared toward their own needs. She wanted to offer yoga classes to newly arrived refugees from Syria who did not have access to food or healthcare!" Kristina says she felt compelled to speak up against what she regarded as an abuse of power that affected the running of the organization. "I confronted

her about her attitude—the harm she was producing by seeing this community of displaced people as objects of charity
rather than complex humans capable of deciding their own
needs . . . and that she was catering to herself rather than
[them]. She cried, called me a racist monster for calling her
out, [and] left the room. The other white women I worked
with told me I needed to stop being sensitive and looking at
race."

Kristina says her job became so stressful she was hospital-
ized and eventually forced to quit, only to then find herself
having similar experiences elsewhere. Increasingly, she found
that white women use their tears to police how she expresses
herself and what issues she can discuss: "I am a trained com-
municator and negotiator [but] I'm labeled as being divisive
or an angry brown woman." In another incident, when she
was part of a Fulbright Fellow cohort that traveled to Turkey,
and one of the few nonwhite women in her group, she found
herself part of a subgroup of four women of color who spoke
up about Islamophobia and racism in the organization only to
be literally labeled the "Angry Brown Girl Club."

"It demerits what we say and overlooks our professional,
academic, and lived expertise. When white women cry it also
makes them able to leave the conversation and choose not
to listen, whereas women of color do not have the ability to
choose to leave a conversation when we have made someone
uncomfortable. White women believe that their womanhood
puts them on the same level of oppression as [us] and that's
where the conversation stops. They seem to believe in equality
to the point that they are more interested in having the same
power and privilege as white men rather than dismantling
oppressive attitudes and systems for all. It's angering because

I'm on their team but I don't understand why our narratives can't bolster each other up."

Kristina sees differences between the United States and Europe: "Germany . . . they have this horrible past and they have more cultural reckoning with their abuse of power from World War II, so there's generally more openness." This openness, however, doesn't seem to extend to her industry: "It's still within the sector, this social impact sector . . . trying to tell people you can't talk about race whatsoever. It still happens. I think in the American context it happens no matter what you're engaging with; here, I feel a bit better because Germans [are] just in many ways more willing to sit through it and listen, whereas in America, we've never had a reckoning with our history of slavery and colonialism, imperialism, you name it, global interventions to this day, so we've never had a chance to look at our own backyard, whereas Germany has."

Another country that hasn't had a reckoning with its colonial foundations is Australia. Rashida arrived in Australia as an Afghan refugee after living in refugee camps with her family. Now in her thirties, she has had similar experiences to Kristina in the nonprofit sector. Despite being Afghan, not Arab, she has frequently found herself to be her organization's media "face" and "voice" for any issue to do with the Middle East—a tokenism that she says has not translated to respect and promotion in the organization. Like Kristina, she has found herself in uncomfortable work meetings in which she is the sole woman of color surrounded by white female colleagues who can't or don't understand why she brings up racism and representation.

❉

This kind of behavior isn't limited to the workplace and can be particularly devastating when it happens between friends. "It completely floored me." Rashida's voice drops in the middle of our phone conversation. For all her frustrations at work, it was an interaction with someone she believed was a good friend—"one of my closest"—that has impacted her the most. At a night out with friends working in the aid sector, one of them, recently returned from India, brought up her "yoga journey and spiritual awakening." Rashida was born in India where her family lived before being granted visas to Australia, so she casually—she thought—asked the friend if she'd ever thought about the direction yoga has taken in the West. "The studios are full of white women and the prices are not really reflective of the ethos I thought yoga was meant to be about," she explains.

"I have never in my life experienced such a level of defensiveness." Her voice cracks. "How *dare* I even question something so important to her in her journey . . . that helps her deal with the stress of her work." Rashida had tried to initiate a general conversation, but her friend's response left her stunned. "I was completely perplexed and the whole conversation spiraled to the point where she just up and left the pub. All my friends there were also white, and they told me I was rude to even bring it up because it was important to her and I was way out of line." Like so many other women of color, Rashida blamed herself: "I thought, okay, it's clearly me. I'm crazy. I should shut the fuck up because I am losing all my friends." Rashida did not want to lose a friend she'd known for more than a decade: "I told myself, I can't make a big deal of this. Our friendship is worth much more than me making an issue out of it." She sent her friend a long letter of apology, which was accepted, but the friend told her she had felt "very attacked." Rashida eventually ended the friendship. "If I can't have this conversation with someone I saw as progressive, as an ally, who had worked in refugee migrant community spaces . . ." Her voice trails off. "The mob mentality backed her up and made me feel like I was totally in the wrong."

The feedback from other people of color was very different: they all told her she had nothing to feel bad about. "Lucky I had PoC friends I could use as a sounding board . . . otherwise I probably would have retreated from my public position." The disbelief and sadness in Rashida's voice is familiar to me, both because I have felt the same thing when trying to unpack my own interactions with white women who I thought "got it" when it comes to race, and because I heard it in the voices of so many other women of color with startlingly similar experiences. It is as though there is a literal textbook.

All of which is to say, her now-former friend's behavior may have come as a shock to Rashida, but it is not surprising that she reacted in this way. The spirituality and wellness scene seems to see more than its fair share of this dynamic. Full disclosure: I have practiced yoga for two decades. I even taught it for a few years back when my writing career was just starting. I have seen yoga's popularity explode across the West and, with it, a distinctive rise in competitiveness and ego, and a fixation on appearance and nailing advanced poses. All of these were once considered anathema even to Western yogis. Nonetheless, many of those drawn to yoga take to heart the idea of spirituality and the desire to be seen as good, ethical people. Since this jars with the scene's reputation for exclusivity and cultural appropriation, it is a breeding ground for conflict between women of color and white women.

"For spiritual white women, their triggers are words like 'tribe' and 'namaste,'" Sharyn Holmes, the diversity consultant in Queensland from Chapter 2 tells me. "Namaste" is a Sanskrit word that has been popularized in Western yoga classes. Although Indians and other Hindus use it as a common greeting, Western yoga has transformed it into something more mystical and seemingly profound. When women of color such as Sharyn point out this kind of thing, "white women use defenses like 'We are all human' and seem ignorant that oppression still exists today." If Sharyn calls them out online, they will often refuse to engage with her directly but will "bring in another white woman as an ally" who will then attack Sharyn, as well as any woman of color who agrees with her. "White women will gaslight us, they will sealion even weeks later," she says. "Sealion" has nothing to do with the marine animal but refers to the online phenomenon of trolling someone by persistently asking for yet more evidence and continuing a debate under a façade of civility. The term comes from a webcomic, "The Terrible Sea Lion" by David Malki, in which a sea lion attempts to troll an unwilling opponent into a debate by following them from place to place, all while faking politeness. "They infantilize themselves. They take on these childlike qualities of 'Oh, I'm being hurt by the big bad wolf' to mask their manipulation and their emotional and psychological abuse against women of color."

Nonwhite women are left with little in the way of recourse. "White women can feel and express the full spectrum of human emotion. But brown and black women can't feel sad that someone has hurt us or feel angry that they hurt us. We have to live life on that line . . . it's so hard to take care of yourself when you are constantly receiving messages that you're not worth it. You start to *feel* like you're not worth it. It is so, so important that we set boundaries, to just say, 'There is the door—can you please leave?'" For her part, Kristina has often tried to take a more diplomatic approach. "I do think there needs to be respect and kindness when you are having these dialogues because the process of unlearning white supremacy is hard," she says. The problem is when white women start talking about things such as "color blindness" in wellness and spirituality. Around the time we spoke, Kristina was meant to feature on a spirituality and wellness podcast to discuss that subculture only to be disinvited after the host began following her on social media. "[She] thought I was too angry. I made her too uncomfortable." I ask whether the host had used those exact words—angry and uncomfortable: "Yeah . . . she just didn't want to move past this discomfort and victimization."

Sharyn no longer second-guesses whether race was a factor in her interactions with white women. "They didn't see me as a woman but as something lower. Their behavior is very strategic and orchestrated." She describes white women as 2IC—second-in-command to white men, a role they know they hold and do not want to relinquish. "They are not willing to give up this power. We see this in how they treat women of color . . . They think they are so superior to us that we can't even see their behavior for what it is. But we know now. Women of color can see. We know the secrets. We just need to build our own platforms, we need to work together as a collective." She pauses, then: "White women just need to wake up. White women, please look at your behavior and how you're treating other people."

Several of the two dozen or so women I spoke to in the course of writing this book told me their ill-treatment by white female colleagues became so pervasive and damaging, they felt they had no choice but to leave their workplace. Any attempt to draw attention to their situation only led to further ostracism. "Being victimized when you're seen as 'strong' is really difficult, because no one believes you," feminist organizer Nadine Chemali, a thirty-eight-year-old Lebanese Australian, sums up. "I was told consistently that I was a problem."

On a few occasions, former coworkers would get in touch months or even years later to apologize and say they finally understood what had been happening. Of course, by then the damage had been done to these women's livelihoods and psychological well-being. Not only had they been subjected to covert, unacknowledged bullying, but they were invariably blamed for it when they tried to bring it up.

Speaking to these women of color in all corners of the globe, I found it startling how the same words were used again and again to describe them and wear them down: toxic, bully, hostile, troublemaker, aggressive, irrational, divisive.

Accusing her of "creating a hostile work environment based on race and gender" is exactly how the two female colleagues who complained about Lisa Benson said they felt about her after the African American journalist posted my article to Facebook (see Introduction). In sharing the article, Lisa's manager claimed she had "made broad, unfair characterizations of white women as a group based on their race and gender, conveyed that white women as a group behave differently than black women, and suggested a bias toward a particular group which undermines the role of a journalist [and] violated the principles of the social media policy."

I have thought long and hard about what to call this phenomenon, this very dangerous performance of womanhood and innocence. In many ways, as Luvvie Ajayi suggests, this weaponization of white women's distress seems a corollary of toxic masculinity, and I wondered if it isn't appropriate to call it simply toxic femininity. Toxic masculinity, though now ubiquitous in feminist theory and popular feminist writing, originated in psychology studies and refers to the stereotypical norms and behaviors adopted by men that are associated with traditional masculinity. They include, explains Michael Flood, "the expectations that boys and men must be active, aggressive, tough, daring, and dominant." Toxic masculinity, he says, is bad both for men and women, contributing to "gender inequalities which disadvantage women and privilege men . . . Narrow and stereotypical norms of masculinity constrain men's physical and emotional health, their relations with women, their parenting of children, and their relations with other men." Poor health, violence, sexism, and homophobia are all linked to toxic masculinity.

But toxic masculinity is not specific to white men, and femininity is not the same as womanhood. While toxic masculinity as we discuss it can help explain the structural inequalities between men and women, it doesn't account for racial inequality and most racial violence (though it certainly impacts on violence against transgender people of color). White privilege applies to white women just as it does to white men. This behavior is certainly toxic, but it is a toxicity of the specific concept of White Womanhood rather than of generalized femininity. Whiteness has ensured that certain norms and behaviors are still implicitly regarded as the domain of white women. And white women's tears are a cynical invocation of a type of womanhood whose historical role was to be not only conventionally and acceptably feminine but the civilizing force in frontier societies, the moral judge, the prototype against which all other women were judged and found lacking—the peak of human evolution.

This behavior is more than just toxic; it is strategic. It's a performance of womanhood that is designed to empower the white woman at the expense of the woman of color for the benefit of white society. It's not about femininity and masculinity and how one should behave to be sufficiently one or the other, but about who counts as a woman and who counts as a man. Who counts as a human. Womanhood and manhood are something you intrinsically either have or do not have, and our settler-colonial history has determined they are something that only white men and white women have. The harms caused by the gender binary can and have filled volumes of books on their own. However, rarely has it been explicitly noted that this binary, not only marginalizes those who don't fall neatly into either category regardless of their race, but is itself one of the ways in which whiteness has maintained its domination.

Strategic White Womanhood makes personal what is political. It reframes legitimate critiques as petty gripes. It takes the onus off the structures and systems that hold back racialized women and places it firmly on the behavior or perceived behavior of these same women. It took me many years to understand what was happening in interactions and conflicts I'd had with white women over the years. I couldn't understand why and how I would end up apologizing to them when I knew they had wronged me and done me harm. I couldn't grasp what would make someone I considered a friend lose her temper with me in a split second and with a contempt so sudden and vicious it left me breathless, and tell me I was being mean to her because I'd simply said that as a white woman she could not know what racism feels like.

More than any other, it was a now-former friend, Anna*, who brought it into focus for me, who set me on this journey of deconstructing White Womanhood and exposing its silent war on women of color. Anna and I had an explosive and—to me—utterly bewildering Facebook interaction. Anna is Anglo-Australian but spent many years in the Middle East, where she met and married an Arab Muslim man before moving back to Australia. Although we'd never met in person (and this is where I caution against assuming that people you know purely in the online world are genuine friends), we'd had many long conversations on Messenger as well as on the phone. With a keen interest in conflict and resolution, she avidly followed the Syrian Civil War and expressed what I still believe were genuine concerns for Syrians, even though I didn't quite share her perspective on the Middle East. Talking about Syria in public has proven to be difficult for me as much of my mother's extended family still live there. It is such a fraught issue that genuine discussion is impossible while smears and misplaced outrage are the norm.

However, on this occasion in early 2018 I felt compelled to say something as it was the day after U.S. president Donald Trump launched strikes on Damascus following an alleged chemical attack on a rebel-held town. Anna expressed support for the strikes in a post, which I found jarring, and I told her—*calmly*—that I was confused given the United States' act signaled a possible escalation of the conflict and further suffering. I was rebuffed as an aggressor who was hurting her and had to be publicly humiliated for it: the damsel requires her retribution. Merely letting Anna know that although I understood she cared for Syrian civilians, her stance was disappointing to me, I inadvertently unleashed a demonstration of strategic White Womanhood that brushed aside the actual issue—the airstrikes—and turned it into a supposed attack on her "just for being white." The result was a torrent of abuse hurled *at me* on a Facebook thread that, with her assuming faux victimhood, told me to watch how I spoke to her, mocked me about previous relationships I had discussed with her in confidence, and accused me of bullying and demonizing a "mother who does not deserve this abuse."

And guess what? Guess which issue didn't get addressed again? It was my query as to why she would support a possible escalation of war in a country not her own. Now, the personal opinions of readers as to which one of us was "right" about the Syrian conflict is not the issue here. The point is, she deflected from my statement on her political position regarding an issue that affects me but not her by turning the tables to implicate my supposed behavior. The political was reduced to the personal. Strategic White Womanhood is a spectacle that permits the actual issue at hand to take a back seat to the emotions of the white woman, with the convenient effect that the status quo continues unabated. White women's tears are fundamental to the success of whiteness. Their distress is a weapon that prevents people of color from being able to assert themselves or to effectively challenge white racism and alter the fundamental inequalities built into the system. Consequently, we all stay in the same place while whiteness reigns supreme, often unacknowledged and unnamed.

It's a familiar scenario for Middle Eastern women when it comes to Western foreign policy, this complete lack of empathy and understanding we routinely receive whenever we broach a discussion of our ancestral lands where, for many of us, members of our extended family still reside. Of course, my conflict with Anna was but a minor example with no bearing on any actual political outcome, even though it was the incident that more than any other provided the light bulb moment that helped me decipher what had actually been occurring all this time in my interactions with white women. More important than this single incident is how similar scenarios play out again and again, everywhere from the virtual pages of social media to the hallowed halls of the highest power. On U.S. TV panel show *The View* in March 2019, Meghan McCain, daughter of the late senator and Vietnam War veteran John McCain, gave a performance of strategic White Womanhood when she claimed that freshman Democrat congresswoman Ilhan Omar had made allegedly anti-Semitic tweets in which she'd criticized the relationship between the United States and Israel. "I take the hate crimes rising in this country incredibly seriously, and I think what's happening in Europe is really scary," McCain trembled. "And I'm sorry if I'm getting emotional." That's when the tears started. "Just because I don't technically have Jewish family that are blood-related to me doesn't mean that I don't take this seriously. And it is very dangerous . . . What Ilhan Omar is saying is very scary to me and a lot of people."

This didn't go down all that well with much of the public,

with some even taking the liberty to link McCain to my *Guardian* article. This was a heartening outcome, indicating we may be approaching a kind of tipping point where we can recognize and rebuke such behavior when we see it. McCain played the victim, assuming persecution that was not her own, and steered the conversation so that it was purely about Omar's alleged vices—completely erasing what Omar had actually said (she had clumsily criticized the pro-Israel lobby) as well as the political context. McCain played the role of the toxic white damsel whose job is to personally exhibit distress so that white society can project its vices onto "scary" women of color and continue on its merry path, unhindered by the implications of its own violence.

Ever since I published my piece on white women's tears and their strategic weaponization to silence women of color, I have seen the issue explode into the public consciousness again and again. Friends and followers continue to send me examples of white women's tears in action, the article is still making the rounds, and one young woman of color, Alana Kingston, even jokingly turned it into a verb on her Twitter account, @filo_pastry, as in: "today I got white women teared by my bf's [boyfriend's] mum." Several women have told me that although they have experienced the exact scenario I laid out, some of them multiple times, they did not really understand what was happening until they read my article. While the weaponization of white women's innocence and distress against men of color—in particular black men—was widely recognized, there was less material linking that behavior to interactions between white women and women of color. "I spend hours and hours talking and fielding (questions) and explaining to white women behind the scenes," Nadine says of the online feminist group she runs. "I wasn't able to identify it, though, until [your article] gave me the terminology."

Anjali*, a Sri Lankan woman in her mid-thirties living in Australia, had a similar experience. "I kid you not: there have been three instances in my life where after each it took me years to come out of a depressive funk, and I had no way to contextualize it," she says, "other than to say, 'You know what? Shitty things really, really happened to me. Why do these things happen to me? Why am I the only person going through things like this?'" By "these things," Anjali means being undermined by the unspoken race politics in the workplace. "It's a zero-sum game. An absolute zero-sum game, where (white women) are not willing to listen . . . For me the critical thing is to help women of color in particular to see it, understand it, and not be crushed by it—because it crushed me, it crushed *you*," she says, referring to me, "and it's about, how do we make sure other women don't get crushed?"

Doing my bit to ensure as many women of color as possible don't get crushed is the purpose of this book.

Anjali describes a recent situation in her workplace where a coworker who was relatively new to the office as well as the country, having moved to Australia from New Zealand, was emotional in a work meeting. While outlining why she didn't wish to work on a particular project with Anjali, she claimed that despite Anjali's more senior position in the organization, she herself had superior experience. "She undermined my authority at every step and my seniority in the organization. I had to step away. Because I knew if I went after her, I'd be attacked [for making her cry]," Anjali recalls. "I had every right to take the pugilistic approach and stand up for myself.

But I was in an audience of two white women. Guess which way that would have gone?"

What Anjali means is that against the tears of a white woman, a brown woman like her stood no chance. The one thing white women have had that sets them apart is their assigned innocence and virtue. But these are purely symbolic, existing not in the world of material reality but in the same world of representation that created the archetypes of Lewd Jezebels, Bad Arabs, and Dragon Ladies. Edward Cope, a prominent American evolutionary scientist in the nineteenth century, once scoffed that if white women were a nation, men would have long ago invaded them too. In a similar vein, bell hooks notes that although white American men in that era appeared to revere the virtue of white women, they didn't seem to like them very much. In other words: it's all a performance, a façade. But it is a façade that white women have insisted on sustaining, to their own detriment as well as ours.

The role of White Womanhood in the maintenance of white-dominated society is far more pivotal than most historians have traditionally granted. The women's public displays of emotion serve a crucial purpose. The Western concept of sex difference is, as Kyla Schuller summarizes, a racialized one, and the role of White Womanhood is to keep white society stable. White dominance is asserted and maintained through biopolitics: the concept that population management rather than direct control over the individual is the key to maintaining the status quo. Schuller calls this the "sentimental politics of life," or the notion that only the feelings of the civilized individual matter. Since the "true" civilized individual is, of course, white, then the fundamental role of White Womanhood in this system is to feel and to express those feelings so that her emotions become the focus of attention, leaving white men free to think—and act.

This history is long and it is brutal. In 1836, a white woman by the name of Eliza Fraser was shipwrecked off the coast of what is now called Queensland and taken in by the Indigenous Butchulla people on K'gari Island. When she eventually returned to white society she claimed to have been kidnapped and ill-treated—until her honor was saved by white rescuers. Her story was not corroborated by fellow survivors who disputed her account, saying they'd been rescued from certain death and treated very well. Nonetheless, Fraser's claims of mistreatment were taken seriously by authorities and were the justification given for the massacre and dispossession of the Butchulla from their traditional home. Most gallingly, K'gari was renamed after her and is now called Fraser Island.

Biopolitics is a deeply academic term. Still, I think people of color need to be acquainted with it, as it answers one of the key questions that white people invested in this system use to try to trip us up: "If racism is so bad, how come you're successful?" The answer is that biopolitics—the structuring of society in a way that favors certain groups over others—creates a society that makes it far easier for certain segments of the population to thrive while others are vulnerable to exclusion. In other words, rather than making it absolutely impossible for people of color to slip through, it makes it just hard enough that most of us cannot. That some of us do "make it" is not a testament to the willingness of white society to accept us but to our own often exceptional ability to navigate a rigged system. This is why people of color, and especially women of color, have to be at least twice as capable as white people in order to get half as far. The system was designed to make it as hard as possible for us but in such a way that white people can pretend the barriers simply do not exist.

Western feminism as it currently stands is simply not equipped to deal with this reality. It is crucial here to understand that the history of Western feminism we have inherited, rooted as it is in the politics of the nineteenth century and the struggle for suffrage, is a tradition that embodies this racial and gendered hierarchy. The white feminist battle is not one that aims to dismantle this hierarchy but merely seeks to ensure white women join white men at its helm by agitating only against those limitations imposed on their sex. After a white woman conflicts with a woman of color, her battle is done for the time being. The woman of color is sufficiently chastened and the white woman turns her attention back to invoking a nonexistent sisterhood in order to keep fighting "patriarchy." But this is a patriarchy they themselves have just ensured will continue, because their weaponized tears are a form and function of it. This kind of behavior is a key way by which whiteness asserts and retains its power. By keeping the old structures in place, white women's innocence and virtue serve as the front line of white civilization.

The insidiousness of this strategic White Womanhood is that it masks power. It is power pretending to be powerless. Women of color have even reported being "white women teared" at work by their managers. "Generally the experience is harder with people who are my superiors . . . the white tears come in full bloom there," says Kristina. By "tearing up," white female bosses can mask their power to their subordinates and use their White Womanhood to continue the charade that is the supposed inherent innocence and goodness of white women and the aggressive nature of brown and black women.

"I really wanted to believe that systemic racism in the workplace did not exist on such a personal or insidious level," Nadine says. "White women had always appeared to be my allies. But I think back to high school where I was called 'mean' for being honest or teased for not understanding some cultural nuance. White women are chipping away at the positives of our identity because we are unable to understand or refuse to assimilate to their way of communicating."

School is also where it began for New Zealand writer Shamim Aslani. The thirty-three-year-old, who is Māori and Iranian, recalls being "reprimanded" for her "aggressive approach" throughout primary and high school. Whenever she tried to assert herself to her white peers, she would make so many "cry" that she eventually internalized their criticisms and blamed her own "inability to communicate softly." The incident she most clearly remembers was at a school camp when, at the age of twelve, she tried to correct some friends' pronunciation of the Māori word *Mahurangi*. "I remember everyone laughing at me," she recalls, "and I responded to a particular friend with 'It's not a white word, it's a Māori word,' and she cried. I was called racist and told off for the tone I used." Shamim was the only student in her class from either a Māori or Middle Eastern background, and the incident hit her hard. "This tactic that essentially derails grievances happens from a really young age. And it's been a consistent theme in my life."

White Womanhood is the vanguard of whiteness. It is through the distress of the damsel that whiteness sustains its dominance. But the claims of emotional pain are only one weapon in its arsenal. Meghan McCain, for example, freely oscillates from strategic tears of distress to cynical outbursts of entitled anger—whatever works best in that moment. Another clip from *The View* in January 2019 shows her slamming her open palm forcefully on the table and shouting over her cohosts, "I am John McCain's daughter! I'm not someone who sits here and is okay with racism in any way whatsoever!"

I call McCain's bluff just as I call the bluff of all white women who claim to be above racism—not necessarily because they are consciously and avowedly racist, but because it is simply impossible for any white woman to be genuinely "not okay with racism" when we as a society have not yet reckoned with the fact that this model of strategic White Womanhood that has been honed and entrenched by centuries of colonialism is itself a racist concept.

There Is No Sisterhood

We are trying to solve the problem with the natives . . . the only thing I can see would [be] to get the children right away from their parents and teach them good moral, clean habits & right from wrong & also industries that will make them more useful.

—Annie Lock, Australian missionary, 1929

No uncivilized people are elevated till the mothers are reached. The civilization must begin in the homes.

—"Mrs. Dorchester," Women's National Indian Association, 1890

On October 6, 2018, the U.S. Senate confirmed Brett Kavanaugh as an associate justice to the Supreme Court of the United States. His nomination had not been without major controversy. A few months earlier, when it was revealed that his name was on the short list, Christine Blasey Ford, a psychology professor, claimed he had sexually assaulted her at a high school party back in the 1980s. Despite two other women stepping forward to allege sexual misconduct by Kavanaugh and a committee hearing in which Dr. Ford gave emotional testimony, he was sworn in with a vote of fifty to forty-eight.

On September 21 a posse of seventy-five seemingly all white women, many wearing "Women for Kavanaugh" T-shirts, had convened in Washington to profess their support for the embattled nominee. Led by his former colleague Sara Fagen, the women held a press conference to denounce Ford's allegations as "false" and inconsistent with Kavanaugh's "character." Kavanaugh, Fagen declared, "is a person of honor, integrity . . . and strong moral character. He is a good father, a good husband and a good friend. He's been a strong mentor and to all of us a good friend." And just like that, we had gone from the damsel in distress to the "damsel in defense." (I owe this wonderful turn of phrase to an anonymous follower of mine on Twitter who has given me permission to use it here.)

These seventy-five women weren't alone. A poll by Quinnipiac University published online on October 1, 2018, revealed that only 46 percent of white women believed Ford compared to 83 percent of black people and 66 percent of Hispanics. The picture gets even starker when white men are added to the tally: only 32 percent of them believed Ford was telling the truth. Although there was no gender breakdown given for nonwhites, the numbers reveal a stunning discrepancy not only between whites and nonwhites overall, but between white women and all people of color. Overall, nonwhites were almost twice as likely to believe a white woman making a sexual assault claim against a white man.

What could make so many white women, in the midst of the #MeToo movement, dismiss out of hand the allegations of an accomplished and respected fellow white woman who said her assault took place when she was only fifteen years old? The Kavanaugh debacle came a year after the almost-election of Roy Moore to the Alabama Senate. Despite numerous credible allegations he'd sexually assaulted underage girls, a stunning 63 percent of white women voted for him (even more than the 53 percent who'd voted for Donald Trump). Moore's narrow defeat was made possible only because of the voting patterns of people of color, most specifically black women, 98 percent of whom voted for his Democrat opponent and the eventual victor, Doug Jones. Then, of course, there is the forty-fifth president of the United States, who one month out from the election was seen on an old video bragging about grabbing women "by the pussy."

These voting patterns of white women have stunned white women and women of color alike. In the aftermath of the 2016 election, many feminists and writers both in and out of the United States (including myself), who were expecting a vastly different outcome, concluded that white women who voted for Trump had chosen to side with their race over their gender, that they prioritized whiteness over sisterhood.

But we were wrong.

These women are not "gender traitors" choosing whiteness over womanhood. Rather, they are *performing* their version of womanhood. White Womanhood, as Kyla Schuller argues, has been a key stabilizing feature of Western civilization, in which the role of the woman is to smooth "over the flow of sensation and feeling that makes up the public sphere, ensuring that white men . . . are susceptible only to further progress."

What exactly does Schuller mean by white women smoothing over the flow of feeling so that white men may progress further? This, perhaps: "I am friends with George Bush, in fact I'm friends with many people who don't share the same beliefs that I have," a defiant though visibly shaken Ellen DeGeneres told her viewers following a backlash after the two had been pictured laughing together at an NFL game in October 2019. Exhorting her critics to be "kind" to those with whom they politically disagree, DeGeneres doubled down by quoting a favorable tweet from a fan declaring, "Ellen and George together made me have faith in America again." This thrilled the studio audience as much as it did her fellow celebrities who took to Twitter to congratulate her on her "kindness" (Orlando Bloom) and her willingness to "Let Love Rule" (Lenny Kravitz quoting his own song title). Of course, they missed the point and it was left to political stalwarts Susan Sarandon and Mark Ruffalo to voice dissent and dispel the notion that the problem with George W. Bush is a mere difference of opinion and not the rather thorny issue of imperialism and allegations of war crimes stemming from the Iraq War. "Sorry, until George W. Bush is brought to justice for the crimes of the Iraq War . . . including American-lead [sic] torture, Iraqi deaths & displacement . . . we can't even begin to talk about kindness," tweeted Ruffalo.

❈

Throughout settler-colonial history, white women have aided and abetted the spread of white supremacy—a fact for which they have all too often been given an undeserved pass. The original edition of *Damned Whores and God's Police*, Anne Summers's withering account of the history of sexism in the Australian colonies, published in 1975, had the subtitle *The Colonisation of Women in Australia*. The book referred only to the experiences of white women. Summers has responded to criticism of her exclusion of Aboriginal women—whose country it is that was actually colonized—by arguing that dialogue between white women and Indigenous women is a relatively recent phenomenon. This may well be true, but who is responsible for this lack of communication? The book gives an important history of the subordination of white women but it chafes against the binary they were placed in—a variation of the virgin/whore dichotomy—by positioning them as either victims of male misogyny or perpetrators who internalized this misogyny and then wielded it like a weapon, not against the Indigenous population but against other white women. Compare this to the work of Aboriginal women writers and academics such as Aileen Moreton-Robinson, who states that from the perspective of Aboriginal women, all white women have benefited from colonization, and Melissa Lucashenko, who argues that white racism, not sexism or misogyny, is the dominant form of oppression experienced by Aboriginal women.

More recently, in *You Daughters of Freedom*, historian Clare Wright takes a deep dive into Australia's suffragist movement to shed light on white women's role in shaping the nation, a role that has been suppressed in our male-dominated history.

Wright does acknowledge the vote for white women came at the expense of Aboriginal and nonwhite immigrant women. The Commonwealth Franchise Act of 1902 that granted white women the vote also explicitly barred all Aboriginal people, Asians, and Pacific Islanders from voting, with the sole exception of Māoris in the vain hope New Zealand, which did not similarly discriminate against its Indigenous population when it came to the vote, would eventually change its mind and join the newly established federation. But, in her clear affection for the subjects of her study, Wright skirts around the central role that white suffragettes played in consolidating white identity at the expense of Indigenous women. Of a post-suffrage Australia, she writes: "It was now a nation that had reverse-colonised the landscape of ideas: the ideas of freedom, representation, and democracy that were the cornerstones of the new twentieth-century democratic state." Apart from its own unfortunate use of "colonised," this sentence is emblematic of a public discourse that does not recognize the inherent tension between Australia's history of violently exclusionary politics and its claims to be a world leader in freedom, democracy, and the "fair go." To put this another way: the struggle for suffrage was part of, rather than merely adjacent to, the crusade for a White Australia. The "freest girls in the world," as Australian suffragettes were called, demonstrate that the gains made by white women all too frequently consolidate white power by further disenfranchising people of color.

It is true to say white women were subordinated in settler-colonial society. It is not true to say they were bystanders to the colonial enterprise, and it is certainly not accurate to imply they were victims of comparable standing to the colonized populations. In fact, white women were often among colonialism's most vociferous proponents. Had Summers widened her scope a little, she would have seen that there was a third role white women played in Europe's colonies: that of the Great White Mother. It was through harnessing the Great White Mother that white women were able to access a form of limited power through maternalistic intervention into the lives of Aboriginal women.

Margaret D. Jacobs uses the term "maternal colonialism" to describe the role played by white women in the removal of Indigenous children from their families in Australia and the American west. Focusing on the sixty years from 1880 to 1940, Jacobs uncovers a history of white women far removed from the usual image of steadfast pioneers who were ignorant of the reality of the colonial project. As in other colonial outposts of empire, white women in Australia quickly learned to navigate European colonialism to their advantage, leveraging their status as both a subordinate class and a privileged class to "simultaneously collaborate with and confound colonial aims." When it came to the removal and institutionalization of Indigenous children, colonialism was "largely a feminine domain, defined primarily around mothering, particularly targeted at Indigenous women, and implemented largely by white women." White women decided that the removal of Indigenous children was "women's work for women."

In the American west and on the Australian continent, Indigenous child removal followed a similar pattern. White women drew on both their own sense of superiority as white Christian mothers and the derogatory representations of colonized women to justify their self-appointed fundamental role in "civilizing" the Indigenous population. Flouting the general rule against white women working outside the home, they argued this work was necessary so that the Indigenous population could be absorbed into white civilization. This double standard lives on today in alt-right figures such as Lauren Southern, the Canadian YouTube star who carved out a lucrative public speaking career before "retiring" from public life at the grand old age of twenty-four, only to rebrand as a moderate a year later. In one clip, despite being only twenty-two at the time, Southern was compelled to address many of her white male critics who felt she should be practicing what she preaches—breeding more pure white babies and serving her husband—rather than cavorting around the globe preaching about the imminent demise of white civilization and the urgency of white motherhood. "I'm not going to get married at twenty-two years old just so that I won't be called a degenerate on the internet," she declares in a video titled "Why I'm Not Married." "I think that people who ignore that there are exceptions to the rule are just as crazy as the people who ignore that there is a rule in the first place." How convenient. "Maybe I will end up a crazy cat lady when I am thirty," she quips (oh, horror of horrors). Southern does have one brief moment of insight: "We're longing for an age we've never lived in, and we're trying to recreate something we've never been taught or understood," she muses before inexplicably blaming this alleged sad state of affairs on the inundation of Marxist propaganda. Therefore, she concludes, conservative women today such as herself cannot be blamed for seeming hypocritical.

Southern is right in more ways than she realizes about her lack of understanding of this mythical golden age longed for by many white conservatives, for this hypocrisy is nothing new. The white women maternalists of old leveraged their roles as white mothers even though many of them were single and child-free. They reasoned that because they were women, they were much better placed than white men to understand and respond to the needs of Indigenous women and their children. This professed valorization of motherhood did not extend to Indigenous mothers, whom they disparaged as sexually immoral and unfit for motherhood. If white women were the only true women, then by the same token white mothers were the only true mothers. They saw their role not as depriving Indigenous children of their families but as "rescuing" and "saving" them from their uncivilized parents. In America, they formed organizations like the Women's National Indian Association to fulfill their aims. In Australia, the Women's Christian Temperance Union—some branches of which were active in the suffragist movement—and the Women's Service Guild appointed themselves spokeswomen for Indigenous mothers without seeking input from those on whose behalf they sought to speak.

Indigenous women "make slaves of themselves for the men," Idaho missionary Helen Gibson Stockdell complained. Similarly, the Australian anthropologist Daisy Bates asserted of Aboriginal communities: "All of their laws were formed for the convenience and well-being of the men only."

In other words, Indigenous society did not properly adhere to white notions of sex difference and sex roles. To white women, Indigenous women did not fit the white model of womanhood, and this made them either victims or perpetrators. They had different cultural norms around sex, which made them immoral. They labored outside the home to help provide for their families, which made them enslaved drudges.

Ironically, the white response to this perceived oppression was to oppress them. Let's repeat that. Because colonized women did not adhere to cultural roles akin to White Womanhood, white women assumed they were oppressed, and this status was used to actually oppress them further. One could fairly say that Indigenous cultures were not oppressive enough of women for the liking of white society. White women criticized everything about Indigenous motherhood, from how they carried their babies to the structure of the homes they raised them in. In the end, the only thing that could "save" these children was for white women to take them. According to Jacobs, between 1908 and 1937, some 58 to 78 percent of workers in Australian missionary organizations were white women, and two of these organizations were founded and run primarily by white women.

"The Indian child must be placed in school before habits of barbarous life have become fixed," declared Estelle Reel, who served as superintendent of Indian education for the Office of Indian Affairs from 1898 to 1910, "and there he must be kept until contact with our life has taught him to abandon his savage ways and walk in the path of Christian civilization." Reel fancied herself such an advocate for the Native American community that she gave herself her own nickname: the Big White Squ*w. Not only did she employ a slur to ingratiate herself as an honorary member of the community she was attempting to destroy, but she threw in an extra insult by alluding to her superior size. Similarly, notorious Australian missionary Annie Lock declared in 1929 that the only hope for the Aboriginal population was to remove their children and put them in service of the white population to transform them into model citizens.

The underlying motive for Indigenous child removal diverged. Americans, writes Jacobs, were keen to end the ongoing wars with Indians who were resisting encroachment on their lands. Australians were motivated to "breed the color" out of "half-caste" children, who were considered to be a "burden" and a "menace" to society. Neither the state nor the Great White Mothers could stop sexual contact between white men and Aboriginal women, so they sought to deal with the so-called "native problem" in two ways: by isolating the "full-bloods" until they died out—which they assumed was inevitable—and by absorbing the "half-castes" to make them useful to white society. The boys were "apprenticed" as laborers and the girls as domestic servants.

Where the two countries did not differ was in the duration of separation of child from mother: in both cases it was to be permanent. By 1911 every Australian state barring Tasmania had enacted some form of legislation permitting forced removal, and by 1921 some 21,500 Native American children were housed in boarding schools or had been placed with white families as laborers. In a remarkable feat of coincidence, I am sure, it turned out that what was best for Indigenous children also happened to involve free labor for white families.

The colonial maternalists encountered resistance from Indigenous women. So much so that Reel complained the Native woman was "much more opposed, as a rule, to allowing her children to accept the white man's civilization, than is her spouse." Those women who fought to keep their children, as well as those children who were taken and later grew up to object to the policy, were condemned as ingrates of "unfortunate character" and "morbid disposition." One such woman, the Nakota Sioux writer, poet, and activist Zitkala-Sa, wrote powerful but poetic critiques in such luminary titles as *Harper's Magazine* and *The Atlantic Monthly* during the first few years of the twentieth century.

> On account of my mother's simple view of life, and my lack of any, I gave her up . . . like a slender tree, I had been uprooted from my mother, nature, and God. I was shorn of my branches, which had waved in sympathy and love for home and friends . . . Now a cold bare pole I seemed to be, planted in a strange earth.

When Reel got wind of Zitkala-Sa's essays, she wrote a chastising rebuttal of her own. After "receiving the greatest care and attention at the hands of many good missionary women and having the Government spend many thousands of dollars upon her education, [she] has seen fit to write an article which has attracted some attention on account of its unjust character and the morbid disposition of the unfortunate girl."

Ingratitude is a common theme in white women's responses to the resistance of colonized women. Turning the tables and accusing the very Indigenous women they were wronging in a catastrophic way, white women used their more powerful status to silence the other women, essentially gaslighting them into submission. In early 1920s Western Australia, fifteen-year-old Daisy Corunna was taken to work as a servant for Alice Brockman, who later removed Daisy's own daughter, Gladdie, and placed her in a children's home at the age of three. Moreton-Robinson quotes from Daisy's testimony: "What could I do? . . . I wanted to keep her with me, she was all I had, but they didn't want her there. Alice said she cost too much to feed, said I was ungrateful. She was wantin' me to give up my own flesh and blood and still be grateful. Aren't black people allowed to have feelin's?"

Apparently not, and certainly not if those feelings clashed with the goals and aims of the state and the white maternalists. Sometimes, as in the case of Estelle Reel, the maternalists were more zealous than the state, while in other cases, particularly in Australia, they pushed back against the authorities. However, this was not out of empathy with the Indigenous mothers: while they supported the removal of Indigenous children, white Australian women generally objected to the rhetoric of "breeding the color out" because, argues Jacobs, "they believed it encouraged extramarital and extra racial sex and sanctioned male sexual privilege." In other words, they built their feminism and empowerment on the backs of colonized women.

Similar to Jacobs's concept of maternal colonialism is what historian Barbara Ramusack termed "maternal imperialism," the name she gave to describe the relationship between British women in colonial-era India—known as *memsahibs*—and local Indian women. In classic Orientalist style, the memsahibs constructed their own womanhood in opposition to the women they were colonizing, either dismissing them as sex-crazed simpletons or pitying them for their perceived inferiority. It was through this comparison that British settler women defined themselves as more enlightened and emancipated, handily asserting both their own superiority over Indian women and European cultural superiority over that of the colonized population as a whole.

We must be wary of any rhetoric from white women that follows the narrative of "rescuing" and "saving" brown and black women and children. Today we can see the aftereffects of white maternalism in the attitudes of white women such as Jenni White, a columnist for the conservative U.S. website *The Federalist*, who penned a baffling column in January 2019 titled "The Worst Racism My Children Have Experienced Came from Black Peers." White claims her two daughters, whom she adopted from Zambia, are being raised in a house that does not see color because "Why would I raise them to identify with a specific race as if being members of the *human* race weren't enough?" As if racism would disappear if only black people would stop calling themselves black. This allegedly hideous racism included merely being asked by their black pastor whether she was educating the girls about their culture. White, who claims to be a "*staunch* believer in Martin Luther King" (emphasis is all hers), says that once her daughters were brought to America, "they became Americans. Not African-Americans, not black girls." Assimilation and absorption into the default that is whiteness continues to be the frame from which many white women view women of other races.

Perhaps no incident has demonstrated this to me more in recent times than the case of Rahaf Mohammed, the eighteen-year-old Saudi Arabian woman who in early January 2019 barricaded herself in a Thai hotel room in an attempt to get to Australia to seek asylum. Rahaf announced via Twitter that she was fleeing the guardianship system that rendered her a permanent minor, and that her parents would kill her if she was forced to return to Saudi. Immediately, activists in the West, led by white women in Australia, started a #SaveRahaf hashtag on social media. White Australian female journalists described Rahaf as "terrified," defining her as a victim rather than as a brave young woman exerting agency and seeking to liberate herself. The prominent white female senator Sarah Hanson-Young tweeted that Australia was morally obliged to offer Rahaf "sanctuary and the chance to live free of discrimination in a country that respects women & girls." Apparently, Hanson-Young was suffering from a bout of temporary and very specific amnesia in which she'd forgotten that she had just penned a book, *En Garde*, detailing the sexism and misogyny she herself had experienced as an elected official at the hands of her own white male political peers—the very men to whom she was now appealing to "save" Rahaf. Yes, women in Australia enjoy more legal rights than their Saudi counterparts, but Hanson-Young's misleading rhetoric implies these rights are far more respected than they actually are. It is one thing to say women in the West are better off, quite another to declare that all live free from discrimination and disrespect. Here, Hanson-Young, whether wittingly or unwittingly, demonstrates both "maternal colonialism" and "maternal imperialism" in action: confounding white patriarchy through her outspokenness about the rampant sexism in politics but then collaborating with the very same male politicians she has implicated by praising them as the only bastions of respect for women. In the process, she reasserts the self-definition of Western women as more enlightened, and therefore perfectly positioned not just to support but to *rescue* the pitiable Arab woman from her inferior culture.

So intense was the media attention that Canada beat Australia in offering Rahaf a refugee visa and, as Australian media responded with characteristically churlish claims she had "snubbed" us, she flew to Toronto. Upon landing, and dressed in a "Canada" sweatshirt, she was immediately flanked by two triumphant white women, including Canadian minister of foreign affairs Chrystia Freeland, who were there to greet and parade her before a rapturous media. An op-ed published in *The Globe and Mail* followed on January 11, 2019, crowing about Canada's "moral leadership," and within days media was monitoring Rahaf's social media, approvingly noting her short skirt, glass of red wine, and breakfast of bacon and eggs. Subtle.

That Saudi Arabia has long been a staunch Western ally and that the weapons the Saudi government uses to oppress its civilians and launch wars on neighboring civilians are sold to it by Western governments became irrelevant. Ditto the fact that less than a year earlier, the Saudi crown prince had himself toured the United States, where he was feted by movie stars and media moguls alike. Although Egyptian American feminist Mona Eltahawy, who championed Rahaf's cause, did try to pay proper respect to the young woman's courage, Rahaf quickly became a symbol of something much more important than her own personal quest for independence: she symbolized the victory of the maternalism of white women, who had rescued her to bring her into the fold of civilization. Once again, the aims of the state and the aims of white maternalists had meshed to ensure the West had won, this time scoring a small but symbolically powerful victory over its old foe, the barbaric Orient. It is most audacious: the West helps make the Saudi government's draconian rule possible and then generously "saves" one Saudi woman from this very oppression, using white women as its mouthpiece.

Also left out of the narrative of saviordom were the

Indigenous women in Canada and Australia who most certainly are not the beneficiaries of "moral leadership" and do not benefit from any chance to live free of discrimination. In 2018, Aboriginal women made up 34 percent of the female prison population in Australia despite Aboriginal people comprising only 2 percent of the overall population. Some of these women are now free, but only because the unpaid fines that landed them in jail have been paid off by a crowdfunding campaign founded by Debbie Kilroy, a former prisoner turned prison abolitionist. Meanwhile, as recently as 2019, Indigenous women in Canada were alleging forced sterilization, and petitioning the government to change the wording of the Indian Act, first written in 1876, which limited First Nations membership to "a male Indian, the wife of a male Indian or the child of a male Indian." This means Indigenous women who married non-Natives found themselves no longer Indigenous under the law. According to *The Guardian*, changes to the law made in 1985 have expanded the definition to include such women and their children, but as of 2018, Indigenous women who marry non-Natives still couldn't pass down their Indigenous status to their grandchildren.

This is part of the reality of life in white society for colonized women that the white women who acted as the faces of the #SaveRahaf movement were complicit in whitewashing. Once again, white women shaped their own identities in opposition to nonwhite women, just as the memsahibs did long before them; this time appropriating the story of a young Arab woman's bid for freedom in order to assert their own enlightened, philanthropic status and present the West as a veritable paradise of women's liberation.

The language of the white savior is not one of liberation

or sisterhood: it is a language of imperialism. Nothing gives away a White Savior Complex like white women rallying to "save" brown women despite the gruesome history of what "saving" has entailed. White women have to free themselves from the lingering notion that white supremacy has socialized them into—that they know what is best for nonwhite women and their job is to save us from ourselves by turning us into mirror images of them. This must occur before they can even begin to think about their membership in a sisterhood that is capable of freeing all women from what we call patriarchy.

In Southern Rhodesia, white women reasserted class, racial, and religious hierarchies as they organized to leverage the Black Peril panics to their advantage. Women's groups such as the Rhodesian Women's League and the Federation of Women's Institutes began to chafe against white male authority not by rejecting racial segregation but by enforcing racial hierarchy and purity. This included supporting laws barring cross-racial relationships in the hopes of curtailing liaisons between white men and African women and improving their own status at the expense of the black population. In the early decades of the twentieth century, there were six thousand white women living in the colony. Of these, twelve hundred—20 percent—signed a petition condemning the legal decision to commute the death sentence of a black man who had been convicted of a sexual crime to life imprisonment. These women's groups also organized against concubinage, denouncing sexual relationships between white men and black women as a threat to white superiority on the grounds that miscegenation led to an erosion of respect for whites among the black population. Some even went as far as pressing for an extension of the death penalty to white men in an attempt to end any and all relations between white men and African women, even if consensual, and even though black female sex workers relied upon such liaisons for income in a white-dominated society that had completely upended their own way of life. In other words, rather than pressing to end unjust persecution of black men and demonization of black female sex workers, white women navigated the system to keep these racial inequalities entrenched while angling for better status for themselves.

Also petitioning the courts as a means of asserting their rights at the expense of other women were female slaveholders in the United States. In *They Were Her Property*, Stephanie Jones-Rogers debunks the long-cherished myth that white women were largely shielded from the day-to-day realities of slavery. Jones-Rogers uses the testimony of formerly enslaved people gathered in the 1920s and 1930s and corroborates their accounts with newspaper records, court documents, and written records by white men and women. She uncovers a history not of benevolent mistresses ignorant of slavery's brutality, but of slave owners who were heavily invested in their "property."

White women, Jones-Rogers discovered, learned from a young age of their future role as mistresses and grew into this role, treating their parents' slaves as both companions and subordinates. Often when a black woman gave birth, the master and mistress would allow one of their own daughters to "claim" the baby as her future servant. White parents often bequeathed human property to their female children, with land usually passing down to the males. Despite the legal custom of coverture, whereby a woman becomes "covered" by her husband much as a bird covers its young under its wings, theoretically subsuming both her identity and property into his, white women went to great lengths to guard their human property. Legal contracts were drawn up before wedding vows were exchanged, determining that she would have "sole and separate use" of her slaves. A white woman would not hesitate to take her husband to court if she felt he was encroaching on her rights as an owner of human property—and she frequently won. She also took charge of the disciplining of their slaves. If she thought her husband was too harsh, she would intervene to stop him. If she thought him too lenient, she would oversee the punishments herself. "Master talked hard words, but Mistress whipped," recalled George C. King of Lexington, South Carolina, whose former mistress would "whip [his] mammy 'til she was just a piece of living raw meat."

When enslaved people could bear no more and attempted to flee, it was often their female owners who placed notices in newspapers offering a reward for their return—with explicit instructions not to return the slave to her husband. Jones-Rogers shares a notice placed by one such woman, Elizabeth Humphreyville of Mobile, Alabama, on March 8, 1846, seeking the return of her pregnant slave, Ann, with a fifty-dollar reward. Suspecting her own husband was responsible for the disappearance and was pretending to be the owner, Mrs. Humphreyville cautioned the public "not to trade for her as the titles to said woman is in me *alone*" (emphasis in original notice). For white Southern women, "slavery and the ownership of human beings constituted core elements of their identities."

The term "mistress" has come to have an almost benign quality that suggests total dependence on a woman's brothers, father, and sons. Jones-Rogers rejects this, arguing that "mistress" as used in the antebellum South was more akin to its original English meaning: "In Western Europe, a mistress was 'a woman who govern[ed]; correlative to a subject or to [a] servant.' She was 'a woman who ha[d] something in [her] possession'...A mistress also exercised 'dominion, rule, or power.'" In other words, from the perspective of slavery a mistress was the equivalent of a master. There were social conventions and legal obstacles, to be sure, but slave-owning white women had legal means to challenge these, and they often won. Like their maternal colonialist counterparts, these female slave owners both confounded and collaborated with the prevailing legal and social customs, navigating their identities as white women both to challenge their subservient role and to leverage it to their advantage.

The sexual abuse of black male slaves by white women, for instance, was far less common than that of black women by white men, but it did exist. Despite the restrictions placed on white women—their sexuality was regulated by both law and culture, with women facing far greater legal penalties for adultery—they still flouted both law and custom, entering into sexual relationships with enslaved black men. Again, whether these can really be considered consensual given the power imbalance is extremely doubtful. In the same way that contemporary feminism frames rape and sexual assault of women by men as an exercise in power and control, this frame can be applied to sexual liaisons between white women and enslaved black men. "I have never found a bright looking colored man, whose confidences I have won ... who has not told me of instances where he has been compelled, either by his mistress, or by white women of the same class, to have connection with them," wrote the abolitionist military commander Captain Richard J. Hinton around the time of the Civil War.

Harriet Jacobs's *Incidents in the Life of a Slave Girl*, written in 1861, also spells it out. The daughters of the plantation owners, she wrote, "know that the women slaves are subject to their father's authority in all things; and in some cases they exercise the same authority over the men slaves." In other words, white women propped up the very system that oppressed them by leaning into rather than rejecting their role of damsel—an inherently subordinate role—in order to exert control over those with less power and status than them. Today, when white women invoke the damsel to silence women of color with unfounded accusations of bullying and aggression, they repeat this very cycle, ensuring we all remain trapped in it.

With this history, it's not surprising that the marginalization of women of color by white women was rife in feminism's first wave. The white supremacy of many of the giants of the suffragette movement is becoming well known. When Elizabeth Cady Stanton gave her famous speech at the first Women's Rights Convention at Seneca Falls in 1848, she demonstrated exactly what she meant by "all men and women are created equal" when she blasted Man for withholding from Woman "her rights which are given to the most ignorant and degraded men—both natives and foreigners." Stanton was an abolitionist and worked alongside the great Frederick Douglass, but that didn't stop her from referring to black men as "Sambo," a derogatory term for someone of mixed Native American and African descent that comes from the Spanish *Zambo*. Furious that the Fifteenth Amendment would ratify black men's enfranchisement before that of white women, she embarked on a Lord Cromer–like tirade in the pages of the newsletter she edited alongside Susan B. Anthony, asking, "What will we and our daughters suffer if these degraded black men are allowed to have the rights that would make them even worse than our Saxon fathers?"

Douglass was invited to speak at the 1848 convention, but no such invitations were extended to black women, setting the tone for the treatment of black women by white suffragettes. In the North, they excluded black women from their meetings and activism on the grounds it would offend their white sisters in the South. At the 1913 suffragist parade in Washington, D.C., black women were asked to march in their own segregated rally—an invitation Ida B. Wells refused. Meanwhile, black-and-white images from a suffragist parade in New York City that same year show what appears to be at least one white woman in a Ku Klux Klan–like cape and pointy hat.

White women were no strangers to the Klan. In her recent book *The Second Coming of the KKK*, which looks at the movement's revival in the 1920s, Linda Gordon coins the term "bigoted feminism," arguing that white women demanded membership in the KKK, seeking their own right to inherit property and be legally protected from domestic violence. At the same time, they supported political figures who advocated for restricted immigration and white supremacy. These women did not see any disconnect between their agitation for their own rights and their denial of the rights of black and brown women. In 1923, national Klan leader Hiram Evans formed the WKKK, which means exactly what you think it means.

Even outside of the Klan, white women defended and propagated white supremacy in both covert and explicit ways. Elizabeth Gillespie McRae notes in *Mothers of Massive Resistance* that it was white women who were at the forefront of the grassroots resistance to school desegregation in the mid-twentieth century. Warning that it presented a threat to the integrity of the white race, white women stoked fears of miscegenation and cautioned that black and white children would mix, socialize, and eventually reproduce.

By this time, the faith of the scientific community in the ability of humans to direct their own evolution had given way to genetic determinism—and white women were at the forefront of the eugenics movement. The nineteenth century was dominated by the scientific belief that humans could acquire new traits from their surroundings that they would then pass on to their children. This led to, among other things, a mild panic in the South that white babies who had a black wet nurse would "inherit" negative traits from her. It also compelled slave owners to whip a heavily pregnant slave by digging a hole for her stomach and forcing her to lie facedown; this, they believed, would prevent actual physical harm to the fetus while at the same time creating a lasting impression that would make the future slave less likely to resist their enslavement. The twentieth century, on the other hand, marked the rise of genetic determinists such as Gertrude Davenport, wife of the more famous Charles Davenport but also an accomplished biologist and avowed eugenicist in her own right. Eugenicists were obsessed with achieving evolutionary perfection. However, they believed this could be reached not by controlling sensations but by controlling the reproduction of "undesirable" women. The women deemed too "unfit" for reproduction were not only those with a degraded racial status but also the white disabled, poor, mentally ill, queer, and/or genderqueer.

The eugenics movement reveals that white supremacy is a project that cuts across all these oppressions. Disturbingly, race science rebranded as "race realism" is making an intellectual comeback. In *Superior*, science journalist Angela Saini reveals that contrary to popular belief, scientific racism did not vanish with the demise of the Nazis and their horrific implementation of eugenics. Rather, it simmered for decades at the fringes of the international scientific community. Confined at first to self-funded peer-review journals such as *Mankind Quarterly* that were shunned by mainstream scientists, race realists doggedly maintained their commitment to race as a biological destiny, awaiting an opportunity to push their dogma back into the mainstream. Saini uncovers links between race realists and high-ranking government officials. She notes that at least one editor of *Mankind Quarterly* has sat on the advisory board of scientific publishers that publish respected journals such as *The Lancet* and *Cell*. And she reminds readers that every so often race realists explode into mainstream consciousness with crossover titles such as *The Bell Curve*. Published in 1994, this hugely popular but largely discredited book by Charles Murray and Richard Herrnstein argued that black people had lower levels of intelligence than whites and that this discrepancy stemmed from innate genetic differences between racial groups. In other words, they claim that white people are simply smarter. *Quillette*, an increasingly influential website founded in 2015 by Australian former postgrad psychology student Claire Lehmann, bills itself as the home of "free thought" and an alternative to "postmodern" irrationality. It also regularly publishes opinion pieces by scientists with links to race realists. Indeed, in June 2019 it published a negative review of *Superior*, cowritten by Noah Carl, a sociologist who'd just been fired from a research fellowship position at Cambridge for sloppy and ideologically driven research that included defending the validity of racial stereotypes. Carl had attended a conference at the London College of Intelligence where eugenics and "race intelligence" were on the schedule. Nonetheless, his review of *Superior* criticized Saini's work as ignorant of science (Saini has two master's degrees), defended *The Bell Curve*, and even put in a good word for phrenology.

No analysis of any form of oppression in a Western context is complete without an analysis of the role played by whiteness. To put this another way, every form of oppression that exists in the Western world—yes, including class—is an oppression of white supremacy and its zealous ambition to scale the peak of human civilization and evolution. The white women of history have been given a pass for their role in colonialism and the institutionalization of white supremacy. We say they were "of their time" and didn't know better, or assume they acted out of either fear or ignorance. The truth is that calling them women "of their time" can be a legitimate excuse only if there were no serious challenges to their racist worldview in their time. Of course there were such challenges. Douglass, upon learning of Stanton's diatribe against the Fifteenth Amendment, responded:

> When women, because they are women, are hunted down through the cities of New York and New Orleans; when they are dragged from their houses and hung upon lampposts; when their children are torn from their arms and their brains dashed out upon the pavement; when they are objects of insult and outrage at every turn; when they are in danger of having their homes burnt down over their heads; when their children are not allowed to enter schools; then they will have an urgency to obtain the ballot equal to our own.

Douglass's words ring like a harbinger of those of Frances Ellen Watkins Harper (Chapter 3), uttered almost twenty years later and also largely ignored by white suffragists. The treatment of Harper demonstrates the extent to which white women deliberately marginalized and excluded their black counterparts. This becomes even more pertinent given we still see this kind of exclusion and appropriation of the work of women of color by white feminists today—perhaps most glaringly when white women adopt a self-serving "intersectional feminist" identity, both as a shield against criticism from women of color and as a weapon with which to silence us by claiming we are causing division in the sisterhood by raising issues of racism within feminism, as though they are intrinsically incapable of it.

There is no sisterhood. How can there be, when white supremacy has done such a thorough job of setting White Womanhood apart from the rest of us? There's a division, all right, but it is not caused by us. Yes, there is much for white women still to fight for, but consider that every single obstacle to their advancement is placed there by white society, by their own people.

Meanwhile, women of color have to not only battle white patriarchy and that of their own culture, but must also contend with colonialism, neocolonialism, imperialism, and other forms of racism. Given white women have never had to deal with racial and colonial oppression, it is not surprising—though it is certainly regrettable—that so many of them still regard feminism as a movement purely concerned with gender, leaving racialized women to keep trying to draw their attention to the ways in which various oppressions affect our lives. Until white women reckon with this, mainstream Western feminism cannot be anything more than another iteration of white supremacy.

White women and white feminism must also grapple with the history of white women's tears being used to demonize black sexuality. At the same time, through such things as disparaging nonwhite women as "slaves for their men" and "easy for the taking," and their involvement in slave ownership and child removals, white women participated in the sexual degradation and oppression of colonized women. This, I believe, is the link white women who agitate to end the sexual violence committed by men against women are missing.

White women continue to reap the benefits of the default to innocence they have been granted—but only when this innocence can be used to bolster whiteness as a system of power. "Women for Kavanaugh" demonstrates the pivotal role White Womanhood still plays in the maintenance of this system, but for some white women this privilege comes at a catastrophic cost. Not believing white women like Ford who make allegations—no matter how credible—against white men has its roots in this tragic and unpalatable history: usually, when white women made rape claims against black and brown men *they were lying*, and white men knew they were lying, because the cry of rape and attempted rape was itself a ruse for justifying white racial violence and fortifying white economic, social, and political domination. Sure, this gave white women a measure of power over black men and over women of color that they lacked in other areas of their lives, but it also ensured they stayed right where they were, sandwiched between white men and men of color in that racial and gendered hierarchy, with women of color lagging below. White men have been socialized by centuries of white supremacy not to believe the sexual allegation claims of white women—unless the accused is a man of color.

The price white women pay for masking the violence of white civilization is to in turn be disbelieved when they too are brutalized by it.

Let's revisit the words of Kavanaugh's damsel in defense, Fagen, who said Ford's allegations had to be false because Kavanaugh "is a person of honor, integrity . . . and strong moral character. He is a good father, a good husband and a good friend." Rape allegations are not and never have been regarded as being about the act of rape at all but about the "character" of the man accused of it—character being a euphemism for race. Men of color were not (and largely still are not) regarded as honorable, moral, good fathers, and good citizens. Punishing them for rapes they may or may not (often not) have committed served as a means of punishing them merely for being who they were, which is none of the things that white men like Kavanaugh and his damsels claim him to be. In a town hall meeting on the 2008 U.S. presidential campaign trail, Republican nominee John McCain responded to an older white voter who said she "can't trust Obama" because "he's an Arab." McCain shook his head, "No, ma'am. He is a decent family man." The unspoken implication, whether explicitly intended or not, is that Arab men are none of these things.

The claims of women of color, on the other hand, are not only disbelieved, they are rarely even noted—because, having "surrendered" their sexuality to white civilization long ago, they have long been positioned as lacking innocence. This applies whether the alleged perpetrators are white men or men of color, as Anita Hill discovered more than twenty years before Ford when she made allegations against Supreme Court nominee Clarence Thomas and had to watch him be confirmed regardless. This is what feminism must reckon with before any notion of a global sisterhood can even be on the table, let alone before white women can accuse us of dividing such a sisterhood.

White women are not like other women not because their biology makes them so, but because white supremacy—colonization's enduring legacy—has determined they are not. White women cannot speak of a sisterhood as long as they indulge white supremacy in its covert as well as explicit forms. Only when—and if—they regain the humanity they lost the moment they started to accept the fallacy that their "race" makes them better than the rest of us can feminism as a truly global project aimed at bettering the lives of all women emerge, be those women white or of color, trans or cis, nonbinary persons, poor or middle class, disabled, neurodivergent. It all leads back to the same place, and that place is the rift that European colonialism deliberately created between women, making white women complicit in the racism they have since been all too eager to blame solely on white men. Because, as Stephanie Jones-Rogers reminds us, white women were not passive bystanders to the racial crimes of white men: "They were co-conspirators."

Pets or Threats

WHITE FEMINISM AND THE REASSERTION
OF WHITENESS

*For as long as any difference between us means
one of us must be inferior, then the recognition of
any difference must be fraught with guilt.*
—Audre Lorde, *Sister Outsider,* 1984

July 2017 saw two big announcements in the world of pop culture. First, following a worldwide search, Egyptian Canadian actor Mena Massoud was cast as Aladdin in director Guy Ritchie's live-action adaptation of the animated Disney favorite. After decades of being relegated to playing terrorists, religious fanatics, machine-gun fodder, and double-crossing agents, an actor from the Arab-speaking world was set to play a bona fide romantic leading man—almost unheard-of in Western cinema since the heyday of Omar Sharif.

Just days later, it was revealed that for the first time in *Doctor Who*'s fifty-four-year history the beloved time-traveling TV alien was to be played by a woman, Jodie Whittaker. This was greeted rapturously by many—mostly white—feminists.

So rapturously, in fact, that the celebration quickly overshadowed Massoud's landmark casting. For weeks afterward, *Doctor Who* dominated social and online media as white feminists raved about how a female Doctor spelled empowerment and representation and *equality for women at last!* I suppose, despite the ample bandying about of words such as "intersectionality" and "inclusion," that it was too much to ask of white women to understand that, for many Arab women, the casting of a Middle Eastern Aladdin could be an equally, if not more, important milestone. Since the days of the silent screen, Hollywood's portrayal of Arab characters has been so relentlessly negative it has completely skewed the perception of Arabs in the Western imagination. This is what people need to understand about representation: it has real-world effects. A positive casting decision like the Aladdin one was more than just a landmark "first": it was a sign that Arabs, seemingly the final diversity frontier in Hollywood, were perhaps finally on the verge of breaking through and breaking down that destructive typecasting. Indeed, a few months previous, an Egyptian American, Rami Malek, was cast as Freddie Mercury in the Queen biopic *Bohemian Rhapsody*, a role for which he'd eventually win an Academy Award.

Frustrated at the lack of traction this significant moment was getting, I watched as, once again, white women triumphantly transformed what was a personal victory for them into a supposed win for all women. More and more, I was wondering whether most, if not all, white feminists—which does not mean "any feminist who is white" but refers to feminists who prioritize the concerns of white, middle-class women as though they are representative of all women—are even listening to women of color when we say we experience race and gender simultaneously rather than as distinct and separate impositions.

Like many other female writers, I am privy to more than my fair share of online trolling, and, as I shared in the introduction, it is the rare occasion when this abuse is not both gendered and racialized. More than once, I've been accosted on social media by white men demanding to know if I still have a clitoris. This kind of misogyny is not only steeped in racism, it cannot be divorced from it. More recently, a troll account on Twitter dispassionately informed me that my "ethnic animus" and "hostility toward feminine women" stem from what must be an overabundance of testosterone. In a throwback to nineteenth-century scientific racism, this gentleman had concluded that the size of my chin was too large to belong to a woman, which meant that I must be at least partly male.

Since I cannot separate my experiences of racism and sexism, sometimes I will identify more with my race than with my gender: in fact, increasingly so. I'm aware the story of Aladdin and his magic lamp is not without problems in its portrayal of the Middle East. Director Guy Ritchie does attempt to redress some of the virulent Orientalism of the film's predecessors, such as editing out some of the more objectionable lyrics referring to the fictional Agrabah as "barbaric." Yes, the story is still a Western construct, but let's analyze it not only on its artistic merit but through Stuart Hall's framework that looks at pop culture as a key site of power and hegemony (see Chapter 2). Watching *Aladdin*, I certainly did not feel I was seeing an authentic Arabian tale but nor did I feel I was witnessing Arabs being mocked and ridiculed, and after one hundred years of consistently degrading cinematic portrayals, this is actually saying something. There is much room for improvement, of course; trusting Middle Eastern filmmakers with the story would no doubt have resulted in a more layered and convincing film, one that perhaps would not have inserted Bollywood-style dance sequences into a story set in the heart of Arabia. Still, the film does represent a step forward. Not least because to me, an *Aladdin* with an actual Arab lead is far more indicative of social progress than a female Doctor, who, let's be honest, was never going to be anything other than white because, whatever barriers are still facing white women, their participation on-screen and in other spheres of public and professional life has been steadily improving.

In this context, the focus on the casting of a female Doctor—and again, let's be real for a moment, a thin, blond, conventionally attractive and youngish woman in a leading role is hardly the first brick of the revolution hurled through the window—left me feeling at first cold and then steadily resentful as white women kept the limelight firmly fixed on their heroine, leaving the *Aladdin* casting with its two brown romantic leads, and a black genie to boot, to drop from the headlines and public consciousness within days.

The *Aladdin/Doctor Who* discrepancy was one of the formative events that led me to conclude that what I was witnessing was more than a white-led feminist movement unsure of how to make room for brown and black women, but something far more destructive. What had been an unpleasant, sinking feeling secretly niggling at me for some time began to formulate itself into an actual question. What if the problem wasn't just that us brown and black feminists needed to speak louder because white women were still not hearing us? What if it wasn't that we needed to spell out our issues more clearly and calmly so as not to alienate them? What if the real problem was that our white feminist colleagues were consciously, deliberately, and loudly talking over us, shouting us down, snatching our microphones, and undermining our progress?

There were other hints. Like many other Aboriginal and black women in Australia and North America, the writer and trade union activist Celeste Liddle, an Arrernte woman from the Central region of Australia, was cautious in her enjoyment of the small-screen adaptation of Margaret Atwood's dystopian feminist treatise, *The Handmaid's Tale*. She liked the show but was put off by the effusive praise from reviewers and lay feminists alike lauding the program's vision of a bleak, bloody future that *might* happen to women. As Liddle noted in a comment piece she cowrote with me for *Guardian Australia*, not only were the bodies of black women mined to perpetuate slavery and colonialism for hundreds of years, but the children of Aboriginal women are still being taken away by the state.

The violence imposed on women's bodies in Atwood's dystopia has already been visited upon the bodies of black and Indigenous women many times over. Atwood herself has revealed that she researched and included only injustices that women have already suffered, so though the storyline is fictional the peculiarities of the misogynist violence are very real. Does misogynistic violence really not count until it is inflicted on the body of a white woman? Given that more women of color are being published than ever before, how can it be that white feminists are still not reading and heeding our work?

❀

Throughout my media career, I've been a big proponent of visibility and diversity. Repeatedly using my columns to critique the lack of brown and black people on television, in the media, in movies, even on the catwalk, I did so not because I view these as important ends in themselves, but on the assumption that more visibility will translate into more access, acceptance, and participation for all people of color. Now I wonder whether I wasn't inadvertently selling something of a false idol. In her 1984 essay collection *Sister Outsider*, the now-iconic black feminist academic and author Audre Lorde warned us not to mistake tokenistic inclusion for material change. Tokenism, she explained, "is not an invitation to join power" but an empty gesture designed to placate and even silence our demands for more equitable treatment. Close to forty years later, I fear we haven't got her message.

As my contention over *Aladdin* and *Doctor Who* indicates, I am well aware of how important representation and diversity are, both to those being represented and, more broadly, as indicators of social progress. What I have observed in feminist circles over the years, however, is that shallow markers of representation and diversity are serving as substitutes in lieu of much-needed progress. It's an illusion I don't think I fully appreciated until I was submerged in the relentlessly giddy and frequently hostile feminist discourse surrounding the 2016 presidential election campaign of Hillary Rodham Clinton.

Because the United States is the world's sole superpower, its internal elections are of more global importance than most. And because the United States has been deeply invested in the Middle East for many decades now, those of us connected to that region have no real option but to be invested in U.S. politics. As secretary of state during Barack Obama's first term,

Clinton continued the interventionist policies of many of her predecessors. Arguably more hawkish than Obama—she voted in favor of the Iraq War, which she later described as a "business opportunity"—Clinton has what I'd call a deeply Orientalist attitude toward the Middle East region. During a campaign speech at American Israel Public Affairs Committee, she boasted about having imposed the "toughest sanctions in history" on Iran during her tenure, and laid the blame for the Israel–Palestine conflict firmly at the feet of the Palestinians. This speech betrays the failure of many Westerners to consider that the primary victims of hard-line foreign policies in the Middle East are not the governments but the civilians. Iranians have suffered greatly under the sanctions, and Palestinians live under intolerable restrictions of their freedom and civil rights in the occupied West Bank, and under such disastrous conditions in Gaza that the small strip of coastal land that has been under siege from Israel and Egypt since 2006 has been described as an open-air prison by the United Nations.

As I tried to outline at the time, I did not see these types of statements as a reason for feminists to withdraw support entirely from Clinton given the alternative. I *did* request many times, to no avail, that feminist writers and leaders (particularly in Australia, where it wasn't even our election!) temper their rhetoric away from excited declarations that a Clinton victory would be a win for the rights of all women and minorities everywhere, which many Arab and other nonwhite women found alienating, and to cease dismissing any critique of Clinton as inherently sexist and therefore irrelevant. It couldn't have been that hard, surely, to support Clinton wholeheartedly without implying her role in imperialism is of no consequence.

As it turns out, white feminism's Middle East problem has quite the history. According to academic Sara Salem, way back in the 1920s frustrated Egyptian feminists who had been drawn to the suffragette movement stopped working with Western feminists when it became clear that resisting imperialism and championing national liberation were not on the latter's list of priorities. Among them was Huda Sha'arawi, most famous for defiantly removing her face veil on a Cairo train platform in protest of women's segregation. Egyptian feminists, writes Salem, felt their Western counterparts "were not putting into practice the democratic principles that they consistently spoke of and encouraged" by failing to speak out against the colonization of Palestine. In fact, some Western feminists were actively supporting the very colonial projects Arab women were attempting to resist. And so, disappointed Arab feminists, for whom gender justice was inseparable from national liberation, turned to African and Asian feminisms, where colonialism was a primary focus.

How sad to see that one hundred years later, this remains the case. White feminists still overwhelmingly approach the oppression of women as one informed primarily if not solely by gender, and, as a result, they cannot seem to conceive of imperialism as a feminist issue—if they think of it at all. The Arab world has been hit with military interventions and political sanctions, both before and after Clinton, which clearly attests to the entrenched nature of Western foreign policy. Clinton was furthering an already existing policy, not creating a new one, but how hard was it, really, to simply acknowledge why some of us couldn't find anything to get excited about when we knew our people were still going to suffer no matter who became president? How difficult could it have been to simply refrain from implying over and over again that all women should be "With Her"?

To do so would have required white women to recognize and acknowledge the role Western women have played in the continued suppression of Arab women's freedom. It would have required them to stop viewing oppression only through the lens of gender and to acknowledge that Arab women, like all racialized women to various degrees, are also inhibited by white racial dominance, and that this means there are times gender is not, as Salem put it, the "master factor" in our decision-making. It would also have required white feminists to accept that they too are marked by racial difference, that they are not raceless, and that their race privilege is predicated on the continued oppression of brown and black women across the globe.

Far easier, of course, was to continue to extol Clinton's virtues, gloss over her vices, and allow feminism itself to be further absorbed into Western power structures. So fraught is this, so fragile is the feminism of white women, that to merely not feel represented by Clinton was interpreted as an attack *on them*. Lina, a thirtysomething Palestinian American from Washington, D.C., tells me she feels "completely alienated from white women in America" even though "on the surface our values may seem aligned." She says her Palestinian identity makes her feel as though there is no place for her in American politics: "The two-party system does not represent me, protect me, or value me, and because of that, I don't have hero worship [of] politicians like Obama or Hillary Clinton." For the most part, she finds liberal white feminists either unwilling or unable to listen to, let alone validate her perspective. "They don't want to hear it, and they certainly don't want to hear about the suffering these politicians have contributed to."

Arab women, in attempting to voice their legitimate fears—and I both witnessed and experienced this firsthand—were left without any recourse as the tables were turned and they found themselves framed as bullies and abusers of white women, who felt victimized "just because they support Hillary Clinton." There was no distinction made between the so-called Bernie Bros, the supporters of Bernie Sanders who blamed Clinton for their own hero's loss, and feminists of color, who were merely requesting not to be forgotten in all the giddiness: we were all sexist and deranged Hillary haters. Days before the election, Van Badham, a *Guardian Australia* columnist, wrote a column called "Time to Hail Hillary Clinton—and Face Down the Testosterone Left," in which she did not deem it worthy to mention that women of color had repeatedly challenged the uncritical support of the presidential candidate. Let's be clear: when Badham writes that Clinton's "tenure as secretary of state was characterised by her unprecedented centralisation of gender equality strategies," she is not only silencing any Arab woman who puts forward a legitimate, thoughtful critique of Clinton, just as her white feminist forebears did to Arab women a century ago, she is channeling the maternalism of those frontier white women who came before her, and the Orientalism of those white men who have always insisted they know Arabs better than we can ever know ourselves. Moreover, she is doing so in a way that voids our voices by erasing our femaleness. Attributing all opposition to Clinton to masculinity, she essentially exiles us from feminism and womanhood altogether. It seems that to whiteness, the size of my chin isn't the only indication of my apparent excessive testosterone.

Perhaps this could all be made more palatable had more feminists taken something away from the 2016 shambles. Instead, it was more of the same in 2020 as white liberal feminists, many of them "Still With Her," shifted focus to Elizabeth Warren and promptly scolded brown and black women who didn't do likewise. When freshman Democrat congresswomen Alexandria Ocasio-Cortez, Ilhan Omar, and Rashida Tlaib endorsed Bernie Sanders, they were chastised in both traditional and social media for throwing their support behind "an old white guy" rather than a woman. How is it that so many white feminists still cannot grasp the many factors that shape the politics of women from such diverse backgrounds? Again, the issue isn't that white feminists threw their weight behind a white female candidate, it's that they continued to expect all other women to fall into line behind them—and treated with contempt those who didn't. When Tlaib, who has repeatedly spoken on how her Palestinian heritage influences her own leftist politics and support for Sanders, was recorded on video jokingly booing Hillary Clinton during the Iowa Caucus in February 2020, incensed liberal feminists seethed at her failure to show the requisite respect to Clinton, to whom she was apparently deeply indebted. Again, we are talking about a woman with Palestinian heritage expected to show deference, if not all-out reverence, to a politician who has shown little concern for her people simply because that politician is a (white) liberal woman. Predictably, Tlaib was hounded online and off until she apologized. Never mind that her own actions came after months of Clinton injecting herself into the 2020 campaign by repeatedly taking swipes at Sanders. These potshots include equating his policies to high school election promises on the Howard Stern radio show and taking the high school *Mean Girls* route herself, claiming in a documentary that, when it comes to Sanders and the Democratic Party, well, "Nobody likes him."

What can be said in response to all this? In *Talkin' Up to the White Woman*, Aboriginal academic Aileen Moreton-Robinson writes that Aboriginal women have been regarded by white feminists as either "assimilated or angry." I believe this restrictive binary applies to other women of color too, as all too often our attempts to challenge white feminists are met with hostility and our disagreement with accusations of divisiveness. There is no denying it: white feminists have learned to silence us by claiming that our pain is hurting them.

Why do white women struggle to read and apply the words of women of color? Lorde answered this question almost forty years ago. "For as long as any difference between us means one of us must be inferior, then the recognition of any difference must be fraught with guilt," Lorde explains. White feminists keep women of color trapped in those old binary archetypes because allowing us to break free is too guilt inducing since any recognition of racism in their own midst necessarily "threatens the complacency of those women who view oppression only in terms of sex." In other words, white women largely ignore women of color because their own self-image can only be maintained by viewing and treating assertive or, God forbid, critical women of color as aggressive and angry bullies who don't appreciate all that feminism has done for them. I would go further than Lorde and argue that white feminism has a vested interest in ignoring the work of women of color not only because ignorance is a shield from feelings of guilt but because as long as they can feign this ignorance, then their white privilege is never seriously threatened. It's not just complacency: it is a deliberate choice to uphold whiteness.

People are fond of describing forward-thinking people as "ahead of their time." This is a mischaracterization that fuels a false belief in an inherently linear social progress where positive change is inevitable. As much as Lorde's words seem prescient today, it would do her a disservice to describe her this way. No one is really ahead of their time. If anything, such people are exactly *of* their time because they have the capacity to diagnose the maladies of their era and prescribe the remedies. The problem is just how stubbornly resistant to this medicine the rest of us are: it's not merely that we are behind them, it's that we all too often resent those bold thinkers for what they tell us about our society and ourselves. And our response is to either ignore or silence them.

What Lorde outlined in *Sister Outsider* is what, a few years later, law professor Kimberlé Crenshaw would define as "intersectionality," which refers to the intricate nature of oppressions that meet to create new, compound forms of oppression that are experienced acutely by those who have more than one marginalized "identity." Like Lorde, Crenshaw made a point to include class in her analysis. Building on the work of black feminists before her, she used the case study of a lawsuit brought against General Motors in 1976 by a group of black women who alleged race and gender discrimination in the car manufacturer's hiring process. At the time, the assembly plant restricted all women and black people to certain—and separate—roles. The problem for black women was that the jobs set aside for women were off limits to blacks, and the jobs open to blacks did not permit women. Black women seeking work at GM were in limbo as there was clearly no job they could even apply for. Even so, they lost the case. According to the judge, only sexism or racism could exist, not both at once.

Mainstream Western feminism claims to embrace intersectional theory, but it may be truer to say it is weaponizing it. Unmoored from Crenshaw's critical analysis of institutional power, it becomes little more than a buzzword and a shield from legitimate criticism. More than once I have been scolded by a white woman who believed that because she identified as an "intersectional feminist," she couldn't be racist.

Perhaps this betrayal was inevitable. It certainly isn't the first time an initiative aimed at improving the lives of racial minorities has been appropriated by whiteness. The closer to power a person is, the less their "identity" is held against them. White women share the same racial characteristics as white men and so are more easily able to transcend gender-based oppression. Their proximity to white men gives them, as Lorde pointed out, access to rewards for identifying with patriarchy when it suits them.

What makes this all the more frustrating is that white women have been able to chip away at the chains that bind them through the tools gifted them by people of color. Perhaps the most obvious example of this is "diversity." The civil rights era made the 1960s counterculture and the second-wave women's liberation movement possible, and affirmative action has long included gender diversity among its aims. Affirmative action is viewed through a racial lens as unfairly benefiting undeserving blacks because of its origins in civil rights. In 2006, Crenshaw described this toxic discourse as "simply a gross distortion of the reality" because "the primary beneficiaries of affirmative action have been Euro-American women." Her claim that white women have most reaped its rewards is supported by evidence from various state departments. In 1995, a report by the California Senate Governmental Organization Committee found that white women occupied 57,250 managerial positions in California, more than those held by blacks (10,500), Latinx (19,000), and Asian Americans (24,600) combined.

For all the "I'm With Her" and "The Future Is Female" high-fiving floating around, it's becoming increasingly apparent that merely having more white women in powerful positions isn't going to result in a more just and equitable world. This reality continues to be glossed over by the rhetoric of "empowerment" and "lean-in" corporate feminism. But liberation is more than equality for some in an unjust system: it necessitates rethinking the entire system itself. Whatever gains white feminism is making for women, liberation is not one of them. Sure, more women are "leaning in" and advancing further and further in positions of power, and many of them are adopting feminist principles, or at least feminist rhetoric. But they are not showing significant signs of any intention to discontinue the same inequitable system. Indeed, despite being its greatest beneficiaries, white women in the United States are the likeliest group to object to affirmative action: the claimants in most U.S. racial discrimination lawsuits resulting from affirmative action are white women.

❖

"White people still run almost everything," *The New York Times*'s Australia bureau intoned in 2018 in a devastatingly brutal report on cultural diversity in Australia's workplaces. The whiteness above is noticed by workers below. Sonia*, a forty-something woman of color (she asked me to omit her ethnicity for privacy reasons), has been employed in the same medium-sized private sector firm for a decade. She is a mid-level manager, a position she only achieved after nine years despite consistently positive performance reviews and above-average results that, she tells me, were frequently better than the men and white women promoted ahead of her. Following a restructure several years ago, she has seen a handful of white women promoted or newly hired into senior managerial positions, disrupting the previously male-dominated leadership team. Any hopes, however, that a more gender-diverse management team would improve her working life were quickly dashed. "It used to be a boys' club," she describes. "It felt like no matter how hard I worked, I wasn't going to break through. I had to get results three times as good as my (male) coworkers just to be considered for a promotion . . . I finally managed to get promoted only to find it is now a white club."

What Sonia says has happened in her rapidly changing workplace is that as the male managers, including the small number of men of color, either left or were let go, many of them were replaced by white women. In that time, the cultural diversity of the entire workplace has shifted, with newly hired employees and contractors being almost uniformly white. Whereas before, women of all races, including white women, were absent from management, now there are white women in leadership positions; however, this newfound power is not trickling down to women of color. Rather, in an apparent display of inverse intersectionality, the privilege of white women is intersecting with the power formerly held exclusively by white men and fusing to create an even more impenetrable, compounded barrier for nonwhites, undermining any prospect of female solidarity in the process. Sonia had hoped that the restructuring would result in an easier pathway ahead for her—she describes her new, white male boss as "very supportive"—but has found her progress stymied by the new management, who, she says, are less likely than ever to reward or even acknowledge her ongoing achievements. Convinced she never would have made it even as far as she has if the company had operated this way when she first joined it, Sonia now feels she is on borrowed time, and is considering her future prospects. "I broke through the boys' club," she says, "but I don't think it is possible to break through this white club."

But how can Sonia break through the white club in her corporate finance world when even feminist organizations fall back on the masters' tools of white innocence, moral superiority, and victimhood when challenged by women of color? "Rage, tears, and confusion," described sociologist Sarita Srivastava back in 2005, is how white feminists respond to even the most tentative discussion of anti-racism. Western feminism has inherited the legacy of presumed moral virtue, innocence, and benevolence that has categorized the Western identity since its settler-colonial foundations. This means that white feminist women whose dominance is questioned by women of color frequently respond in ways that demonstrate this attachment, and Srivastava quotes women of color who found themselves repeatedly frustrated by white women crying "all the fucking time." One noted that the indignant tears, anger, and foot stomping were not only common but standard responses in any organization discussion of anti-racism. So standard, that it was only after it happened in every single organization she has worked for that she finally "realized it wasn't about me . . . after a while." Meanwhile, white feminists Srivastava interviewed spoke of their "fear" and "terror" that "at any second" they might be accused of racism, echoing the common position that being accused of perpetuating racism is somehow worse than being subjected to it. These feminists responded to any anti-racist challenge mounted, not as an organizational or analytical problem that can be discussed and rectified, but as a personal attack that goes to the core of their being and brands them as "racist" for life. By turning the tables, they use their strategic innocence both as a shield from criticism and as a weapon to get what they want from women of color: "I'm feeling attacked," "You are calling me a racist; how can you?" "But I'm the one who's been a victim all my life," are typical emotional responses. In this way, their self-image as good people is restored, and the woman of color is once again silenced.

I can understand why white feminists do not want to be seen as "bad." Feminism is, after all, a movement concerned with rights, justice, and tolerance. But the historical foundations of white society, built as it is on a racism and colonialism that claimed to be acting in the best interests of those it oppressed, do not just magically disappear because people want to be "good." The answer is not to fall back on defensive tears that disempower and silence women of color because the very existence of these tears aimed in our direction is both an indictment and our punishment. White feminists have to do what they expect of men: to separate the act from the person and look at racism as they look at sexism, as a structural problem that can only begin to be solved when they stop putting their hurt feelings ahead of our material harm. It is not enough for white women to have their hearts in the right place or to claim they don't see color and treat everyone equally. Feminism must commit to an explicitly anti-racist platform. And that means severing themselves from their historical and emotional attachment to inherent innocence and goodness.

As it is, white feminists keep apologizing whenever we raise these issues, telling us they will listen, they will improve, but they never do. And women of color are losing patience. Because white women can't not know. After all the years of viral articles, hashtag movements, and marches instigated and led by women of color, white women simply cannot claim they do not know what it is they are doing to us that is driving us away from them. All too often, we are expected to be content with getting our ideas out there only to see them quickly appropriated by white women as they join white men in the halls of power—the very same halls that oppress and exclude us.

There is no recourse for women of color who have been burned by white feminism. Internet call-out culture, often accused of "silencing" powerful white voices, is far more likely to be successfully utilized to further ostracize brown and black women. Those of us who attempt to make our grievances public—myself included—are met not with empathy and support but with derision and "blacklisting." This is how whiteness reasserts itself: through a white feminist movement that aligns itself with diversity and inclusion to get white women through the door but then slams it shut in brown and black women's faces.

White supremacy is not a left/right issue. It is the very foundation, the structure, the roof, and the contents of our society. Racism is not so much embedded in the fabric of society as it *is* the fabric. For all their differences, progressives and conservatives will often unite in tacit displays of white solidarity when it comes to ensuring people of color do not threaten whiteness to any significant extent. Think of how Alexandria Ocasio-Cortez and Ilhan Omar are so strongly rebuked by their own party as well as the Republicans (the accusations of anti-Semitism leveled at Omar did not gain mainstream traction until they were endorsed by Chelsea Clinton on her Twitter account). The right sees us as threats and their scorn is relentless unless we assimilate, disavow our own cultural heritage, and pledge allegiance to "Western civilization." The left claim to be our "allies," but only as long as we implicitly accept an inferior position and never attempt to get ahead of ourselves, let alone ahead of them. As long as we play the part of their pets. And that means allowing our hair to be stroked or playing the passive silent victim or acting the role of the nonthreatening sassy sidekick.

Feminism is not immune to this. For should we fail to keep up our end of the unspoken bargain, should we tug at the invisible leash that whiteness and white feminism have secured around our necks, then that solidarity is revoked and White Womanhood ensures it is always us, and never them, who pay the price for speaking out. Turns out, they too saw us as threats all along.

The Rise of Righteous Racism

FROM CLASSWASHING TO THE LOVEJOY TRAP

"Sister, I will give my child to you, that I will never have back again."

"This child will be claimed; as soon as possible; how soon I do not know."

"Oh cruel poverty!"
—Notes pinned to the clothes
of newborns left on the steps
of the New York Foundling, c. 1870s

J anuary 26 is a date that is becoming increasingly contentious in Australia. Whereas the Fourth of July marks the
date that the United States won independence from Britain, "Australia Day" celebrates the very day in 1788 that the
First Fleet of British ships sailed into what became known as

Sydney Harbor. Unsurprisingly, Aboriginal people, for many of whom the day is one of mourning, have been vocal in their opposition to the national holiday and every year nationwide protests organized by Aboriginal activists grow larger and louder as more and more Australians come to think of January 26, 1788, as Invasion Day.

Of course, every significant protest movement must contend with an equally loud backlash, and so it is with this one. In 2019, a striking photograph taken at one of the huge rallies made the rounds on social media. I shared this image of an oversized Aboriginal flag set against a cloudless blue sky to my public Facebook page without any additional commentary of my own, preferring to let the photo and the organizers of the protests do the talking. Nonetheless, an account I did not recognize and had never before interacted with took exception to the picture. Calling me a "vile bitch" who used Aboriginal issues to "fuel hatred against whites," the troll told me to "calm [my] Arab ass down" (not that I'd actually said anything) before asking me, "What have you done for Aboriginal people? When was the last time you went to these remote communities?"

This is an ethical bait and switch. What this internet troll had done, in addition to invoking the Angry Brown Woman by scolding me to tone it down despite the fact I had literally not said a word, was to target me as a non-Indigenous person attempting to support a movement run by Indigenous activists. Baiting me by accusing me of not doing enough for Aboriginal communities, he then switched the focus of the debate entirely: suddenly we weren't even discussing Australia Day—I was defending myself against accusations of being inhumane, hypocritical, and blithe to the "real suffering" of

Aboriginal people, most especially that of children. As an added bonus to himself, he got to occupy some sort of moral high ground by doing nothing but accusing me of not doing enough. This is a tactic that I am seeing play out more and more online, in the media, and in the political sphere. Indeed, just days after this online exchange, the same taunt was used by a prominent Australian daytime television host, Kerri-Anne Kennerley. On live morning television, Kennerley vented about the "hypocrisy" of activists who attended the Invasion Day marches but who have never been to remote Aboriginal communities where "five-year-olds are being raped and their mothers are being raped." The implication being that Aboriginal children and women need to be saved from Aboriginal men.

I call this type of bait and switch the Lovejoy Trap. Helen Lovejoy, of course, is the prim cartoon wife of Reverend Timothy Lovejoy on *The Simpsons*, and the star of an enduring meme for her performatively anguished wail emitted during a community debate on whether or not to reintroduce prohibition: "Won't somebody please think of the children?" The Lovejoy Trap is a means of neutralizing challenges to the status quo by taking the onus off the actual issue at hand, in this case the insensitive celebrations taking place on the very day that began the ongoing dispossession of Aboriginal people from their land, by not only accusing those making the challenge of being uncaring hypocrites but by implicitly positioning Aboriginal people as responsible for their own suffering. Funnily enough, exhorting well-meaning people to "think of the children" is exactly how this trap first took hold.

In the mid-nineteenth century, Reverend Charles Loring Brace was a young social reformer with a feverish wish to cleanse New York City's Lower East Side of its so-called "dangerous classes," also rather tellingly referred to as "street Arabs"—Eastern European immigrant children from impoverished families. He also had a fervent belief in the power of transforming these unwashed street vagrants of the rapidly industrializing city into useful domestic laborers. In 1853, Brace founded the Children's Aid Society (CAS), which would go on to become the most prominent and praised child welfare organization in the United States. Its crowning achievement was its "placing out" plan, in which up to one hundred thousand Irish, German, and Italian American children were sent on "orphan trains" out west to serve as laborers in rural homes. Around half of these children had at least one living parent, indicating that "orphan" was less a state of material reality and more a state of Brace's mind.

Kyla Schuller argues that Brace's audacious vision, ostensibly a program to lift the children out of poverty, was in fact an example of the prevailing scientific belief that humans could direct their own evolution. Poverty was seen not as a consequence of capitalism and industrialization, but as a moral failing on the part of the child's parents. Removing them from that toxic environment and exposing them to good, hardworking American families would not only satisfy capitalism's endless requirement for cheap labor, it would transform them into worthwhile members of the community.

It would make them white.

By now, it will likely surprise you not an iota to learn that anyone who objected to this white-ification of almost-white immigrant children was accused of not caring about lifting the kids out of poverty or of cleaning up the crime-ridden tenement neighborhoods of the city. The real aim, however, was to redesign the demographics of the Lower East Side. That so many of those children did not fare very well in their new homes was largely irrelevant: this was a project that aimed at repairing capitalism's growing reputation for callousness and at bringing young Irish, German, and Italian children into the bosom of white civilization. The program was so successful that many CAS-inspired child welfare organizations popped up with similar programs, which ran until the late 1920s.

Brace's pioneering use of the Lovejoy Trap shifted the entire frame of the debate in favor of the CAS. Before his intervention there was antipathy toward removing children from their free parents (there were, of course, no such qualms when it came to children of the enslaved). He is now generally praised as a radical and a progressive by social welfarists, but Schuller carefully outlines how his philanthropy was fueled less by humanitarianism and more by his desire to turn these "street Arabs" into productive, "civilized" humans. His vision served as a prototype for the Indigenous child removals that became official policy in Australia and the United States. By cloaking it in the rhetoric of child welfare, Brace was able to counter any objections with his own accusation that his critics did not care about the well-being of children. What did it matter that some children still had living parents when it was their future that was at stake—a future that could be spent as a productive member of white society rather than following in the footsteps of their primitive parents? He was doing it for their own sake, you see. *Won't somebody please think of the children?*

Well, somebody did. By the 1870s poverty was considered so shameful that poor families were voluntarily surrendering their newborn infants to the wicker cradles set up for this very purpose on the steps of charity organizations across the city. Many pinned heartbreaking notes to their baby's clothing, promising to return and collect them when they could afford it. Brace's vision had successfully convinced poor white parents that their poverty-stricken status meant they had forfeited their parental rights to their own children.

The case of Charles Loring Brace and his orphan trains demonstrate the fluidity of whiteness and its contingency on capitalism. White people are not united by a shared ethnicity: they are united by access to institutional power. Historically, being white—by which I mean Western European—was a necessary characteristic for admission into white society, but it was not sufficient. And that means that some who we would easily categorize as "white" today were excluded from white society, including sex workers, criminals, and the working class. Over time, white power structures have adapted to the resistance of the white working class in much the same way as they did to suffrage and feminism: by granting them admission into the white club but without really addressing the conditions that made poor whites poor. For lower-income whites this proximity to power is little more than an illusion that promises upward mobility and opportunity if they are prepared to "work hard" and lift themselves "up by their bootstraps." This reward rarely materializes but nonetheless elicits loyalty to the system and a willingness to blame "outsiders" for their economic conditions. Brexit and the political demise of former Labour leader Jeremy Corbyn in the 2019 U.K. election demonstrate just how powerful this identification with a white national identity can be. Corbyn's working-class-friendly platform included the repeal of austerity measures and keeping the National Health Service (NHS) completely in public hands, but he was still no match for his conservative Tory competitor and prime minister Boris Johnson who campaigned and won a landslide victory on the back of the nationalistic slogan "Get Brexit done."

This means that there has always been ripe potential for solidarity between people of color and those more marginalized whites, and that such a solidarity could undo white supremacy. And whiteness knows this. This is why our governments expend so much money to detain asylum seekers in detention and lock their children in cages. It is why white workers are encouraged to blame immigrants for both stealing jobs and simultaneously lounging around on welfare. It is why immigrant, black, and Indigenous populations are blamed for the bulk of everything from social security fraud to sexual crime. Not only does invoking and stoking racial differences prevent solidarity from taking effect, it backfires and keeps class divisions as well as racism alive. The rise of socially conservative, anti-immigrant groups on the left, such as Blue Labour, which emerged in the wake of Corbyn's defeat, sadly indicates that many writers and activists on the white left are aware of how race is manipulated to foster these divisions. But all too often, the overwhelming response has been to pressure people of color to tone down their talk of racism in favor of a singular focus on "the real oppression," which is class. Apparently, it is our insistence on resisting racism that is to blame for racism. How many people of color reading this have been admonished for supposedly driving working-class white people into the arms of the populist right and causing the election of Donald Trump? I know I have—and I am not even American.

This line of thinking does not and cannot account for the destructive power of racialization. We think race and racism are natural now, but these classifications were deliberately constructed in order to permit and justify exploitation of brown and black people. Over time, we have collectively forgotten this in favor of assuming that it's always been this way. Responding to claims of racism by pointing to the economic conditions of the white working class—what I call classwashing—may be tempting, but there are at least three massive problems with this. Classwashing excludes people of color from the working class, it makes racism a working-class problem, and it frees them and white society in general of responsibility for racist voting habits. Classwashing is an attempt to absolve and deny the existence of racism at all strata of society by turning the tables to admonish people of color that it is unfair to talk about racism at the polling booth because the white working class is disenfranchised. Or they are uneducated. Or they just don't know any better. We need to hear them out and then we will see their racism will dissolve as soon as their economic needs are met. On and on it goes.

But this is a tale as old as colonialism. There is a reason why the first blackface minstrel shows are believed to have taken hold in those slums of New York City populated by poor Irish immigrants. In *Black Like You*, historian John Strausbaugh argues that, seeing the social acceptance of the middle and upper classes as their only route out of poverty, the Irish used blackface to align themselves not with their similarly impoverished black neighbors but with the elite WASPs. "They are using blackface as a way of saying to white Protestant New Yorkers and other people in the urban settings, 'We're as good as you, we're white like you—we're making fun of black folks, that makes us white like you,'" Strausbaugh told *The Guardian* in a 2019 interview. Who says "identity politics" is the preserve of people of color?

In 1997, well before identity became the hot-button issue it is today, renowned Egyptian feminist Nawal El Saadawi wrote an essay called "Why Keep Asking Me About My Identity?" In her sixties at the time, she was astonished that, having regarded herself as both Arab and African all her life without controversy, Western colleagues with their own national identity firmly secured, began to ask why she considered Egyptians to be Arab or Egypt a part of Africa. "[Now] I should say my identity is Middle Eastern . . . Now I no longer know the continent in which Egypt can be found, nor do I know if I am Arab, or African, or whether I should be here at all." She places the struggle over history and the struggle over identity as part and parcel of the struggle for power: "It is those who possess military and nuclear power and economic power, those who invade us and take away our material and cultural sustenance, those who rob us of our own riches and our labour and our history, who tell us what our identity is."

The antipathy toward "identity politics," which now seems to describe any mention of race whatsoever, from across the political spectrum betrays this entitlement to categorizing identity, as if it is the prerogative of white society alone to decide what other people are and can call themselves. To be a person of color, especially a woman of color, was never something that those who set about racializing the world saw as anything to be proud of. Our claiming and taking actual pride in what was meant to be an insult has seen white society once again attempt to set the standards for humanity by dismissing our attempts to define and advocate for ourselves as divisive posturing. For conservatives, "identity politics" supposedly divides the population by inhibiting national cohesion. This is merely a euphemism for assimilation into the white default. For progressives, "identity politics" divides the left by shifting the focus away from a class consciousness. This is a false allegation that belies the link between race and class. Settler-colonial societies were built on Indigenous dispossession, literally seizing ownership of land and all its resources from its traditional and rightful owners. Their labor was then exploited and, when this was not enough to fill the coffers of colonizers, enslaved labor was imported from Africa to ensure white society continued to prosper on stolen land. It is not so much a matter of race *versus* class, but of recognizing that race is integral to class. In the words of Stuart Hall, "Race is the modality through which class is lived."

Since the defeat of social democrat Bernie Sanders to Hillary Clinton in the 2016 primaries, this antipathy to "idpol," as abbreviated in internet parlance, has seen a new breed of millennial socialist emerge. Giving themselves the moniker "dirtbag left" to indicate their rejection of faux civility, they take particular aim at those sections of the left they deem to be "woke scolds": essentially any progressive who doesn't center class in every analysis or who "lectures" others on aspects of identity. These "class scolds" as my friend Brendan jokingly named them, arose out of the (sometimes justifiable) resentment toward the Clinton campaign's use of gender politics. However, in the same way as white feminism places the white woman as the universal norm of womanhood, the dirtbag left similarly centers the needs of the white worker. What this means in practical terms is, just as white feminists accuse women of color of dividing the sisterhood, the dirtbags similarly locate the lack of a cohesive leftist movement on people of color who dare talk about race—even those of us who analyze racism as a form of structural oppression intrinsic to Western capitalism. This is significant because, as black studies professor Kehende Andrews argues, Marxism fundamentally fails to accept this central role played by the exploitation of brown and black people in Western capitalism. Like other white people who subscribe to myths about the inherent goodness of Western civilization, Marxism also minimizes the role of racism in society. To Andrews, the traditional Marxist understanding of class, far from being a challenge to oppression, is actually key to perpetuating whiteness because "the idea that poor Whites suffer equally to or worse than Black communities allows issues of racism to be obfuscated."

Nawal El Saadawi warned that the separation of culture, class, gender, and other forms of identity from politics is not an accident nor is it benign. Rather, it strips culture of its history and turns identity into a performance by undermining its connection to time, place, and self-determination. The struggle for identity, she insists, is a "total struggle" and this depends as much on our material existence as our cultural traditions. To separate identity from economics and land rights and language turns culture into little more than those exhibitions found at arts festivals and multicultural events, a spectacle that exists for others to enjoy and consume. Aboriginal academic Tyson Yunkaporta makes a similar observation more than twenty years later. If you are an Aboriginal person in Australia, he writes, "you perform and display the paint and feathers, the pretty bits of your culture, and talk about your unique connection to the land while people look through glass boxes at you, but you are not supposed to look back, or describe what you see." To counter this, El Saadawi calls for global alliances between people of color living in the West and those in the global south, alliances that recognize and respect cultural differences between them but that can also unite in a common struggle against oppression. In other words, we need to look back out from within the glass box, to write what we see—and to act accordingly. The Combahee River Collective, a 1970s black feminist movement, also knew this. They organized to articulate and advocate for "the real class situation of persons who are not merely raceless, sexless workers, but for whom racial and sexual oppression are significant determinants in their working/economic lives." While the collective was primarily concerned with conditions facing black women, like El Saadawi they also recognized the importance of a collective outlook. "The inclusiveness of our politics makes us concerned with any situation that impinges upon the lives of women, Third World and working people . . . We might, for example, become involved in workplace organizing at a factory that employs Third World women or picket a hospital that is cutting back on already inadequate heath care to a Third World community." For the collective, the most effective means of organizing came out of their own identity as black women, not because they only cared about black women but because such is their degraded status that if black women were free everyone else would also be free.

This is why women of color are the easiest to discredit: silencing us ensures that race, class, and gender continue to be widely accepted as disparate concepts, and this conveniently keeps the system ticking along, pointing the finger back at us for daring to name it. In my own case, for years I was able to withstand the attacks from white supremacists and other racists on my social media accounts that seem to come with the territory of writing for public consumption. What finally led me to shut down my almost decade-old Twitter account in late 2019, however, was a campaign of relentless harassment, smearing, and abuse from a group of Australian wannabe dirtbag leftists determined to push me—and my work—out of the public discourse. They almost succeeded.

Like the class scolds, those who resort to the Lovejoy maneuver also seek to turn the tables against people of color. Whereas class scolds hide their racial hostility behind appeals to class solidarity, the Lovejoys cynically and effectively mask their economic and political imperatives by invoking the suffering and well-being of children to neutralize any objections because that is where our humanity is most easily tested. What kind of *monster* doesn't want to protect children? However, this maneuver is not limited to invoking the plight of children. In fact, it is becoming a particularly effective tactic when it comes to the sexual assault—both real and imagined—of women of color, albeit only in very specific circumstances. It seems the one time settler-colonial societies are concerned enough about gender-based violence to do or say much about it is when (as the Black Peril moral panics that swept Southern Rhodesia in the early twentieth century demonstrated) the alleged perpetrators are men of color and the proposed solution involves an intervention into those men's communities and countries. As Gayatri Spivak famously put it, "white men are saving brown women from brown men." This phenomenon has long been used to rationalize intervention in the "Middle East," as in the case of Lord Cromer's adventures in Egypt (see Chapter 2). More recently, since the 1990s, Western wars against Arab, Balkan, and Central Asian nations have been pinned to the pretext of saving brown women from sexual violence. Ironically, at the same time there has been growing recognition of the feminist argument that rape itself is a weapon of war. What this means is that by "saving" brown women from sexual violence, Western countries staging interventions and incursions have actually been exposing the women to greater risk of same.

In November 2001, First Lady Laura Bush gave a radio address linking the "war on terror" and the U.S. invasion of Afghanistan, begun on October 8, to the "severe repression against women" in that country. "[The] fight against terrorism is also a fight for the rights and dignity of women," she declared. While her words may sound feminist, what numerous scholars and authors have pointed out since is that they demonstrate how governments can and do appropriate "feminist rhetoric without undergoing legitimately feminist transformations." There was something missing from the first lady's speech, and from subsequent reports from the U.S. State Department, and from media reports with such sensationalistic and familiar titles as "Lifting the Veil," which focused on the repressive policies of the Taliban—including the denial of education to girls and women and the denial of freedom of movement and access to health care. What was missing was the historical context of how the Taliban had come to power, and the role that Western powers had played in their rise. The Taliban emerged from former U.S. allies the mujahideen ("holy warriors"), who were partly funded by the United States in order to counter the Soviet invasion in 1979.

There is a Western tendency to view Islamist extremism as intrinsic to Islam and as popular among Muslims, but groups such as the Taliban enjoyed only very minimal support from the Afghan population before the war against the Soviets. Ten years and ten billion U.S. dollars in military aid later, when the United States walked away from the country immediately after the defeat of the Soviets, the stage was set for the Taliban to take charge, and they did. Without this crucial context, including the willingness of Western powers to look the other way when it came to human rights abuses of their allies, the blame falls to Muslims themselves, and the subsequent demonization creates more, not less, suffering for Muslim, Afghan, and Arab women. On one level, it is not surprising that there is such widespread fear and antipathy toward Islam when politics and history are omitted from the official narrative. In the absence of information, the gaps are filled with religion: if this is happening, it must be because Muslims have an inferior and violent culture. Or so the thinking shaped by centuries of Orientalism goes. The 2001 invasion may have deposed the Taliban officially, but not only do many of their repressive policies survive, they are also still active in two-thirds of the country and control significant swathes of it.

More ironic still is that the status of women in Arab- and Muslim-majority countries is used as a rationale for military intervention even though the military itself continues to be less concerned about sexual assault in its own ranks. Sexual assault reports in the U.S. military have risen every year since 2012 but Western and Western-allied soldiers are still framed as the saviors of brown women. As sociologist Josh Cerretti argues, not only is rape a weapon of war, it is a weapon of warriors: an endemic issue that has simply not been taken seriously by the military. On the relatively rare occasions when sexual assault by U.S. servicemen has been prosecuted, whether the victims were their own peers or civilians, it is overwhelmingly black servicemen who have been charged and convicted. The problem those of us who attempt to shine a light on this selective justice face is that it becomes almost impossible to object to such disproportionate punishment without opening yourself up to accusations of defending rapists: if the military is staging an intervention in order to rescue brown women from sexual abuse, then objections to this intervention can and are very easily framed as not caring about the protection of women. If this sounds familiar, it should—it is the same rationale given for lynching during Segregation.

Cerretti focuses primarily on incidents involving the U.S. military in the 1990s, but the selective and self-serving prosecution and condemnation of men of color for sexual crimes against women of color—again, whether real or imagined—also played out in Australia in the lead-up to World War II. In 1936, a series of outraged newspaper reports detailed the "poaching" of Aboriginal women by Japanese pearlers. Here, there was much consternation and outrage that Japanese fishermen were engaging in sexual liaisons with Aboriginal women and paying for the services of Aboriginal sex workers. Apparently keen to preserve the entitlement they felt to the bodies of Aboriginal women, white men accused the Japanese of sexual exploitation and abuse, previously the prerogative of white men. Once again, pointing out the hypocrisy of demonizing Japanese men when white men had been doing this very thing for decades would only have led to accusations of defending forced prostitution and the abuse of Aboriginal women. There was such a scandal that Australia closed its waters to all foreign pearling craft and established a base off the Northern Territory from which Japanese luggers were shot at with machine guns to prevent them entering Australian territory. Historian Liz Conor notes the hypocrisy of the sudden flurry to "protect" Aboriginal women from alleged abuse from Japanese pearlers given there had been "decades of unheeded reports of violence toward Aboriginal women by white pearling masters." Whereas any accusations made against white men had long been dismissed through the rhetoric of "black velvet" that regarded Aboriginal women as incapable of virtue and chastity, no such defense was mounted for the Japanese men. The authorities intervened in such a way that positioned the bodies of Aboriginal women as their property. Once again, white people set the standards that ensure their victory.

It seems like a no-win situation. Not only does the Lovejoy Trap divert the focus of conversation entirely, it perpetuates the myth of the demonic and insatiable sexuality of brown and black men, a myth that permeates all our cultural artifacts even where you may expect it the least.

The Hunting Ground (2015), an award-winning documentary directed by Kirby Dick, produced by Amy Ziering, and—ironically—distributed by the Weinstein Company, exposed the shocking pervasiveness of sexual assault across U.S. college campuses. It featured on-camera interviews with survivors from a diverse range of socioeconomic and racial backgrounds, some of whom had been assaulted by their peers at the most prestigious colleges in the country. For obvious reasons, the film did not feature either interviews or images of the alleged perpetrators. Except for one.

Toward the end of the film, one survivor recounts her alleged assault at the hands of a former star quarterback for the Florida State Seminoles. He is black and his accuser is white. This, of course, does not mean he didn't do it, and I'm not commenting on the allegations themselves or even the outcome. Rather, it's the power of representation and history that comes into play. Against the historical backdrop discussed throughout this book, and toward the end of a film that has spent well over an hour showing the pervasiveness of sexual assault and the reluctance of authorities to take serious steps against it, the filmmakers chose to show moving images of only one of the accused: a black man. *Representation matters.* And how people are represented matters most of all. People believe what they see more readily than what they hear. What we "saw" in *The Hunting Ground* was that black male college students were menacing their white female peers, despite the fact that most of the other perpetrators were white. That may not have been what was intended, but as we should all know by now, intention and outcome are not the same thing. It's Black Peril all over again.

This optic was repeated a couple of years later in the fictional *Riverdale* TV series, a live-action adaptation of the classic *Archie* comics. In a nod to the #MeToo movement, an early storyline revolved around the harassment and assault of female students at the hands of the school football team. Again, although many boys from various racial backgrounds, including white, were implicated, only one was shown both taking advantage of a (brown) girl and getting his comeuppance. In the revenge scene, the virginal blond Betty Cooper, dressed for some reason as her own "evil"—and therefore dark-haired—doppelgänger, traps said black football star in a hot tub and comes close to drowning him. Again, he was not the only accused, but he was the only accused we saw with our own eyes; and we saw him both humiliating a girl and getting punished for it—by a white woman.

This imagery cannot be divorced from the context of white settler colonialism. It cannot be separated from the violent history of slavery and segregation and lynching, the history of Emmett Till, and the damsel in distress, and the white savior. Yes, black men do assault women, but this does not negate the fact that such repetitive imagery taps into a long, bloody history and serves to perpetuate the biases and fears of white society: that black and brown men pose an outsized threat to the safety of women. This is why the Lovejoy Trap works so well. The hidden recesses of our collective unconscious already position black and brown men as violent, sexual threats. The main difference now is that the frame has widened from white men to include white women *also* saving women of color from men of color.

Rape survivors are never going to get the uniform justice they deserve until we unmoor the abuse of women's bodies from these colonial-derived prejudices and ambitions. In our public discourse, rape is often less about the crime itself and more about its usefulness to institutional power. Does it serve power to prosecute the rape or to ignore the rape?

To reward the rape or to deny the rape? The answer all too often depends on where it lies in relation to current—i.e., white—power structures. Bilal Skaf, the Lebanese Australian ringleader of the notorious Skaf Gang, who assaulted several young women in Sydney in 2000, was sentenced to more than fifty-five years in 2001. The presiding judge described the crimes as "events you hear about, or read about, only in the context of war-time atrocities." Hardly. Only six years prior, Anglo-Australian rapist Geoffrey Michael Haywood was sentenced to just six years for leading the gang rape of a teenager in Burnie, Tasmania. The victim, known only as "Leia," told media Haywood had put a knife to her throat and said, "I should kill you, you slut," before threatening to make the then sixteen-year-old schoolgirl dig her own grave. She survived Haywood's assault only because the pickup truck in which they were traveling to what he intended to be her burial site crashed into a tree. Skaf's victims, despite coming from a range of ethnic backgrounds including Anglo, Greek, and Aboriginal, were depicted in the media as innocent, white victims of racially motivated crimes. Leia, on the other hand, was degraded in court as a drug-taking liar who was fabricating the allegations to avoid being punished by her parents.

To grasp just how cynical the Lovejoy Trap really is requires an understanding of settler-colonial history. After centuries of the abuse, exploitation, objectification, dehumanization, and assault of women of color as both a tool of colonialism and a justification for it, and with the effects of all this not yet in the past, the apparent urgent concern of otherwise apathetic or even hostile white people for the safety of children and women of color is something to behold. The hypocrisy is astounding, and the self-serving sense of righteousness is almost impressive in its audacity.

Even worse is how well it works.

In white societies, people of color are used as a wedge. Immigrants are given promises of acceptance and assimilation that come with implicit and sometimes explicit threats of ostracism if we don't comply. At the same time, we remain excluded from the inner circle as the lack of people of color in leadership positions attests. This "two birds with one stone" approach is just one of the ways in which white domination maintains itself. What is saddening is how often and how deeply people of color buy into it. Across the world, whiteness has become so attached to the symbols of privilege, wealth, and status that it no longer even needs European-derived white people themselves to perpetuate it.

The Privilege and Peril of Passing

COLORISM, ANTI-BLACKNESS, AND THE YEARNING TO BE WHITE

[On] September 10th I went to bed a white guy; September 11th, I woke up an Arab.

—Dean Obeidallah,
Arab American comedian, 2007

If there is one thing I am grateful for regarding my 1990s adolescence, it is that hair-straightening irons hadn't yet been invented. No doubt I'd have destroyed every last follicle on my head if they had. As it was, forced to consider other ways to make my natural curls conform, I settled on spending hours at a time in front of the television brushing my hair as straight as I could get it. Eyeing with envy the suitably straight-haired residents of mid-1990s Summer Bay, the fictional coastal town setting of long-running Australian soap opera *Home and Away*, I'd begin when the curls were still wet from the shower. Then I'd methodically repeat the motions, pulling every last stubborn curl straight until they were dry and hung down to the middle of my back rather than their usual position just below my shoulders. To the untrained eye it looked like I had dead-straight hair.

I don't remember how many times I put on this personal performance, but I do recall very clearly the fervent hope it would work *this time*, that somehow this time my hair would stay straight and neat and bouncy. Looking hopefully into the mirror, I'd shake my head vigorously from side to side but, rather than cascade down my shoulders, my stubborn locks would surround my head like a brown halo of bouffantness. I'd managed to brush the curls out, but that wasn't going to change my hair's stubborn inclination to fly away and volumize. Another personal failure.

When I think of that young girl, I am struck not only by her patience (it takes hours to brush long wet hair straight!) but by her completely unfounded hope that she could change a fundamental physical feature just by brushing it away. Back then, I didn't really think much about why straight hair was so desirable and my own thick brown curls that seemed to cover every bit of space on my scalp were not, just as I never questioned why Angel and Bobby in Summer Bay didn't have to brush their hair straight for hours or agonize over the shape of their nose. Whiteness was invisible. White people just were. They set the standard and we had to try to meet it. If we couldn't meet it, well, that meant there was something wrong with us; it was our fault, not theirs. We were the ones who had to change.

Whiteness is more than skin color. It is a system that privileges those racial, cultural, and religious identities that most resemble the typical characteristics associated with the white

Western Europeans who created the system in their image. And this system of white supremacy is now so ingrained it can exist without white people. Colorism—the discrimination and prejudice against darker-skinned people of color (often from within their own communities) and in favor of those whose physical features are closer to those set by Western beauty standards—plagues virtually all communities across the globe.

My own fair-skinned Syrian mother still acts horrified when I let my olive skin see any sun: *samra*—brown—is not considered attractive. A few years ago a Latina woman in the United States whom I interviewed for a story on colorism explained that among Latinx immigrants, darker skin was seen as an indicator of poverty. "There is an incredible amount of shame about being a migrant farmworker," she told me. "My mom didn't want us getting *prieta*—dark-colored or tanned. We would wear a long-sleeved shirt with a long-sleeved dress shirt over that, heavy blue jeans, gloves, a large hat, and sunglasses. And the temperature would be in the hundreds." Years later, this woman took up waterskiing and her mother would still get upset, just as mine does. "Every time I would visit her, she would make an awful face and say I 'look so *prieta*.'"

Samra. Prieta. It seems there's a tacitly derogatory word for it in every language. In India, antipathy toward darker skin is so rife that a recent study found that 70 percent of both male and female respondents wanted to date a fair-skinned partner. According to the research team at Hindustan Unilever, the British-Dutch-founded corporation behind Fair & Lovely, India's most popular skin-whitening product, "90% of Indian women and girls view skin lightening as a 'high need'" because "it is aspirational, like losing weight. A fair skin is like education, regarded as a social and economic step up." But why would so many South Asian women come to think this way? At least part of this yearning to be fairer can be put down to the aggressive marketing of such products. Typical marketing shows potential suitors choosing fairer-skinned partners over their darker rivals, and it doesn't stop at merely promoting lighter skin. The implication is that these products can transform their users' entire lives.

Indian actor Abhay Deol wrote an op-ed for the *Hindustan Times* in 2017 criticizing advertising that "preaches that we would get a better job, a happier marriage, and more beautiful children if we were fair. We are conditioned to believe that life would be easier if we are fairer." In 2014 the Indian Advertising Standards Council banned television ads depicting darker-skinned people as inferior, but the products persist, as do their campaigns, and they remain wildly popular. Although most users of lightening products are women between the ages of twenty-one and thirty-five, there are reports of girls as young as twelve using Fair & Lovely. Its availability throughout the subcontinent and even as far as Southeast Asia and Australia has seen the Asia-Pacific region become the biggest market for skin-whitening products. There are even products designed to lighten the skin on the labia and, alarmingly, inside the vagina. The adverse health effects are significant and well known even to many of the products' users, with skin cancer, permanent pigmentation, liver damage, and mercury poisoning just some of the potential consequences. And yet, according to Zion Market Research, the global skin-whitening products market was worth approximately U.S. $4.5 billion in 2017 and is projected to reach more than U.S. $8.5 billion by 2024. The main driving factor behind this phenomenal growth? "[I]ncreasing consumer consciousness regarding their physical appearance." Other key markets include parts of the African continent, where 77 percent of Nigerian women, 59 percent of Togolese women, and 27 percent of women in Senegal use creams and lightening agents such as Whitenicious.

Marketing alone, however, cannot explain the obsession with lighter skin. Where advertising is most effective is when it taps into already existing insecurities and desires. This, after all, is why sex is used to sell everything from cars to clothes to real estate: that desire has to come from somewhere. Colorism has a long relationship with colonialism, with each fortifying the other. Skin color has been associated with both attractiveness and status for two reasons. First, it implicitly signifies a life not spent laboring in the fields under the hot sun, and second, it was the color of the ruling class. Like many people, I was long under the impression that Indian colorism was rooted in the caste system, with lower castes being darkest and higher castes lightest. However, Indian scholars such as Neha Mishra, head of legal studies at the University of Bangalore, dispute this, arguing that the earliest classifications we associate with the caste system were based on job occupation rather than skin tone, since skin coloring itself varied from region to region. Over time, the four original caste classifications outlined in the Rig Veda, the collection of ancient Sanskrit hymns dating back to at least 1500 B.C., spawned thousands more castes and subcastes, leading to a vastly more oppressive system in which, rather than castes being arranged according to skin tone, preference was given to light skin across all castes. So while some castes are higher than others, in each individual caste those with lighter skin fare better than those with darker skin.

Mishra argues that pre-colonization India showed no visible prejudice based on skin color, citing the "dark-skinned heroes" of the Rig Veda as evidence. Even after the Muslim Mughal conquest and empire, the status of the lighter-skinned ruling classes was based on their preexisting Arab and Persian ethnicity rather than their skin color: having been persistently ruled by fairer-skinned foreigners for hundreds of years, Indians came to associate lighter skin with status, wealth, and privilege. It was not, however, until European colonization that discrimination according to skin color became discernible, rife, and institutionalized. European colonialism consolidated this by—in contrast to their Mughal predecessors—claiming "themselves to be a 'superior' and 'intelligent' race; consequently, they were born to rule the 'inferior' and 'black colored' Indians who were more akin to crude animals than humans." According to Mishra, Indians became excluded from restaurants and schools, and jobs were distributed to lighter-skinned locals first, essentially founding a segregation system based on Western ideals of beauty and intelligence. The foundations for this system were laid down as far back as the mid 1600s, when the British East India Company founded its Fort St. George settlement. They gave it the name White Town, distinguishing it from the nearby Indian settlement that was named, yes, you guessed it, Black Town. And so the binary was born.

Colorism brought violence to the Indigenous population in Australia under a converse rationale where it was the lighter-skinned children who were targeted for separation from their families and forced into assimilation into white society, which usually meant laboring and domestic servitude. Today, Indigeneity is determined not by skin color but "by heritage, acceptance by an [I]ndigenous community, and active participation in the affairs of that [I]ndigenous community." Aboriginal people report experiencing colorism and social exclusion from both non-Indigenous and Indigenous people who judge their Indigeneity solely on their skin color. Social exclusion is a key factor in determining overall mental health, and, as a 2016 study by the Australian College of Mental Health Nurses found, when the authenticity of their identity is questioned, the resulting feelings of belonging neither here nor there can exacerbate the preexisting psychological distress caused by "unresolved grief that is associated with multiple layers of trauma that span many generations." Mental health distress is significantly higher in Indigenous communities than it is in the non-Indigenous population, both in Australia and globally, manifesting in higher morbidity rates, a health and income gap, and criminalization.

Too black or not black enough: colorism does not always directly involve black people, but at its core it is driven by anti-blackness, by the yearning to distance oneself from blackness in order to be included in whiteness.

Colonialism ravaged Africa in a multitude of ways, one of which was the growth of a mixed-race population who were regarded as particularly threatening due to their aesthetic proximity to whites, and punished all the more for it. In Southern Rhodesia, human beings were taxonomized. To be white was a status determined not solely by skin color, and white-skinned people who lived in poverty were also excluded from white society, regarded as an embarrassment and potential contagion. The children of an African mother and a European father were isolated, referred to as "half-castes," and usually resided with their mother unless the father wished to have them educated, in which case they were separated from their mother permanently.

The children of "half-castes" were categorized as "coloreds," and it was they who were perceived as a particular threat to white society. Regarded as neither black nor white, they often formed their own communities. Sometimes, those with paler skin were able to mingle with white society and deny their links to the African population, and many coloreds attempted to attain the status of whiteness by disavowing their links to blackness. Schools were opened specifically to segregate coloreds, and those mixed-race couples who sought to enroll their children in white schools were treated with disdain and anger. White parents threatened to pull their children if a child suspected of being colored was permitted to enroll, no matter how white-skinned the child appeared. Since there was often no way to visibly tell if a child had mixed-race lineage, if a family were known to associate with any coloreds this was held as proof of their own identity, and their children were barred from schools attended by white children. Mixed-race parents, even those who were well-off financially, who wanted to educate their children had an uphill climb and resorted to denouncing their African lineage in order to do so. One such parent, Mrs. Maggio, mother of Grace Maggio of Ardbennie, admitted to having colored grandparents but nonetheless felt it would "be a disgrace to the British to put a child of English and Afrikaner persons into a Coloured school." So internalized was her racism that Mrs. Maggio opted to end her daughter's education rather than see her enrolled in such a school, which was perceived to be a hotbed of future criminals. The supposed propensity to criminality of blacks and coloreds made white-skinned children with mixed lineage social outcasts if their status was discovered, perceived as they were as carriers of "a racial inheritance which made their misclassification a danger to their classmates."

The term *colorism* was coined by African American writer Alice Walker, and in North America its origins are firmly rooted in slavery. In the antebellum South, skin tone began to dictate the slavery experience, with lighter-skinned slaves more likely to be assigned less physically taxing work in the house but also more likely to be hired out as "fancy girls" and sold into sex slavery markets. The lascivious Jezebel archetype ensured they were not seen as trafficked and abused prostitutes but as willing competition for virtuous white women.

In June 1864, *Harper's Magazine* ran a feature aimed at a Northern audience whose enthusiasm for the Civil War was waning as they questioned whether they had a stake in it all. Under photographs of newly freed child slaves, the caption read "Emancipated Slaves White and Colored"; it served as a reminder to those Americans who still associated slaves only with black skin that children born to enslaved women, although fathered by white men across two or more generations, were also legal property. "[They] are as white, as intelligent, as docile, as most of our own children," the copy read. The images were turned into postcards and sold to shore up support for the war and to fund homes for the now-free children. Some children even embarked on tours of the North alongside famous Abolition figures such as the Reverend Henry Ward Beecher, who, with newly emancipated six-year-old Fanny Lawrence, whom he'd adopted, standing beside him, thundered to his audience at Brooklyn's Plymouth Church: "The loveliness of this face, the beauty of this figure would only make her so much more valuable for lust. Let your soul burn with fiery indignation against the horrible system which turns into chattels such fair children of God! May God strike for our armies . . . that this accursed thing may be utterly destroyed!"

Post-Abolition, these "white" slaves meant two things: that there were white-passing former slaves with black heritage mingling with white society, and that those who could pass for white often had to divorce themselves from the black community, as in Southern Rhodesia, in order to avoid the wrath of those "real" whites who were still seething about losing the war. Those known to be or suspected of trying to "pass" were discriminated against nonetheless.

Passing had markedly different connotations then from what it does now. To pass now does not refer to "falsely" pretending to be white, but to benefit from privilege on account of having lighter skin, whether or not one's racial heritage is known. It is also a process that is actively encouraged by the dominant white society keen to assimilate "problem" ethnic communities. In the post–Civil War United States, however, fearful whites who abhorred the thought of sharing their wealth and status with anyone with "black blood" sought to ensure that didn't happen. White people who socialized with black and "colored" people were regarded with suspicion, and black and colored people who socialized with whites were regarded as fraudulently "passing" in order to access white entitlements and privileges that they did not deserve.

That outwardly appearing white people could be enslaved or otherwise excluded from white society is not as surprising as it may now appear to some of us. The intervening centuries have so cemented the association between race and skin color that the history tends to be obscured: racialization was a deliberate process, not an organic one. And in some rare cases, just as apparent whites could be excluded, nonwhites could find their way into whiteness.

A few years ago I tutored an undergraduate course in global history and one of the case studies in the textbook was that of a European travel writer's visit to the colonies in what is now South America sometime in the eighteenth century. The racial hierarchy in Spanish America was so rigid that there were no less than sixteen categories in the *casta* system. Where a person fell in the system affected everything from their occupation to their social status to their marriage prospects. At the top were the *peninsulares* (Spaniards or other Europeans born in Europe), followed by the *criollos* (Spaniards born of European parents in the colonies). *Mestizos* were of mixed Native and European descent, *castizos* were mostly European with some Native, and *cholas* were mostly Native with some European. *Pardos* were mixed European, Native, and African, and, it will likely surprise no one to note, on the bottom rungs were *mulattos* (mixed African and European), followed by *negroes* (blacks). The existence of such an intricate taxonomy implies the difficulty inherent in crossing economic and social boundaries. This was a system designed to protect privilege and wealth and keep people firmly in their place. The system in Brazil was somewhat looser, designed to allow some mobility for lighter-skinned mixed-race people but keep those with darker skin on the bottom rungs. Nonetheless, the European visitor in the textbook was stunned to come across a dark-skinned mulatto official in a small town in what is now Brazil. Even more surprising was the lack of scandal caused by this clear transgression of the racial boundary. "Isn't your governor a mulatto?" he asked some locals. "He was but he isn't anymore," his hosts replied. "How can a governor be a mulatto?"

I still marvel every time I think about this anecdote. The rhetorical question put to the scandalized European wasn't "How can a mulatto be a governor?" since this would indicate the impossibility of a biracial man ever attaining the position, but "How can a governor be a mulatto?" This means that even racial classification for visibly black people in Latin America in the eighteenth century was not an intrinsically biologically fixed category: by sheer virtue of becoming a governor, he was no longer considered a mulatto. He had somehow transcended his inferior status.

Dig a little deeper into this history, and we discover that the racial categories we take as a given and obvious feature of our world were themselves brought into being by a process of deliberate racialization. At the beginning of the transatlantic slave trade, Europeans did not go to Africa to enslave Africans because they were black but because, as historian Paul Lovejoy (no relation to our friend Helen, of course!) argues in *Transformations in Slavery*, it was a source of supply with an already existing trade. Domestic slavery across the

African continent had already been ongoing for centuries before Europeans muscled in on it. It was not, however, racialized. Over the centuries, and as new laws were written and rewritten to justify their enslavement, black Africans came to be seen as a slave class. The categories of white and black were invented to justify slavery, rather than slavery being justified by virtue of the enslaved people being black.

Slavery in Africa goes back much further in history than the transatlantic trade. In fact, it began almost a millennium before the Portuguese and Spanish turned up on the African coast, with slavery in North Africa and sub-Saharan Africa already a feature of life. Domestic African slavery differed greatly from transatlantic slavery, but it was no less devastating for those who became enslaved, either by other Africans or by the later Middle Eastern traders. There were, however, two key differences between domestic African and Middle Eastern slavery on the one hand, and the later transatlantic slave trade on the other: racialization and economic rationalization. Before the Europeans, no one had justified slavery either on the grounds of racial inferiority or economic necessity. Though slaves were certainly already exploited for their labor, it was not yet so ingrained that entire economies depended on it.

That does not make the preexisting slave trades benign. The trans-Saharan trade associated primarily with Arab traders was not as brutal or as prolific as the transatlantic trade, and in many cases slaves were afforded a significant amount of mobility that was simply impossible in the Americas. However, these differences meant little to the victims of it, such as the sixteen hundred captured Africans who died of thirst in a single trip when their caravan hit trouble crossing the Sahara;

they would certainly contest any claim that non-Atlantic slavery was "not so bad." Likewise, separation from family and kin for the purposes of forced labor or military service was hardly a pleasant experience, regardless of how specifically physically brutal some trades were over others. For those who were caught up in it, kidnapped in raids, or captured as spoils of war, their destiny was to be taken from their families and communities, denied their kinship, and forced to live at the mercy of others, often for the remainder of their lives. Nonetheless, it is those important differences that affect the impact slavery's legacy has today. Over the 1,250 years of the trans-Saharan trade, some 2,500 enslaved Africans per year were transported to what are now North Africa, the Middle East, and the Mediterranean, first by Indigenous North Africans and then by Arab traders. This is roughly the same number that were exported in the 300 years or so that the trade to the Americas operated—which indicates just how prolific American slavery was and how it changed the course of history. But statistics can't tell the whole story of slavery's legacy.

The trans-Saharan trade was begun in pre-Islamic times by Indigenous North African dealers and was continued after the Islamic conquest. In Africa, writes Lovejoy, "Africans owned Africans." However, they did not enslave their brothers: "they enslaved their enemies." There was not yet any notion approaching a Pan-African identity, which, like Pan-Arabism, eventually came about as a response to colonialism and an attempt to resist it. Domestic slaves were usually prisoners of war but could also be captured in raids, and were usually destined for the military or agricultural labor. After the Islamic conquest of North Africa, the trans-Saharan trade continued and was used primarily as a way to widen Islam's reach and circle of influence. Slavery was regarded as an opportunity to educate and convert pagans to Islam, upon which they would (theoretically but not always) be freed. It was illegal to capture and enslave Muslims (as well as Christians and Jews, who were regarded as "people of the book"), although this did happen.

This process of emancipation or manumission was also a feature of domestic African slavery, where being enslaved did not necessarily indicate an inherently degraded moral status. Female slaves were generally used as concubines and upon having their master's child would be in a kind of semi-enslaved state, unable to be sold again but technically not free until their master died. Their children were born free. Other enslaved Africans ended up either in the military or, for those especially unlucky, as eunuchs. Eunuchs fetched a high price because the surgery was so brutal that only one in ten survived it.

By the nineteenth century, slavery was rife across all of Africa, was still going in parts of the Middle East, and had spawned a minor trade across the Indian Ocean to the subcontinent. But it was the transatlantic trade and slavery in the Americas that historians call "a particularly heinous development." The key features setting European slavery apart were not just the sheer volume or the generally more sadistic aspects: in the Americas, slavery had a racial and economic imperative that was lacking elsewhere. These two factors—race and capitalism—mean that it is the legacy of transatlantic slavery that most impacts the modern world, as race and uneven distribution of wealth and resources continue to benefit the Western world over the global south.

The racialization of slavery and its pecuniary place in American society meant it wasn't a minor feature but what that society was constructed around. As Stephanie Jones-Rogers writes, Southern society was a slavery society not just in the sense that slavery existed, but in that it was fundamental to how white people perceived themselves: as slave owners. The submissive status of blacks became not just acceptable but both necessary and right in order for white people to live their lives. Their identity as white people hinged on slave ownership and white superiority.

The diaries and personal letters of female slave owners reveal emotional reactions to the Emancipation Proclamation. "Slavery was done away with and my faith in God's Holy Book was terribly shaken," wrote one. "This is a most unprecedented robbery," wrote another. Some white women who knew their wealth and status depended on slavery wept even as their former slaves celebrated. "I hope you starve to death," one sulked, "for it's going to ruin me to lose you." Some took the extraordinary step of simply not telling their slaves they were free; on remote plantations, owners continued to extract free labor for years after Abolition. Others took their slaves and ran. One white couple fled to Cuba, where they opened a sugar plantation and forced their slaves to work there until Cuba too abolished what had become known as "the most peculiar institution."

The point of all this is not to rehash the past for the sake of it, or to score points in a misguided debate. We need to understand how and why the past still affects us so deeply. Slavery occupied a fundamental place in the economic and social life of the Americas that it did not elsewhere. The economic dependency on slave labor, and the racialization that structured society in relation to blackness, are its two enduring legacies, and these legacies now permeate the entire globe. Over time, the racialized perspective on slavery penetrated Arab attitudes also. Despite the fact that in the peak years of slavery in the Middle East region slaves were sourced from a multitude of places—including Europe—Arabs and Persians came to see slavery as a black issue too. Racism and colorism are now shamefully huge problems in the Middle East, and the pejorative for *black person*—*abeed*—is also the word for slave.

The aftereffects of slavery on Africa are untold. Millions of its young people were forcibly migrated both domestically and internationally, with those bound for the Americas utilized against their will not only to extract wealth for their owners but to cement the capitalist system as the global one. It was their transportation and forced labor that created the conditions for the Industrial Revolution and the ascendency of Europe. As international traders increased their demand for slaves, the nature of slavery within Africa also changed as more and more were used on American-style plantations and to mine resources, and as African warlords used slavery to consolidate their power. The economy of Africa became so dependent on slavery that when it was abolished, it left the continent—the last to be colonized by Europe—weak and unable to deflect the Scramble for Africa.

Ironically, abolitionism helped Europe to conquer Africa, with Europeans using the abolition of domestic African slavery as a rationale for colonizing that continent. Africans born under colonial rule were "born free," according to the colonial rulers, and could not be enslaved. Missionaries and reformers used abolitionist rhetoric to appeal to Africans, and the formerly enslaved who escaped their bondage often returned to their homes as Christian converts. It was not, as many ahistorical revisionists like to claim, empathy or a moral desire to end slavery that turned Europeans into abolitionists: it was the incompatibility of African slavery with capitalism, as industrialization sought to transform the global economy from an agrarian one to one based on a wage labor system. Paradoxically, the legal abolition of slavery in Africa signified not liberation for all but submission to colonial rule.

Although slavery absolutely still exists today, its legality does not; it is no longer an institution. Its legacy, however, lives on in the Middle East as it does across the West. In recent years the Dutch character Zwarte Piet (Black Pete) has come under fire. The companion of Sinterklaas (Saint Nicholas) is traditionally played in festivities throughout the Netherlands by a white performer in blackface and a bright Moor costume, reflecting Piet's status as a servant from Muslim-era Spain. As controversy grows over the character, who remains hugely popular with schoolchildren, defenders claim his blackened face is merely meant to signify soot from climbing down the chimney to deliver presents. One wonders why, in that case, St. Nick himself never has such a problem or, indeed, why Piet's clothing is not similarly stained, or why he has big red-painted lips. Cries of "What about the children?" are used by adults to defend the practice. Less known than Piet is the Iranian character of Haji Firuz, who makes his annual appearance at Narooz, or Iranian New Year, dressed in bright red clothing and with a painted black face. Iranians claim he acquired his black face as a result of his role as a

Zoroastrian fire keeper. Like the Dutch, Iranian defenders of Firuz seem unwilling to admit he could be black because he represents an enslaved African, even though he has his own rhyme that includes the lines, "My master hold your head up high / My master, why don't you laugh?"

Whiteness can and does exist even in the absence of white people. The inauguration in January 2019 of Jair Bolsonaro as president of Brazil, who immediately marked the Indigenous population for erasure if they refused to adapt to capitalism and accept logging and mining on their land, is a continuation of the elitism in Latin America that has long worked in tandem with whiteness. During the post–Mexican War period, even as other Mexicans were being lynched, many Mexican elites—descendants of the "pure" Spanish *peninsulares*—were marrying white Anglo-Americans to form and consolidate power over *mestizos*, *cholas*, and Afro-Latinx. We can be both targets of racial abuse and perpetrators of it. Kim Crayton, the founder of #CauseAScene, a podcast and initiative advocating for racial diversity in the U.S. tech industry, says two of her worst experiences of being "white women teared" happened with other nonblack women of color. "I know all women of color get it from white women," she told me during a Skype conversation, "but we get it from everyone. It comes from everywhere."

Like internalized misogyny, internalized racism is real, and it causes enormous damage to ourselves and to others as we strive to present ourselves as white as possible in order to access the privileges associated with whiteness. Appealing to whiteness is intrinsically antiblack. When we veer toward one end of the binary structure, whether deliberately or not, we implicitly but necessarily devalue the other side of the pole. And eventually it will catch up with us. Prior to 9/11, Arab American comedian Dean Obeidallah did not see his Palestinian heritage as pertinent to his life; he felt and was treated as "white." Following the attacks, however, his Arab heritage became an issue for others if not for him, prompting him to perform a stand-up routine on how he "went to bed a white guy" the night before 9/11 and "woke up an Arab" the morning after. Identity may be about how we see ourselves, but racism is always about how others see us, regardless.

There is an inherent peril in passing as white or almost white: this apparent inclusion can be revoked at any time. One young, white-passing Arab woman told me she'd worked for a couple of years in an office without her race coming up, where she felt like one of the gang of almost all white colleagues, but after she casually mentioned her Lebanese heritage, she turned up one day to find her desk had been unexpectedly moved. I'm cognizant that on a day-to-day basis my own olive skin tone has inoculated me from some of racism's more virulently explicit forms that take aim at dark skin. Arabs, like some other racial minorities, can slip under the radar but it requires never bringing up our heritage, never demanding more or challenging the negative depictions of other Arabs, lest the ire be turned toward us.

I'd be lying if I said I knew how to reconcile all this. I'm well aware of the racism and colorism in Arab societies, of the Filipina and other Asian maids mistreated by their rich employers in the Gulf states who regard them more as indentured servants than hired help. It did not escape my notice on a trip back to Lebanon that the workers cleaning the windows and washing the dishes in the hotel were darker than the receptionists and the waiters. Yet I am also aware of the tendency to collapse all Arab societies into one and all of Arab histories into one singular, ahistorical narrative. Arabs have a complicated and often contradictory relationship to whiteness, in which the antipathy toward us is based less on our perceived biological characteristics and more on our supposed cultural deficiencies. In this era of the "clash of civilizations" in which Islam and the Middle East are held up as a unique threat to the West, individual Arabs living in the West occupy a strange position where racism against us is not necessarily always overt or visible, depending on how close to white we present and how far we are prepared to assimilate. But the flip side of that is we are often left flailing without much support from "allies," as though we are not white enough to be white but not quite brown enough to be "real" people of color. "Am I too ethnic or am I not ethnic enough?" is how Egyptian American actor Rami Malek put it. The U.S. State Department still lists Arabs and other Middle Easterners as "white." This sometimes feels like the worst of both worlds: we are subjected to racism and discrimination, often implicit and difficult to prove, but without the solidarity from progressives that other people of color can turn to.

The litmus test here is how progressives react when an Arab woman disagrees with them. Some of the most personal and vicious online abuse I have experienced has come from progressives and even socialists, who, furious that my perspective on the Middle East does not align perfectly with theirs, will mock everything from my heritage ("a troll who claims to be Syrian") to my character ("vile, toxic human being [who] exploits other people's suffering for profit"). These kinds of attacks from people I'd have expected to be supportive of women like me, given their professed leftist sentiments, have become so frequent it feels pointless for me to even ask them what exactly they are referencing. Even worse is that they so rarely get pulled up on their behavior.

This isn't a pity party, nor am I suggesting that Arab women have it the "worst." I'm only pointing out the inconsistencies and contradictions. Just as it morphs over time, racism shifts across situations, takes different shapes, depending on who it is being directed against and why. An Arab woman who wears a hijab or otherwise presents as visibly different will almost certainly experience overt racial vilification, be it at work or on the street. Arab women such as myself who are more ethnically ambiguous and less easily identifiable as Middle Eastern are more likely to escape this explicit daily bigotry, but we are also more likely to be dismissed or demonized in progressive circles that pride themselves on tolerance, diversity, and inclusion, precisely because we are not quite different or other *enough*. I've seen Arab women shouted down by white women online simply for challenging a white woman on derogatory language she has used to describe Arab men and Arab culture. The subtext here is that we are not sufficiently victim-like to warrant recognition. Following a bizarre altercation in which a Palestinian Australian journalist had taken exception to me using my Twitter account to promote my own work (?!), a young white self-described socialist took great pleasure in telling me I had been "put in [my] place" and he "wouldn't want to undo the good work of a Palestinian woman." A good Arab victim does not talk back to or challenge her white saviors. She is a pet not a threat, be that perceived threat a physical one or, more likely these days, an intellectual one. She is also willing to seek white approval by cosplaying the damsel in distress and attacking other women of color in a misguided attempt to make her way up that racial hierarchy, until she too crosses that invisible line and is discarded. Our relatively fair skin means Arabs are often disparaged for being "white," but this pseudo-whiteness is bestowed only on select individuals rather than the collective. Moreover, it is both conditional and revokable: one wrong move and you're on the scrap heap. This too is part of the privilege and peril of passing.

Arab is not even a racial or ethnic category; rather, it denotes a supposed shared culture and language. But the dialects and cultures vary significantly across the region, making the word *Arab* itself, as an identifier, a testament to the inadequacy of our racial literacy and vocabulary. It doesn't allow for these differences in power and identity or history. What does it mean to be an Arab when there are so many dialects and variations of the language? (There are some thirty modern varieties.) What does it mean to be an Arab when the notion of a pan-Arab identity did not exist until the early decades of the twentieth century? This was when, led by Egyptian president Gamal Abdel Nasser, countries in North Africa and the Levant, whose populations had not previously identified as "Arab" despite speaking the language, became Arab almost overnight, as national liberation efforts intensified and secular leaders sought to both confound Western powers and contain the burgeoning Muslim Brotherhood. What does it mean to be Arab when you come from a line of people indigenous not to the Arabian Peninsula but to the Levant, when you still carry the DNA of the long-dead Canaanite culture even though you speak Arabic and your people long ago converted to the Arab-founded religion of Islam or to Christianity? What does it mean to be an Arab in a region where persecution is often based not on race or ethnicity but on religious sect? What does it mean to be an Arab when your lands were colonized first by the Arabians, then by the Ottomans, then by the Europeans, and finally, along with the rest of the world, by capitalism itself?

What, then, is an Arab? Do we even know who we are anymore? Sadly, and ironically, this impossibility of pinpointing what constitutes an Arab makes it all the easier to essentialize us, to regard us as one heaving, swarthy, generic mass. Seen one Arab, seen them all. Perhaps the most astounding comment posted under one of my articles (and I've seen plenty) was one in which, responding to my claim that white people struggle to feel empathy with Arabs, the commenter scoffed that neither he nor the majority of readers cared "what splinter of Arab [I] identify as or want others to be identified as." Once again, I was reminded of Edward Said's critique of T. E. Lawrence's adventures in the Middle East: "We are to assume that if an Arab feels joy, if he is sad at the death of his parent or child, if he has a sense of the injustices of political tyranny, then those experiences are necessarily subordinate to the sheer, unadorned, and persistent fact of being an Arab."

When we are not being reduced to our race, we are being excluded from it. Ever since Rachel Dolezal, the white woman who "identifies" as black, imposed herself on our consciousness, I have noticed white people increasingly attempting to dismiss lighter-skinned people of color as "transracial," as if we too are white but pretending to be something else. It is something I see most frequently leveled at Aboriginal women in the public eye, as well as something I've personally experienced. After so many decades of being told to go back to where I came from, of being ridiculed for my hair or my eyebrows, the size of my eyes or shape of my nose, I am now increasingly told that, actually, I am white. Too Arab or not Arab enough. Reducing us to our race or erasing us from it altogether. Threat or pet. It's not logical but it works.

It is these kinds of experiences that make living in a white society as a nonwhite person feel like we are in an abusive relationship from which we cannot escape. And as in all "good" abusive relationships, one of the key tools of abuse is gaslighting, or the deliberate subversion of someone's reality to make them question their own experiences, interpretations, and, eventually, sanity. It is gas-whiting to take the focus away from the abuser's racism. This denial of our racial difference, even as we are simultaneously vilified for being different, means we receive very little empathy when we are on the receiving end of rather horrific abuse.

There are many more intricacies to unpack, but at the least, colorism, anti-blackness, and the shame of slavery are reminders that, although we share many similar experiences, racism manifests differently depending on our racial heritage. The African slave trades were not only a European affair, and the trans-Saharan and Indian Ocean slave trades also affected the course of Africa's history. Those of us who are not African must likewise contend with this history and where we fit into it. It may be the peculiar legacy of Euro-American colonialism and slavery that cemented racism and capitalism in the global consciousness, but our ancestors played a role too. This role lives on in the anti-blackness and colorism that also manifests outside the Western world, and eventually turns itself back on us. Those of us who are nonblack and non-Indigenous people of color cannot divorce the racism inflicted on us in the West by white people from the anti-blackness and colorism that live on in the lands our parents left behind.

Our world is only getting smaller, and as the West continues to set the standards for wealth, success, beauty, and status, then the rest will continue to chase what the West has. And this means they will continue to adopt whiteness, if not white skin itself, as an ideology in the misguided hopes of catching up.

Brown Scars

*Without your article I would simply have been
another black woman who filed a racial discrimination lawsuit—and lost.*

—Lisa Benson

It was late in the Sydney evening of February 8, 2019, when a
friend of Lisa Benson, the reporter terminated from her contract after sharing my article on Facebook, tweeted from Kansas City to let me know the jury had begun deliberating the two
lawsuits Lisa had filed against her former employer, KSHB–TV
Channel 41. Throughout the trial, the defense had kept referring to my white tears piece as "an attack on white women."
Lisa's former employers, with whom she had worked for four-
teen years and who'd sent her flowers when she gave birth to her
son, depicted her in court as angry, hateful, and violent.

The jury of eight included no black jurors and only one of
color. They found against Lisa in her original racial discrimination suit but, in something of a twist, they found in her favor
in the claim of retaliation she had filed against KSHB–TV's
parent company, E. W. Scripps. Lisa's lawyer, Dennis Egan,
had argued that her termination was not about the article

at all but was simply retaliation for filing the original claim, and the jury agreed. Though disappointed for her to lose the main case, I was buoyed that the undue punishment she'd received was rebuked. Retaliation for asserting ourselves is something women of color are well acquainted with, but it is not often that such punishment is even acknowledged let alone penalized. The jury finding she was "wrongfully terminated" means, once the legal process is complete, Lisa should be compensated for lost income.

But as if to prove progress is neither smooth nor linear, in early April, just weeks after the trial concluded, Christa Dubill, one of the two women whose complaint led to Lisa's termination, was promoted by KSHB-TV to evening newscaster.

"I still to this day don't understand why this article was so offensive," Lisa told reporter Toriano Porter of the *Kansas City Star* shortly after her trial. "I believe this particular article shared a viewpoint of women of color that we're not having conversations about, but we should be having conversations about." Lisa is doing just that. She runs anti-racism workshops and has self-published a book, *Anchored in Bias*, about her experience. "My goal now is to help normalize discussions about racism," she wrote via email. "I'm not 100% completely sure of *how* I'm going to do it but I truly believe it is part of my purpose." Like many women of color, Lisa understands that race is not tangential to other factors in our lives. Rather, it has been the key means through which white society secures and maintains its privilege. From the lynching of Mexicans in the mid-nineteenth century to Black Peril in Southern Rhodesia to black velvet in Australia, to the transatlantic slave trade, to the contemporary rise of the far right across the Western world, to Brexit, to Trump, race has been used first to cement the economic disempowerment of people of color and then to divert attention away from the cause of this disempowerment by rooting it in biology.

This does not mean our racial identity is all that matters about us, nor should it mean that we confine ourselves only to our "lane." Our lives do not run parallel. Neither, if we want to be exact, do they intersect: they are irrevocably enmeshed. Critics of my work will sometimes accuse me of such things as "identity politics at its most feral," but I've never suggested race can be divorced from material analysis. Nor have I advocated for a public discourse where only members of certain groups can talk about issues affecting those groups. To say, for instance, that only Arabs can talk about Arabs will not get us out of this box that relegates us to either pet or threat, because the flip side of "only Arabs can talk about Arabs" is "Arabs can only talk about Arabs." What I *do* advocate for is for all groups to have a say in how our society functions, and most of all, for each to shape how they are represented, for us to be believed when we show the world who we really are.

Race and racism have always been about identifying, exaggerating, and even inventing points of difference to justify brute power and economic oppression. Whiteness is and has always been fluid: to be white is less a state of biology and more a state of proximity to formal power, of access to an exclusive club. And every step of the way, White Womanhood has been key to perpetuating white supremacy. It has acted as a buffer between white male power and the rest of the population. It has whitewashed the crimes of whiteness, from Indigenous child removals to the rationalization of imperialist wars. In short, White Womanhood has functioned as the maternal arm of empire. "White women civilised," writes

Aileen Moreton-Robinson, "while white men brutalised."

White Womanhood ensures that women of color cannot break free of the box fashioned for us by the binary archetypes constructed as our placeholders without our consent or consultation. White women have never been mere bystanders to white history: they have played a pivotal role, adopting first the persona of the damsel in distress in need of white male protection, and then pivoting to the defense of white society whenever its authority is even slightly challenged. Today, white women continue their role by gas-whiting women of color, accusing us of attacking them, of dividing the sisterhood, of doing the work of patriarchy. These accusations are all manipulations designed to disempower our resolve and cause us to question ourselves. Then there is the anger, punishment—both seen and unseen—and sometimes, perhaps most biting of all, silence and marginalization: the ultimate invalidation is when they simply pretend we are not there. This too is power in all its brutality.

When white women silence women of color, they act not only in their own defense but in defense of whiteness. Damsels in distress and damsels in defense are one and the same, and both are illusions. White society has constructed representations of racialized people that serve whiteness, casting women of color as Lewd Jezebels, Dragon Ladies, China Dolls, black velvet, Native drudges, Bad Arabs—and all the rest, and it is to these representations that white people react in their interactions with women of color. They don't see us; they see only the caricature they have constructed in our stead. This means that the opposite must also hold true. If white people regard and treat us as mere caricatures, filled not with human complexity but with all the vices that white people insist they do not themselves have, then they too are also constructions, representations of what they would like to be that they have come to accept as true. White people assign themselves all the virtues they deny us—goodness, morality, intelligence, civilization, innocence—and will viciously defend this innocence against anyone who dares to challenge it. But, as academic Sara Salem noted, this innocence is not defensible and is not even innocent. "To remain innocent means to remain ignorant; and this is a wilful, active process, not an accidental passive one."

White society is all about these constructions. The façade. The image. The words. The pretense. No tangible distinction is made between reality as a physical, sensory experience and its representation of reality through words and images. People of color have never systematically oppressed white people, but this has little meaning to whiteness, which, having never experienced it, regards racism as existing in nothing else but words. This is how white people can accuse people of color of antiwhite racism with a straight face: the actual deeds of a racist society become somehow irrelevant, it's only what is said that counts and a frustrated person of color sarcastically calling a white person "mayonnaise" or even simply "white" can be regarded as a transgression akin to the N-word.

Despite all its complexity, the world is presented to us filtered and interpreted through the reductive lens of the white imaginary, which was designed and implemented to benefit white people. This is why, as I wrote, "whether angry or calm, shouting or pleading, [women of color] are always perceived as aggressors." Until these constructions and archetypes are brought crashing down nothing will change, because unless they make a conscious effort to reject it, white people filter reality through this lens, whether or not they admit to doing so.

More troubling yet is when people of color do the same. Any change must start with two things. First, women of color must become aware of the limitations forced on them, that these limitations are designed to keep us on the lowest rung of the hierarchy, and that we need to collectivize to bring them down. "Without your article," Lisa told me, "I would simply have been another black woman who filed a racial discrimination lawsuit—and lost."

Second, white women have to acknowledge the unfair advantage their race has given them not just in the sense they have white privilege, but in the sense they have participated in a system where their womanhood is itself a privilege and a weapon. Only then can the process of dismantling the archetypes begin. Judging by the research I uncovered in writing this book, I fear the opposite may be true: white women are more powerful than ever but they still cling to the role of the damsel in order to both exert and deny this power. Think of how many white feminists adopt antiracism discourse to denounce "mediocre white men" and "white male supremacy," allowing them to temporarily distance themselves from white power. Perhaps it's time to stop taking concepts such as *white man* and *white man's burden* too literally. Since *man* was and remains a catch-all for all genders, then surely *white man* and *white man's burden* refer not only to white males but to white society as a whole. White women also took on the "burden" to civilize and subjugate the inferior races of the world, often with great enthusiasm.

In a way, I can see why the damsel persists: it would require an enormous amount of humility to view the history of white society for what it really is—and to reject the legacy it bestows upon them. And whiteness is not exactly known for its humility. Trying to reason with whiteness is akin to reasoning with a clinical narcissist who refuses to go to therapy: frustratingly impossible because the untreated narcissist simply does not have the requisite tools to see themselves as anything other than "good," and this ensures it is those around them who suffer.

Throughout *White Tears/Brown Scars*, I have used words that suggest women of color are repeatedly traumatized both consciously and unconsciously by white women. I hold to this. The status of women of color can fairly be described as an emotionally abusive relationship with whiteness more broadly but especially with white women, who pivot from professing sisterhood and solidarity with us based on gender identification, to silencing and oppressing us by weaponizing their White Womanhood to keep us boxed into the binary. Historically and right through to the present day, white society has used and abused women of color for its own ends. We cannot even conceive of let alone manifest a world without white supremacy if we don't see it for what it is: a persistent group delusion that externalizes all the characteristics of itself that it doesn't like—and from which feminism is not exempt.

In his insight into Aboriginal cultural and intellectual tradition, *Sand Talk: How Indigenous Thinking Can Save the World*, Aboriginal academic Tyson Yunkaporta puts down much of humanity's travails to "an ancient seed of narcissism that has flourished due to a new imbalance in human societies." That "ancient seed" is the one that leads some of us to see ourselves as better, more deserving, more entitled than others; as conquerors and owners of land rather than its custodians. To Yunkaporta, the binary of "good" and "evil" that permeates so much of our thinking is our way of retelling history in an attempt to grapple with its legacies and consequences.

Yunkaporta's words remind me of a conversation I had with a neuropsychologist a few years ago while working on a series of longform articles on mental health and personality disorders. We were discussing how some patients with antisocial and narcissistic personality disorders are unwilling or unable to admit they have a problem and may use therapy as a means of improving their manipulation skills. I wondered how he would know if this was the case and he replied, "You watch what happens over time." If there is no significant improvement in how they treat others, then it is reasonable to conclude they are gaming the system. This is a fitting analogy for whiteness. Watching what has happened over time, it is clear that though there have been some adjustments, whiteness as a system of power is as strong as ever. Moreover, it is becoming increasingly apparent that a great deal of white women do not want it to change, that they will support women of color only so long as we do not threaten their position above us on that false hierarchy. To oscillate wildly between kindness and cruelty, allyship and marginalization, feminism and racism in this way betrays their exploitation of the power white feminists still refuse to admit they hold.

To be clear, I am not suggesting every single white person is a narcissist and I do not use this analogy lightly. The concept of whiteness and racism as a form of pathological narcissism that manifests in some individual white people has a long research history. In 1980, Carl Bell, a clinical psychiatrist and professor of psychiatry, outlined how the hallmark symptoms associated with narcissistic personality disorder, such as grandiosity, entitlement, and lack of empathy, apply to individual racists. More recently, in 2016, assistant professor of education Cheryl Matias described whiteness as narcissistic because its emotional nature insists on positioning itself as the center of the discourse, "especially when one is trying to push it to the margins." What I am adding here is that in order to understand how we got here as a global society and why it is proving so difficult to get us out, we must shift focus from the behavior of individual white people for a moment and recognize that whiteness as a system of power is not based on the logic and rationality that white society claims to embody. Rather, it is scaffolded by delusions and denials that must be cherished and defended so that whiteness does not implode. And that elicit rage toward anyone who dares to point them out. In her book on Dutch "white innocence," Gloria Wekker concludes that white society is incapable of admitting to its own atrocities so it consistently seeks to exonerate itself by projecting the blame onto its victims, and this often happens at the level of the subconscious.

It is this dissonance between reality and perception that gives rise to white tears. This irrational commitment to maintaining an illusion at all costs is the essence of narcissism, and the cost of white tears is brown scars. White settler-colonial society could not bear to face its own history, so it invented an entirely new one instead. In this tale of good versus evil, colonialism is transformed from a traumatic invasion into a benign settlement that brought the gift of civilization. That same psychologist defined a narcissist to me as "someone whose inner world feels inadequate and so they overcompensate with grand displays of wealth or prowess or kindness. They are overcompensating in the external world to fill in the interior hole, and sometimes that results in exploitation of others." Narcissism, then, is a misunderstood disorder, for it is not necessarily intentionally malicious nor is it born of true love of the self but almost the complete opposite; it is the ostentatious performance of self-love as a mask for insecurity, shame, and doubt. Is this not white fragility? And how can there not be an inadequate inner world at the core of white society when it has been lying to itself as well as to us for so long? When white identity is based on a false construct that emerged from colonization and instilled in white people the mass delusion they are innately superior and completely innocent, despite their legacy of oppression and denial of the humanity of others?

Are white people alone in having a history of violence? Not at all. But they do seem uniquely incapable of admitting to it. And while other cultures and civilizations have also engaged in war and conquest, none has done so in such a way as to span the entire globe and become so dominant that their entire identity, as both a civilization and as individuals, hinged on perpetuating the divide between themselves and those they have conquered.

Throughout settler-colonial history white women have had a choice either to uphold this disorder we call white supremacy and with it their own subordination, or to reach across and take the hands of women of color in order to work toward the liberation of all. Not only have they, as a group, invariably chosen the former, but they have done so with at least as much gusto as their white male counterparts. Jock McCulloch writes that in Southern Rhodesia, the arrival of white women in the colony coincided with increased competition for land, wage labor, and urbanization, leading many historians to, unfairly in his opinion, blame the women for increased social tension and segregation. Likewise, Ann Stoler notes that the entry of white women into colonial communities enforced racial privilege and segregation: "The presence and protection of European women was repeatedly invoked to clarify racial lines. It coincided with perceived threats to European prestige, increased racial conflict, covert challenges to the colonial order, outright expressions of nationalist resistance, and internal dissension among whites themselves."

When I read such analyses, I wonder whether these historians are being overly kind or overly cautious. Is it more likely that this was coincidental, or that when white women join white men in the ranks of power, whiteness coalesces, hardens, and metastasizes? It's not that the women are any more racist than the men, it's that White Womanhood consolidates white domination. To succeed, colonialism needed white women to adopt the "angel in the house" persona as a moral justification for its existence, and clearly enough of them did. When they began to agitate for their own rights, chafing against the restrictions placed on them on the pretext they needed protection from the swarthy colonized hordes, they did so without addressing—and in some cases even exploiting—this racism. In effect, white feminists have only attempted to foil one half of the equation that is their own subordination. Sexism and racism go hand in hand in the West: as long as the myth of sex-crazed, aggressive, inferior subject races is allowed to fester, then so too will the implication that white women need to be protected from them.

This attempt to sever race and gender has slowed white women's progress but it has by no means stopped it. Today, we see white women joining white men, and in some cases overtaking them, in the halls of power. U.S. voters may have missed out on a female president in 2016 but since then four of the top five weapons manufacturing firms in the United States appointed white women CEOs. White women head the top three CIA directorates, including director Gina Haspel, who, under the CIA's extraordinary rendition program during the George W. Bush administration, oversaw a secret prison in Thailand that used torture techniques such as waterboarding to interrogate suspects. White women have senior leadership roles in Homeland Security, National Intelligence, and the FBI. The head of the National Nuclear Security Administration, responsible for building and maintaining the country's nuclear weapons is a white woman. The undersecretary of state for arms control and international security affairs, who oversees billions in U.S. arms sales and negotiates and implements international weapons agreements, is a white woman. In the 2018 midterm election campaign, and in a far cry from the ethos of "Born in the USA," another Bruce Springsteen song, "The Rising," provided the soundtrack for a Democratic advertisement featuring "women rising," consisting of, with one apparent exception, white female Democratic congressional candidates who had served in the military in the Middle East. Why the Middle East has to suffer for women in the West to "rise" is a question still in need of an answer.

Are we to say that white women are rising in these ranks at a time when the United States just happens to be involved in several conflicts in the Middle East, or is it more likely that white women are once again leveraging imperialism for their own advancement and calling it equality? It seems society is perfectly content to have powerful white women in its midst but still prefers them to take a back seat to men when it comes to visibility. What does it mean for the rest of us that white women can quietly control almost all of the weapons belonging to the world's most powerful country and still claim to be oppressed in the same way as other women? Can white women and women of color find common ground when the conditions each live under are so fundamentally different? What long-term benefits can we hope for from #MeToo when white women have not yet accounted for the history of their tears being used to condemn innocent men of color—how do we move on from centuries of white women weaponizing their tears against us to a future where we believe all women? And finally, can white women understand and identify with us when they don't know what it means to be crushed by white supremacy? These are not rhetorical questions, and my challenge to white women is that they start answering them.

We are at a critical juncture. Women, specifically white women, are more visible and powerful than ever and yet these entrenched stereotypes remain. I invite feminists to seriously contemplate why the majority of white Americans continue to struggle with the idea of a female Democratic president. Is it simply that the bulk of the population has no appreciation at all for qualified, capable women, or is that even powerful white women are expected to perform femininity and patriotism in a certain way? The proper white damsel, the vessel for true womanhood, the raison d'être for the subjugation of the colonized, can also be a trap for white women. My prediction, if I may be so bold, is that should the United States elect a female president in the foreseeable future, she will almost certainly be a perfectly coiffed, antiabortion Republican with all-around hawkish politics, a bowl full of perfectly ripe fruit on the kitchen bench, and a traditional nuclear family that she will probably claim to personally cook for every night. An angel in the White House. When you perpetuate an archetype for your own ends, don't be too surprised when it is used against you.

All the structural problems white women face—even climate change—are caused by their own society. But environmental degradation is yet another predominantly white-caused problem for which nonwhite communities bear the brunt. In March 2019, NPR reported that "air pollution is disproportionately caused by white Americans' consumption of goods and services, but disproportionately inhaled by black and Hispanic Americans." A few weeks later, the Women's Agenda website boasted that "when women make decisions the environment benefits," referencing a study of environmental management organizations in Tanzania, Indonesia, and Peru. So, in other words, when *women of color* make decisions, the environment benefits.

This is a common strategy of white feminism: to align with women of color when it suits, trumpeting a nonexistent sisterhood as a mask for appropriating our work to advance the myth of a better world run by women. The truth is, it is women of color, *most especially Indigenous women*, who are at the forefront of environmental rights because their own rights are inseparable from the battle for the environment. According to the World Resources Institute, protecting Indigenous lands is among the most successful methods of fighting deforestation and climate change: remove such protections and environmental catastrophe is unavoidable. The battle for land rights is deadly. From 2002 to 2015, some 1,237 eco-activists were killed for defending (mostly) Indigenous lands. 2017 was the deadliest yet with around four activists killed per week. Indigenous women on the front lines who lost their lives include Berta Cáceres, Lesbia Janeth Urquía, and Efigenia Vásquez. To dress this up as a warmhearted girl power story not only trivializes their work, it erases the danger such women are in. "Sometimes I feel we Indians are alone in this fight to protect our nature—everyone's nature," Brazilian land rights and environmental activist Maria Valdenice Nukini told Reuters in 2015.

Sometimes I wonder when we reached the point of no return that led us so far from home, both figuratively and literally. We are not at home in this racialized, globalized world. We are all living the wrong life. Surely the fact we are destroying this planet that sustains us is evidence enough of this.

As I write this in the first days of 2020, much of Australia remains engulfed in unprecedented wildfires that have decimated more than 20 percent of heritage-listed forests and killed more than a billion wild animals. More than a dozen human lives and counting have been lost, thousands of homes destroyed, and for months many towns and cities have been swamped in a thick smoke haze said to be the equivalent of smoking a pack of cigarettes a day and that can be seen and felt as far away as New Zealand and parts of South America. For weeks, the front pages of newspapers and the television news have been dominated by apocalyptic scenes of crimson skies and flames several stories high. With more than half the summer still ahead of us, significant rainfall not predicted until late January, and beleaguered people fleeing to the shore and hopping on boats to escape the flames, this scenario feels at once a glimpse into a dystopian future and the arrival of a new kind of normal. In just over 230 years of colonization, this continent that had thrived for tens of thousands of years under the careful custodianship of the First Nations is on a fast track to becoming almost uninhabitable. Amidst this tragedy I fantasize whether there was some event in the past that could have gone differently so that European colonialism did not get the traction it needed to sweep the globe and unleash this devastation in its wake. What if Queen Isabella of Spain had not funded Christopher Columbus? What if the Indigenous Taino people on the island of Guanahani had killed Columbus on sight rather than make the mistake of trusting and agreeing to trade, only to be so fatally betrayed?

Then I try to imagine what the world could have looked like if we hadn't been blown so wildly off course. I'm not suggesting we'd be in a utopia or that everything was all roses before white people took it over. What I am saying is the world would look vastly different. In the modern era, Western civilization developed without the persistent interference and domination of external powers; the rest of the world did not. The economic backwardness and draconian laws against, among other things, homosexuality that are associated with the so-called third world are a result of colonialism. Europe drained the global south of its resources and implemented a penal code that many have now come to mistakenly think is cultural and cling to as a form of defiance. How ironic. Where would we be if Western Europe had not taken it upon itself to confer subhuman status on us in order for it to subdue the entire world? Well, for starters, we would not see these kinds of out-of-control wildfires. For many millennia, the Indigenous population managed the land with techniques of controlled burning such as fire-stick farming that lasted until Europeans invaded and erroneously decided what they saw here was nothing but unruly bush. Over in the Middle East, there would be no ISIS and no fundamentalist theocracy in Iran; the latter was a consequence of the Western-instigated coup that toppled Iran's secular prime minister Mohammad Mosaddegh in the 1950s and the former emerged from the ashes of the second Gulf War. The Saudi monarchy that white women are so keen to "save" Arab women from would not have had the financial and diplomatic means it needed to spread its punitive interpretation of Islam across the Muslim world, decimating local practices and traditions in the process. In the 1980s, Arab American academic Laura Nader wrote that the status of women in the West has been used by Arab and Muslim patriarchs to further restrict the rights of women: presenting white women's status as one of wanton degradation, they hold Muslim women to a virtuous and unattainable ideal of chastity and modesty. Are we going forward or backward?

We can't go back and try again, but we can commit to forging a different future from the one we are screeching into like a trackless train. At various points throughout history, it has been somewhat understandable if deeply regrettable that white women chose to remain tethered to whiteness. They were isolated in the colonies. They had a lack of legal rights. They were subjected to puritanical Christian morality. This is no longer the case. There is no reasonable excuse that remains for white women to continue to betray women of color. White women have a choice. It is a choice they have always had to some degree, but never before have they been in such a strong position to make the right one. Will white women choose to keep upholding white supremacy under the guise of "equality" or will they stand with women of color as we edge ever closer to liberation?

Time is running out. We live on a finite, fragile planet, and as economic downturns merge with environmental catastrophes and escalating human conflicts, and public health crises, the white Western obsession with singular power, cultural superiority, and racial purity will only become more unsustainable. White supremacy has led us into this freefall but it falls to all of us to try and get us out. We need not a new kind of feminism, but a whole new—or as Tyson Yunkaporta suggested, a very ancient—way of thinking, a way in which we not only reconcile with each other but reintegrate into the environment on which our lives depend. To return to the metaphor of the narcissist, it usually takes a great shock to compel them into therapy, something that rocks their very core and forces them to face who they are and decide that this is not what they want to be. It may well prove to be the shock of climate change that will provide the "therapy" that can help shake white people out of the thrall of whiteness, but the irrationality of white supremacy means we can't afford to hope we can reason enough of them out of it. We also need to act. To this end, though women of color are still listening to white women just as we always have, we are no longer waiting. As the women featured in this book demonstrate, women of color are refusing to keep walking on eggshells. We are forming collectives and creating our own platforms. We are forging new paths and finding new ways to resist. We are not taking our oppression lying down. The scars inherited from our ancestors have fused with our own to make us stronger; it is through their true grit as well as our own that we will get louder and bolder as we transform this society that for so long has hinged its success on ensuring our failure.

For five centuries white society has forced women of color to dwell in its shadows. But our true lives are calling us and no longer will we be denied our place in the sun. The road will be long and not all of us will get there, but never will a journey be more worthwhile. White women can dry their tears and join us, or they can continue on the path of the damsel—a path that leads not toward the light of liberation but only into the dead end of the colonial past.

Acknowledgments

This book would not have been conceived let alone written if not for the suggestions and encouragement of many women of color, in particular black women in the United States, whom I'd never met. I'd first had an inkling that "that" piece was different from everything I'd written before when one of these women, the writer Clarkisha Kent, shared it on social media with the quip, "Never thought I'd see White Women Tears on a wheat-y platform like the *Guardian*. But lo and behold, here it is. Good morning. Let's shake the table like Ruby Hamad today." Within days, many women were urging me to seize the moment and turn it into a book. It would not have otherwise occurred to me that there was a book in this and that I could be the one to write it, but to echo Clarkisha, lo and behold: here it is.

To my editors at *Guardian Australia*, Gabrielle Jackson and Svetlana Stankovic, I want to say there was no other editor at that time that I would have pitched that article to, and perhaps none who would have published it. Thank you for your willingness to look ahead. Much credit also to my agents Rachel Crawford from Mackenzie Wolf in New York and Alex Adsett in Australia, who took a chance on a first-timer and pushed me past what I thought I was capable of achieving. Rachel, between you and me, I almost gave up just trying to get the proposal to what you always knew it could be.

I began this book in a starkly different political, economic, and social climate than the one in which I finished it. In such turbulent and uncertain times, I am humbled that my publisher Catapult did not waver in its passion for this project. Books like this are never easy to write, but they would be impossible without a team of people as committed as the author is to its message. Many thanks especially to my editor Megha Majumdar, for taking me on and showing me the perfect balance of trust and challenge throughout, and managing editor Wah-Ming Chang, for seeing me through the crucial final stages when it became so hard to keep focus. To the publicity and marketing teams, Megan Fishman, Rachel Fershleiser, and Carla Bruce-Eddings, your enthusiasm was palpable from the start even from the other side of the world, and I knew instantly that I and my book were in good hands. And to designer Na Kim and creative director Nicole Caputo, you've given *White Tears/Brown Scars* the kind of stunning and apt book cover authors usually only dream about.

My family, especially my sisters Mariam, Rania, and Zehna, have ways been my sounding boards, my biggest fans, and my most honest critics. Their words and wisdom are also contained within these pages. Thanks also to the friends who've managed to put up with me despite the lack of familial obligation. Amal Awad, the sageness of your advice is matched only by the kindness with which it is delivered. Morgan Bell, more than any other it was you who got me from there to here. Juliet Porter and Lynette O'Boyle, you are the two I will always come back to. And thank you to Dr Sofia Eriksson for the chats that have informed so much of my professional progress.

Finally, this book stands on the shoulders of giants, some of whose vital words I quote within, and many others who have been all but erased from history. To all the women of color who have been mocked, bullied, blamed, tokenized, ostracized, blacklisted, ripped off, shut up, let down, and left behind: I see you, I hear you, I am you. This book has ended but our stories continue, so let's shake the damn table—let's wake the world.

Notes

19   Epigraph 2: Henry Lawson c. 1900, "Ballad of the Rouseabout," retrieved online 01/05/2020.

20   Hunger Games: tweets sourced from Holmes 2012, *The New Yorker*, March 30.

23   "she did not lead men and children to God": White 1985, *Ar'n't I a Woman?*, pp. 28–29.

24   "When he make me follow him into de bush": D'Emilio and Freedman 1998, *Intimate Matters*, pp. 101–102.

24   "the nakedness of the female slave": hooks 1985/2015, *Ain't I a Woman*, p. 18.

24   "Slavery is terrible for men": Jacobs 1861. *Incidents in the Life of a Slave Girl*, retrieved online 01/06/2020.

26   "The enslaved victim of lust and hate": Northrup 1855, *12 Years a Slave*, p. 189.

26   "Under slavery, we live surrounded by prostitutes": Chesnut 1981, *Mary Chesnut's Civil War*, p. 29.

27   "participants perceived black girls": Epstein, Blake and González 2017, *Girlhood Interrupted*, p. 8.

27   force black girls into adulthood before their time: Ibid.

29   "From the time white men invaded our shores": Moreton-Robinson 2000, *Talkin' Up to the White Woman*, pp. 165–66.

30   In her essay . . . was part of the deal: McGrath 1984, "Black Velvet."

31   "The black woman understands only sex": Ernestine Hill cited in Jacobs 2009, *White Mother to a Dark Race*, p. 118.

31   "Bound to one who loves thee not": Louisa Lawson c. 1905, "The Squatter's Wife," retrieved online 06/01/2020.

32   In his classic critique: Said 1978/2003, *Orientalism*.

32   The only countries: Fisher 2015, *Vox*, February 24.

33   "charming creatures . . . made for love": Jean Dumont

cited in Simons 2003, "Orientalism and Representation of Muslim Women As Sexual Objects."

33   "to display, to conceal, to promise": Edmondo De Amicis cited in ibid.

33   "entire liberty of following their inclinations": Mary Montague cited in ibid.

34   "This domination over the native women": Simons 2003, p. 24.

34   "thought of my nights in Paris brothels": Flaubert 1980, p. 117.

35   "see or imagine the relative sexual freedom of the other": Simons 2003, p. 27.

38   "it is unacceptable that a non-Indian who chooses to marry a Native woman": Indian Law Resource Center (ILRC) website, retrieved online 01/06/2020.

38   Add to that data from seventy-one U.S. cities: Statistics on violence on Native/Indian women from Hudetz 2018, *AP News*, September 20.

43   "When women's sexuality is surrendered": Said 2003, *Orientalism*, p. 207.

CHAPTER TWO: ANGRY SAPPHIRES, BAD ARABS, DRAGON LADIES

45   Epigraph: Salma Hayek quoted in Oldham 2018, *Variety*, May 13.

46   More unexpected was the revelation in a *Politico* report: All quotes about AOC from Democrats from Bade and Baygel 2019, *Politico*, January 11.

48   "It is a well-known fact": Salma Hayek quoted in Oldham 2018, *Variety*, January 11.

51   "No one has so had their identity socialized out of

existence as have black women": hooks 2015, *Ain't I A Woman*, p. 7.

53 "The Sorceress": All quotes on Soong Mei-ling from Fenby 2003, *The Guardian*, November 5.

56 Racial violence occurred before the ink was barely dry: Statistics and information on lynching of Mexicans in the Southwest, including Josefa Segovia, from Carrigan and Webb 2003, "The Lynching of Persons of Mexican Origin or Descent in the United States, 1848 to 1928."

56 "It's always there . . . It's inherited loss": Norma Longoria Rodríguez quoted in Muñoz Martinez 2018, *The Injustice Never Leaves You*, p. 117.

57 "I'm not wild! I am just Lupe": Lupe Velez quoted in Rodríguez-Estrada, "Dolores del Rio and Lupe Velez: Images on and off the Screen, 1925-1944," p. 476.

57 "one of the sites where this struggle": Hall 1981, "Notes on Deconstructing the Popular," p. 239.

59 "Men I have gone on dates with": Gonzalez 2017, *Hip Latina*, November 25.

59 As Richard Dyer said: Dyer 1977, *The Matter of Images*.

60 "caricatures . . . not human beings with their own language": Bird 1999, "Gendered Construction of the American Indian in Popular Media," p. 64.

60 "that'll give you an idea": Suzan Harjo quoted in Adams 2000, *The Straight Dope*, March 17, retrieved online 01/06/2020.

61 "They can't see that our system has any advantages": U.S. Department of the Interior quoted in Merskin 2010, "The S Word: Discourses, Stereotypes, and the American Indian Woman," p. 350.

61 "I really didn't think it would be this hard": Teara Farrow

Ferman quoted in Pérez-Peña 2015, *The New York Times*, March 28.

61   "It degrades our females": Jonathan Buffalo cited in Merskin 2010, p. 351.

62   "part of the normal assumptions": Ahmed 2011, *A Quiet Revolution*, p. 43.

65   "its ability to restrain animalistic impulses": Schuller 2018, *The Biopolitics of Feeling*, p. 36.

68   "dethrone woman from that position of gentle yet commanding influence": Lord Cromer cited in Ahmed 2011, p. 31.

69   It is also supported by more stringent research: Shaheen 2003, "Reel Bad Arabs: How Hollywood Vilifies a People."

70   "heartless, brutal, uncivilized, religious fanatics": Ibid., p. 171.

70   Not enough has changed since *Reel Bad Arabs*: Statistics on Middle East and North Africa representation on U.S. television from MENA Arts Advocacy Coalition 2018. *Terrorists and Tyrants: Middle Eastern and North African (MENA) Actors in Prime Time and Streaming.* Retrieved online 06/01/2020.

71   but the show's reported problem with female writing staff: On *Ramy's* portrayal of Arab women see: Ibrahim 2019, *The Atlantic*, April 23. On the show's troubles with female writing staff see: Sippell, *The Wrap*, September 18.

72   "Crazy Poor Middle Easterners": Friedman 2018, *The New York Times*, September 4.

72   studies have found that negative depictions of Arabs: See for example: Chahdi 2018, "Revisiting Binarism:

Hollywood's Representation of Arabs," and Saiffudin & Matthes 2016, "Media representation of Muslims and Islam from 2000 to 2015: A meta-analysis."

73 "It's not 'Western' to want love": Awad 2017, *Beyond Veiled Cliches*, p. 59.

75 The "hooker with a heart of gold" film character: Rhymes 2007, *Black Agenda Report*, May 2.

75 *Politico* followed up with an article: Otterbein 2019, *Politico*, December 27.

CHAPTER THREE: ONLY WHITE DAMSELS CAN BE IN DISTRESS

77 Epigraph: Harper 1861, *We Are All Bound Up in One Bundle of Humanity*, retrieved online 01/06/2020.

77 The lady of the house was in a right pickle: Unless otherwise stated, all references to Black Peril are sourced from McCulloch 2000, *Black Peril, White Virtue: Sexual Crime in Southern Rhodesia*.

84 "protecting this property was a key": Bardaglio 1994, "Rape and Law in the Old South."

84 "If a female possesses beauty": Letter to *The Rosebud* quoted in, Allain 2013, "Sexual relations between elite white women and enslaved men in the antebellum south: A socio-historical analysis." Retrieved online 01/07/2020.

87 "men and women in the South": Wells 1892, *Southern Horrors: Lynching in All Its Phases*. Retrieved online 01/07/2020.

88 "a slanderous and dirty-minded mulatress": *The New York Times* quoted in Smith 2018, *The Guardian*, April 27.

88 "White men used their ownership of the white female":

Carby 1986, "On the threshold of woman's era: Lynching, empire, and sexuality in black feminist theory," p. 270

89   "no longer do we see a black man": Fanon 2008, *Black Skin, White Masks*, p. 147.

90   "The frequency with which these revelations occurred": Ferber 1998, p. 39.

90   White women had little to no contact . . . than those of white men: McCulloch 2000.

91   In Papua . . . paternalism and racism blended into a toxic stew: Inglis 1975, *The White Women's Protection Ordinance: Sexual Anxiety and Politics in Papua.*

91   "all colonized men of color were potential aggressors": Stoler 1989, "Making Empire Respectable: The Politics of Race and Sexual Morality in 20th-Century Colonial Cultures," p. 642.

92   "We are all bound up . . . it is the white women of America": Harper 1866.

94   "Women want security. Women don't want that caravan": Donald Trump quoted in Davis and Rogers 2018, *The New York Times*, November 3.

94   "America is being invaded": *The New Order March* 1979, cited in Ferber 1998, p. 100.

CHAPTER FOUR: WHEN TEARS BECOME WEAPONS

106   "on everything from my historical competence": Beard 2017, *Times Literary Supplement*, August 7.

106   "genteel patrician racist manner . . . progressive end of the spectrum": Gopal 2017, Medium, February 18.

108   "When White Women Cry . . . defined by two layers of oppression": Accapadi 2007, "When White Women

Cry: How White Women's Tears Oppress Women of Color," p 209.

114 "toxic working culture" at Amnesty International: McVeigh 2018, *The Guardian*, February 6.

120 "The Terrible Sea Lion": Malki 2014, *Wondermark*. Retrieved online 01/07/2020.

123 "the expectations that boys and men must be active . . . and their relations with other men": Flood 2018, *Voice Male*, October 15.

130 if white women were a nation, men would have long ago invaded them too: Edward Cope cited in Schuller 2018, *The Biopolitics of Feeling*, p. 61.

130 although white American men in that era: hooks 1985/2015, *Ain't I a Woman*.

130 "the sentimental politics of life": Schuller 2018, p. 15.

CHAPTER FIVE: THERE IS NO SISTERHOOD

135 Epigraph 1: Annie Lock quoted in Jacobs 2005, "Maternal Colonialism: White Women and Indigenous Child Removal in the American West and Australia, 1880-1940," p. 454.

135 Epigraph 2: "Mrs. Dorchester" quoted in Jacobs 2005, p. 462.

136 A poll by Quinnipiac University published online: Malloy 2018, retrieved online 01/07/2020.

137 "over the flow of sensation . . . to further progress": Schuller 2018, *Duke University Press Blog*, January 11.

139 from the perspective of Aboriginal women, all white women have benefited from colonization: Moreton-Robinson 2000, *Talkin' Up to the White Woman*, p. xxv.

139 white racism, not sexism or misogyny: Melissa Lucashenko cited in Moreton-Robinson 2000, p. 175.

140 "It was now a nation that had reverse-colonised the landscape of ideas . . . twentieth-century democratic state": Wright 2018, *You Daughters of Freedom*, p. 451.

141 "largely a feminine domain . . . women's work for women": Jacobs 2005, p. 456.

143 "make slaves of themselves for the men": Helen Gibson Stockdell quoted in Jacobs 2005, pp. 462–63.

143 "All of their laws were formed for the convenience and well-being of the men only": Daisy Bates quoted in ibid.

144 "The Indian child must be placed in school . . . walk in the path of Christian civilization": Estelle Reel quoted in Glenn 2012, *Forced to Care*, p. 49.

144 the only hope for the Aboriginal population was to remove their children: Annie Lock quoted in Jacobs 2005, p. 454.

146 "On account of my mother's simple view of life": Zitkala-Sa quoted in Jacobs 2005, p. 470.

146 "receiving the greatest care and attention at the hands of many good missionary women": Estelle Reel quoted in ibid.

146 "What could I do?": Daisy Corunna quoted in Moreton-Robinson 2000, p. 22.

147 "they believed it encouraged extramarital and extra racial sex": Jacobs 2005, p. 466.

147 "maternal imperialism": Barbara Ramusack quoted in Ghose 2007, "The Memsahib Myth: British Women in Colonial India," p. 125.

148 "The Worst Racism My Children Have Experienced

Came from Black Peers": White 2019, *The Federalist*, January 10.

149 White Australian female journalists described Rahaf as "terrified": ABC News Australia 2019, January 9 (no byline).

150 crowing about Canada's "moral leadership": Momani 2019, *The Globe and Mail*, January 11.

150 within days media was monitoring Rahaf's social media: Hunter 2019, *Toronto Sun*, January 16; Rahman 2019, *MSN News*, January 17.

151 Aboriginal women made up 34 percent of the female prison population: Australian Law Reform Commission 2018, January 9.

151 Native women in Canada were alleging forced sterilization: Rao 2019, *Vice*, September 9.

151 change the wording of the Indian Act: Kassam 2018, *The Guardian*, April 19.

152 In Southern Rhodesia, white women reasserted class, racial, and religious hierarchies: McCulloch 2000, *Black Peril, White Virtue*, p. 120.

154 "Master talked hard words, but Mistress whipped": George C. King quoted in Jones-Rogers 2019, *They Were Her Property*, p. 72.

154 Jones-Rogers shares a notice placed by one such woman: Jones-Rogers, p. 40.

154 "slavery and the ownership of human beings": Jones-Rogers 2019, p. 183.

155 "In Western Europe, a mistress was": Jones-Rogers 2005, p. xv.

155 "I have never found a bright looking colored man":

Captain Richard Hinton cited in Foster 2011, "The sexual abuse of black men under American slavery," p. 449.

156 "know that the women slaves are subject to their father's authority": Harriet Jacobs 1861.

156 "her rights which are given to the most ignorant and degraded men": Elizabeth Cady Stanton, speech delivered at Seneca Falls in 1848.

157 "What will we and our daughters suffer if these degraded black men": Elizabeth Cady Stanton quoted in *NPR Morning Edition* 2011, July 13.

157 Meanwhile, black-and-white images from a suffragist parade: Staples 2018, *The New York Times*, July 28. Retrieved online 01/07/2020.

160 a negative review of *Superior*, cowritten by Noah Carl: Winegard and Carl 2019, *Quillette*, June 5.

160 Carl had attended a conference: Adams 2019, *The Guardian*, May 2.

161 "When women, because they are women, are hunted down through the cities of New York": Frederick Douglass quoted in Staples 2018, *The New York Times*, July 28.

165 "They were co-conspirators": Jones-Rogers, 2019, p. 205.

CHAPTER SIX: PETS OR THREATS

166 Epigraph: Lorde 2007, *Sister Outsider*, p. 118.

170 As Liddle noted in a comment piece: Hamad and Liddle 2017, *Guardian Australia*, October 11.

171 "is not an invitation to join power": Lorde 2007, p. 118.

172 "toughest sanctions in history": Clinton 2016, AIPAC Speech, retrieved online 01/07/2020.

173 "were not putting into practice the democratic principles": Salem 2018, "White innocence as a feminist discourse," retrieved online 01/07/2020.

175 "Time to Hail Hillary Clinton—and Face Down the Testosterone Left": Badham 2016, *Guardian Australia*, November 2.

177 "Nobody likes him": Hillary Clinton quoted in Rose 2020, *The Hollywood Reporter*, January 21.

177 "For as long as any difference between us . . . view oppression only in terms of sex": Lorde 2007, p. 118.

178 law professor Kimberlé Crenshaw would define as "intersectionality": Crenshaw 1989, "Demarginalizing the intersection of race and sex."

180 "simply a gross distortion of the reality . . . have been Euro-American women": Crenshaw 2006, "Framing Affirmative Action," p. 129.

180 a report by the California Senate Governmental Organization Committee: Massie 2016, *Vox*, June 23.

181 "White people still run almost everything": Cave 2018, *The New York Times*, April 10.

182 "Rage, tears, and confusion": Srivastata 2005, "You're calling me a racist?" p. 29.

183 "all the fucking time": Srivastata 2005, p. 42.

183 All anonymous quotes from Srivastata 2005, pp. 43–45.

CHAPTER SEVEN: THE RISE OF RIGHTEOUS RACISM

186 Epigraph: Cited in Schuller 2018, *The Biopolitics of Feeling*.

188 Reverend Charles Loring Brace was a young social reformer: PBS, *American Experience: The Orphan Trains*.

189 Kyla Schuller argues that Brace's audacious vision: Schuller 2018, pp. 135–36.

193 "They are using blackface as a way of saying": John Strasbough quoted in Lartey 2019, *The Guardian*, April 9.

194 "[Now] I should say my identity is Middle Eastern . . . tell us what our identity is": El Saadawi 1997, "Why keep asking me about my identity?" p. 128.

195 "Race is the modality": Hall et al., 1978, *Policing the Crisis*, p. 394.

196 "the idea that poor Whites suffer equally to or worse": Andrews 2017, "The Psychosis of Whiteness," p. 449.

196 "total struggle": El Saadawi 1997, p. 122.

196 "you perform and display the paint and feathers": Yunkaporta 2019, *Sand Talk*, p. 59.

197 All quotes from the Combahee River Collective 1974, *A Black Feminist Statement*, retrieved online 01/05/2020.

199 "white men are saving brown women from brown men": Spivak 1993, "Can the Subaltern Speak?" p. 93.

199 "[The] fight against terrorism is also a fight for the rights and dignity of women": Laura Bush quoted in Wallace 2001, George W. Bush Presidential Center, February 1.

199 "feminist rhetoric without undergoing legitimately feminist transformations": Cerretti 2016, "Rape as a Weapon of War(riors)," p. 795.

199 "Lifting the Veil": Lacayo 2001, *TIME*, December.

201 As sociologist Josh Cerretti argues: Cerretti 2016.

202 "decades of unheeded reports of violence toward Aboriginal women": Conor 2013, "Black Velvet and Purple Indignation," p. 56.

205 Bilal Skaf, the Lebanese Australian ringleader: Davies, 2013, *The Sydney Morning Herald*, January 19.

205 Anglo-Australian rapist Geoffrey Michael Haywood: Lockett 2019, *The Sun*, April 7.

CHAPTER EIGHT: THE PRIVILEGE AND PERIL OF PASSING

207 Epigraph: Dean Obeidallah quoted in NPR 2007, July 5.

209 In India, antipathy toward darker skin is so rife: Phoenix 2018, *The Conversation*, August 17.

209 "90% of Indian women and girls view skin lightening": Merchant and Luce 2003, *Financial Times*, March 20.

210 "preaches that we would get a better job": Deol 2017, *Hindustan Times*, May 23.

210 global skin-whitening products market was worth approximately U.S. $4.5 billion: Zion Market Research 2019, *Skin Lightening Products Market by Type*, retrieved online 10/10/2019.

211 "[I]ncreasing consumer consciousness": ibid.

211 Other key markets include parts of the African continent: Adinde 2018, *Stears Business*, December 12.

211 the earliest classifications we associate with the caste system: Mishra 2015, "India and Colorism: The Finer Nuances," p. 725.

212 Colorism brought violence to the Indigenous population in Australia under a converse rationale: Doyle, Hungerford, and Cleary 2016, "Study of Intra-racial Exclusion Within Australian Indigenous Communities Using Eco-Maps," pp. 129–30.

214 "be a disgrace to the British to put a child of English": Grace Maggio quoted in McCulloch 2000, *Black Peril, White Virtue*, p. 177.

216 "The loveliness of this face, the beauty of this figure":

Reverend Henry Ward Beecher quoted in Mitchell 2002, "'Rosebloom and Pure White,' or So It Seemed," pp. 392–93.

217 The racial hierarchy in Spanish America was so rigid: Strayer 2012, *Ways of the World*, p. 633.

218 it was a source of supply with an already existing trade: Lovejoy 2012, *Transformations in Slavery*.

221 "a particularly heinous development": Ibid., p. 8.

222 All diary and letters quotes from Jones-Rogers 2019, *They Were Her Property*.

224 the incompatibility of African slavery with capitalism: Andrews 2016, *The Psychosis of Whiteness*, and Lovejoy 2012.

225 many Mexican elites . . . were marrying white Anglo-Americans: Carrigan and Webb 2003, "The Lynching of Persons of Mexican Origin or Descent in the United States, 1848 to 1928."

226 "went to bed a white guy . . . woke up an Arab": Dean Obeidallah quoted in NPR 2007.

230 "We are to assume that if an Arab feels joy": Said 2003, *Orientalism*, p. 230.

CONCLUSION: BROWN SCARS

234 Christa Dubill, one of the two women whose complaint: "Tony" 2019, *Tony's Kansas City*, April 10.

234 "I still to this day don't understand why this article was so offensive": Lisa Benson quoted in Porter 2019, *The Kansas City Star*, February 17.

236 "White women civilised while white men brutalised": Moreton-Robinson 2000, *Talkin' Up to the White Woman*, p. 172.

237 "To remain innocent means to remain ignorant": Salem 2018, "White Innocence as a Feminist Discourse."

237 "whether angry or calm": Hamad 2018, *Guardian Australia*, May 7.

239 "an ancient seed of narcissism": Yunkaporta 2019, *Sand Talk*, p. 3.

241 "especially when one is trying to push it to the margins": Matias 2016, *Feeling White*, p. 71.

243 "The presence and protection of European women was repeatedly invoked": Stoler 1989, "Making Empire Respectable," pp. 640–41.

243 four of the top five weapons manufacturing firms: Brown 2019, *Politico*, January 2.

246 "air pollution is disproportionately caused by white Americans' consumption": Lambert 2019, *NPR*, March 11.

246 "When women make decisions the environment benefits": Hislop 2019, *Women's Agenda*, March 25.

246 According to the World Resources Institute: Stevens 2014, *World Resources Institute*.

246 The battle for land rights is deadly: Watts 2018, *The Guardian*, February 2.

246 "Sometimes I feel we Indians are alone in this fight": Maria Valdenice Nukini quoted in Reuters 2015, December 2.

249 In the 1980s, Arab American academic Laura Nader wrote: Nader 1989, "Orientalism, Occidentalism, and the Control of Women."

Bibliography

ABC Australia (2019). "Rahaf Alqunun 'Was Terrified,' Says Reporter Who Was Locked in Room with Saudi Asylum Seeker." *ABC News Australia*, January 9.

Accapadi, Mamta Motwani (2007). "When White Women Cry: How White Women's Tears Oppress Women of Color." *The College Student Affairs Journal* 26(2), p. 209. (PDF available online files.eric.ed.gov/fulltext/EJ899418 .pdf.)

Adams, Cecil (2000), "Is 'Squaw' an Obscene Insult?" in *The Straight Dope*, March 17. www.straightdope.com/columns /000317.html

Adams, Richard (2019). "Cambridge College Sacks Researcher over Links with Far Right." *The Guardian*, May 2.

Adinde, Stephannie (2018). "Nigeria's Skin-Bleaching Epidemic." *Stears Business*, December 12.

Ajayi, Luvvie (2018). "About the Weary Weaponizing of White Women Tears." *Awesomely Luvvie*, April 16.

Ahmed, Leila (2011). *A Quiet Revolution: The Veil's Resurgence, from the Middle East to America*. New Haven: Yale University Press.

Ahmed, Saifuddin, and Jörg Matthes (2016). "Media

Representation of Muslims and Islam from 2000 to 2015: A Meta-Analysis," in *International Communication Gazette* 79(3), pp. 219–44.

Allain, J. M. (2013). "Sexual Relations Between Elite White Women and Enslaved Men in the Antebellum South: A Socio-historical Analysis." *Inquiries Journal* 5(8).

Andrews, Kehinde (2016). "The Psychosis of Whiteness: The Celluloid Hallucinations of Amazing Grace and Belle." *Journal of Black Studies* 47(5), pp. 435–53.

Australian Law Reform Commission (2018). *Pathways to Justice–Inquiry into the Incarceration Rate of Aboriginal and Torres Strait Islander Peoples* (ALRC Report 133), January 9.

Awad, Amal (2017). *Beyond Veiled Clichés*. North Sydney: Penguin Random House.

Bade, Rachael, and Heather Caygle (2019). "Exasperated Democrats Try to Rein Ocasio-Cortez." *Politico*, January 11.

Badham, Van (2016). "Time to Hail Hillary Clinton—and Face Down the Testosterone Left." *Guardian Australia*. November 2.

Bardaglio, Peter W. (1994). "Rape and the Law in the Old South: 'Calculated to Excite Indignation in Every Heart.'" *Journal of Southern History* 60(4), pp. 749–72.

Beard, Mary (2017). "Roman Britain in Black and White." *Times Literary Supplement*. August 7.

——— (2017). *Women and Power*. London: Liverlight.

Bell, Carl Compton (1980). "Racism: A Symptom of the Narcissistic Personality." *Journal of the National Medical Association* 72(7), p. 661.

Bird, S. Elizabeth (1999). "Gendered Construction of the American Indian in Popular Media." *Journal of Communication* 39(3), pp. 61–83.

Brown, David (2019). "How Women Took over the Military-Industrial Complex." *Politico*, January 2.

Carby, Hazel V. (1986). "'On the Threshold of Woman's Era': Lynching, Empire, and Sexuality in Black Feminist Theory." In Henry Louis Gates Jr. (ed.), *Race, Writing, and Difference*. University of Chicago Press.

Carrigan, William D and Webb, Clive (2003). "The Lynching of Persons of Mexican Origin or Descent in the United States, 1848 to 1928." *Journal of Social History* 37(2), pp. 411–38.

Cave, Damien (2018). "In a Proudly Diverse Australia, White People Still Run Almost Everything." *New York Times*, April 10.

Chahdi, Chadi (2018). "Revisiting Binarism: Hollywood's Representation of Arabs," in *International Letters of Social and Humanistic Sciences* 83, pp. 19–30.

Chesnut, Mary Boykin (1981). *Mary Chesnut's Civil War.* Edited by C. Vann Woodward. New Haven: Yale University Press, 1981.

Cerretti, Josh (2016). "Rape as a Weapon of War(riors): The Militarisation of Sexual Violence in the United States, 1990–2000." *Gender and History* 28(3), p. 795.

Clinton, Hillary (2016). Speech to AIPAC. Transcript published March 21. time.com/4265947/hillary-clinton-aipac-speech-transcript/

Combahee River Collective (1974). *A Black Feminist Statement.* americanstudies.yale.edu/sites/default/files/files /Keyword%20Coalition_Readings.pdf.

Conor, Liz (2013). "'Black Velvet' and 'Purple Indignation': Print Responses to Japanese 'Poaching' of Aboriginal Women." *Aboriginal History* 37, pp. 51–76.

Crenshaw, Kimberlé (1989). "Demarginalizing the Intersection of Race and Sex: A Black Feminist Critique of Antidiscrimination Doctrine, Feminist Theory and Antiracist Politics." *University of Chicago Legal Forum*. Vol 1989, Issue 1, Article 8, pp. 139–67.

——— (2006). "Framing Affirmative Action." *University of Michigan Law Review First Impressions*. Vol. 104, Issue 1, Article 4, pp. 123–33.

Davies, Lisa (2013). "What We Learnt from Skaf Case." *Sydney Morning Herald*, January 19.

D'Emilio, John, and Estelle B. Freedman (1988). *Intimate Matters: A History of Sexuality in America*. New York: Harper and Row.

Deol, Abhay (2017). "Let's Talk About Racism: Our Job Ads Preach We Will Get Jobs, Find Love If We Are Fairer." *Hindustan Times*, May 23.

DiAngelo, Robin (2018). *White Fragility*. Boston: Beacon Press.

Doyle, Kerrie, Katherine Hungerford, and Michelle Cleary (2016). "Study of Intra-racial Exclusion Within Australian Indigenous Communities Using Eco-Maps." *International Journal of Mental Health Nursing* 26, pp. 129–41.

Dyer, Richard (1977). *The Matter of Images*. London: Routledge and Keegan Paul.

——— (1997). "The Matter of Whiteness," from Richard Dyer (ed.), *White: Essays on Race and Culture*. London: Routledge.

El Saadawi, Nawal (1997). "Why keep asking me about my identity?" *Nawal El Saadawi Reader*. London: Zed Books.

Epstein, Rebecca, Jamilia J. Blake, and Thalia Gonzalez (2017). *Girlhood Interrupted: The Erasure of Black Girls' Childhood*. Georgetown Law Center.

Fanon, Frantz (2008). *Black Skin, White Masks*, 2nd ed. New York: Grove Press.

Fenby, Jonathan (2003). "The Sorceress," *The Guardian*, November 5.

Ferber, Abby L (1998). *White Man Falling: Race, Gender, and White Supremacy*. Lanham, MD: Rowman & Littlefield.

Fisher, Max (2015) "European Colonialism Conquered Every Country in the World but These Five," *Vox*, February 24.

Flaubert, Gustave (1980). *The Letters of Gustave Flaubert 1830– 1857*. Cambridge, MA: Harvard University Press.

Foster, Thomas A. (2011). "The Sexual Abuse of Black Men Under American Slavery." *Journal of the History of Sexuality* 20(3), pp. 445–69.

Friedman, Thomas (2018). "Crazy Poor Middle Easterners." *The New York Times*, September 4.

Ghose, Indira (2007). "The Memsahib Myth: British Women in Colonial India." In C. R. Daileder et al. (eds.) *Women and Others: Perspectives on Race, Gender, and Empire*. New York: Palgrave MacMillan.

Gillespie McRae, Elizabeth (2018). *Mothers of Massive Resistance: White Women and the Politics of White Supremacy*. Oxford: Oxford University Press.

Glenn, Evelyn Nakano (2012). *Forced to Care: Coercion and Caregiving in America*. Cambridge, MA: Harvard University Press.

Gonzalez, Irina (2017). "Stop Fetishizing My Anger by Calling Me a 'Spicy' Latina." *Hip Latina*, November 5. hiplatina.com /stop-fetishizing-my-anger-by-calling-me-a-spicy-latina.

Gopal, Priyamvada (2018). "Response to Mary Beard." Medium, February 18.

Gordon, Linda (2017). *The Second Coming of the KKK: The Ku*

Klux Klan of the 1920s and the American Political Tradition. New York: Liveright Publishing Corporation.

Hall, Stuart (1981). "Notes on Deconstructing the Popular," in Raphael Samuel (ed.), *People's History and Socialist Theory.* London: Routledge & Keegan Paul.

Hall, Stuart, Chas Critcher, Tony Jefferson, John N. Clarke, and Brian Roberts (1978). *Policing the Crisis: Mugging, the State, and Law and Order.* London: Macmillan.

Harper, Francis Ellen Watkins (1866). "We Are All Bound Up Together." Speech given to the Eleventh National Women's Rights Convention, New York. Available online at awpc .cattcenter.iastate.edu/2017/03/21/we-are-all-bound-up-together-may-1866/.

Hislop, Madeline (2019). "When women make decisions, the environment benefits." *Women's Agenda*, March 25.

Holmes, Anna (2012). "White Until Proven Black: Imagining Race in the Hunger Games." *The New Yorker*, March 30.

Hunter, Brad (2019). "Saudi Teen: Starbucks, Bacon, Eggs, and Bare Legs." *Toronto Sun*, January 16.

Hamad, Ruby (2018). "How White Women Use Strategic Tears to Silence Women of Colour." *Guardian Australia*, May 7.

Hamad, Ruby, and Celeste Liddle (2017). "Intersectionality? Not While Feminists Participate in Pile-ons." *Guardian Australia*, October 11.

hooks, bell (1981, 2015). *Ain't I a Woman? Black Women and Feminism.* Boston: South End Press.

Hudetz, Mary (2018). "U.S. Doubles Tribal Funding to Fight Violence Against Women." Associated Press, September 20.

Ibrahim, Shamira (2019). "What *Ramy* Gets Wrong About Muslim Women." *The Atlantic*, April 23.

Indian Law Resource Center. "Ending Violence Against Native Women." indianlaw.org/issue/ending-violence-against-native-women.

Inglis, Amirah (1975). *The White Women's Protection Ordinance: Sexual Anxiety and Politics in Papua.* London: Sussex University Press.

Jacobs, Harriet (1861). *Incidents in the Life of a Slave Girl, Written by Herself.* Available online: docsouth.unc.edu/fpn/jacobs /jacobs.html.

Jacobs, Margaret D. (2005). "Maternal Colonialism: White Women and Indigenous Child Removal in the American West and Australia, 1880–1940." *Faculty Publications, Department of History* (University of Nebraska). Vol. 11, pp. 453–76.

———— (2009). *White Mother to a Dark Race: Settler Colonialism, Maternalism, and the Removal of Indigenous Children in the American West and Australia, 1880–1940.* Lincoln: University of Nebraska Press.

Jones-Rogers, Stephanie (2019). *They Were Her Property.* New Haven: Yale University Press.

Kassam, Ashifa (2018). "'Legal Discrimination Is Alive and Well': Canada's indigenous women fight for equality." *The Guardian*, April 19.

Kivel, Paul (1996). *Uprooting Racism: How White People Can Work for Racial Justice.* Gabriola Island, BC: New Society Press.

Lacayo, Richard (2001). "Lifting the Veil." *TIME*, December.

Lambert, Jonathan (2019). "Study Finds Racial Gap Between Who Causes Air Pollution and Who Breathes It." *NPR*, March 11.

Lartey, Jamiles (2019). "'Reasserting White Power': Behind

the Psychosis That Gave Rise to Blackface." *The Guardian*, April 9.

Lawson, Henry (c. 1900). "Ballad of the Rouseabout." *Australian Poetry Library*. Available online: www.poetry library.edu.au/poets/lawson-henry/poems/the-ballad-of -the-rouseabout-0022016.

Lawson, Louisa (c. 1905). "The Squatter's Wife." *Australian Poetry Library*. Available online: www.poetrylibrary.edu.au /poets/lawson-louisa/poems/the-squatter-s-wife -0016020.

Lockett, Jon (2019). "Knifepoint Rape: Schoolgirl, 16, Raped at Knifepoint and Told to Dig Her Own Grave Finally Reveals Her Ordeal as Ringleader Dies." *The Sun*, April 7.

Lorde, Audre (2007, 1984). *Sister Outsider*. Berkeley: Crossing Press.

Lovejoy, Paul (2012). *Transformations in Slavery: A History of Slavery in Africa* (3rd ed.). Cambridge University Press.

Malki, David (2014). "The Terrible Sea Lion," *Wondermark*. Available online: wondermark.com/1k62/.

Malloy, Tim (2018). "More U.S. Voters Say Don't Confirm Kavanaugh, Quinnipiac University National Poll Finds; More Voters Believe Ford Than Kavanaugh." *Quinnipac University Poll*, October 1. poll.qu.edu/national/ release-detail?ReleaseID=2574.

Massie, Victoria (2016). "White Women Benefit Most from Affirmative Action—and Are Among Its Fiercest Opponents." *Vox*, June 23.

Matias, Cheryl E. (2016). *Feeling White: Whiteness, Emotionality and Education*. Rotterdam: Sense.

McCulloch, Jock (2000). *Black Peril, White Virtue: Sexual*

Crime in Southern Rhodesia. Bloomington: Indiana University Press.

McGrath, Ann (1984). "Black Velvet," in Kay Daniels (ed.), *So Much Hard Work: Women and Prostitution in Australian History.* Sydney: Fontana Collins, pp. 233–97.

McVeigh, Karen (2019). "Amnesty International Has Toxic Working Culture, Report Finds." *The Guardian,* February 6.

MENA Arts Advocacy Coalition (2018). Terrorists and Tyrants: Middle Eastern and North African (MENA) Actors in Prime Time and Streaming. Available online at www.menaartsadvocacy.com.

Merchant, Khozem, and Edward Luce (2003). "India Orders Ban on Advert Saying Fairer Equals Better for Women." *Financial Times,* March 20.

Merskin, Debra (2010). "The S Word: Discourses, Stereotypes, and the American Indian Woman," in *The Howard Journal of Communication,* Vol. 21, pp. 345–66.

Mishra, Neha (2015). "India and Colorism: The Finer Nuances." *Washington University Global Studies Law Review,* 14(4), pp. 725–50. openscholarship.wustl.edu /law_globalstudies/vol14/iss4/14.

Momani, Bessma (2019). "By Granting Asylum to Saudi Woman, Canada Shows Its Moral Leadership." *The Globe and Mail,* January 11.

Moreton-Robinson, Aileen (2000). *Talkin' Up to the White Woman: Aboriginal Women and Feminism.* Queensland University Press.

Muñoz Martinez, Monica (2018). *The Injustice Never Leaves You: Anti-Mexican Violence in Texas.* Cambridge, MA: Harvard University Press.

Nader, Laura (1989). "Orientalism, Occidentalism, and the Control of Women." *Cultural Dynamics*, July 1, pp. 323–55.

Niall Mitchell, Mary (2002). "'Rosebloom and Pure White,' or So It Seemed." *American Quarterly* 54(3), pp. 369–410.

Northrup, Soloman, and David Wilson (1855). *Twelve Years a Slave*. New York: Miller, Orton and Mulligan.

NPR (2007). "Muslim Comedian Aims at Breaking Stereotypes." July 5. Transcript available online: www.npr.org/templates/story/story.php?storyId=11746247.

NPR Morning Edition (2011). "For Stanton, All Women Were Not Created Equal." NPR, July 13.

Oldham, Stuart (2018). "Salma Hayek Says Harvey Weinstein Only Responded to Her and Lupita Nyong'o's Harassment Claims Because Women of Color Are Easier to Discredit." *Variety*, May 13.

Otterbein, Holly (2019). "AOC for President? The Buzz Has Begun." *Politico*, December 27.

PBS (2006). "American Experience: The Orphan Trains." PBS, www.pbs.org.

Pérez-Peña, Richard (2015), "Tribes See Name on Oregon Maps as Being Out of Bounds." *The New York Times*, March 28.

Phoenix, Aisha (2018). "Colourism—How Shade Bias Perpetuates Prejudice Against People with Dark Skin." *The Conversation*, August 17.

Porter, Toriano (2019). "Former KSHB reporter challenged the system and won—sort of." *The Kansas City Star*, February 17.

Rahman, Khaleda (2019). "Saudi Teen Granted Asylum Enjoys a Glass of Red Wine and Bacon as She Continues to Enjoy Her New Freedoms." *MSN News*, January 17.

Rao, Ankita (2019). "Indigenous Women in Canada Are Still Being Sterilized Without Their Consent." *Vice*, September 9.

Reuters (2015). "Proposed Law May Remove Indigenous Land Rights in Brazil." *Reuters*, December 2.

Rhymes, Edward (2007). "A 'Ho' by Any Other Color: The History and Economics of Black Female Sexual Exploitation." *Black Agenda Report*, May 2.

Rodríguez-Estrada, Alicia I. "Dolores del Rio and Lupe Velez: Images on and off the Screen, 1925–1944," in *Writing the Range: Race, Class, and Culture in the Women's West*. Elizabeth Jameson and Susan Armitage (eds.). Norman: University of Oklahoma Press, 1997, pp. 475–92.

Rose, Lacey (2020). "Hillary Clinton in Full: A Fiery New Documentary, Trump Regrets, and Harsh Words for Bernie: 'Nobody Likes Him.'" *The Hollywood Reporter*, January 21.

Said, Edward (2003). *Orientalism* (3rd ed.). London: Penguin Books.

Saini, Angela (2019). *Superior: The Return of Race Science*. London: 4th Estate.

Salem, Sara (2018). "White Innocence as a Feminist Discourse: Race, Empire, and Gender in Performances of 'Shock' in Contemporary Politics." Paper uploaded on Academia.edu: www.academia.edu/37735749/White_Innocence_as_a_Feminist_Discourse_Race_empire_and_gender_in_performances_of_shock_in_contemporary_politics.

Schuller, Kyla (2018). *The Biopolitics of Feeling: Race, Sex, and Science in the Nineteenth Century*. Durham, NC: Duke University Press.

——— (2018). "The Trouble with White Women." *Duke University Press Blog*, January 11.

Shaheen, Jack (2003). "Reel Bad Arabs: How Hollywood Vilifies a People," in *The Annals of the American Academy of Political and Social Science* 588, Islam: Enduring Myths and Changing Realities (July), pp. 171–93.

Simons, Hazel (2003). "Orientalism and Representation of Muslim Women as 'Sexual Objects.'" *Al-Raida*, Vol. XX, No. 99.

Sippell, Margeaux (2019). "Former 'Ramy' Staff Writer Says No Women Writers Were Asked Back for Season 2." *The Wrap*, September 18.

Smith, David (2018). "Ida B. Wells: The Unsung Heroine of the Civil Rights Movement," *The Guardian*, April 27.

Spivak, Gayatri (1993). "Can the Subaltern Speak?" in *Colonial Discourse and Post-Colonial Theory: A Reader*, eds. Patrick Williams and Laura Chrisman. New York: Harvester Wheatsheaf, pp. 66–111.

Srivastava, Sarita (2005). "'You're calling me a racist?' The Moral and Emotional Regulation of Antiracism and Feminism." *Journal of Women in Culture and Society* 31(11), pp. 29–62.

Stanton, Elizabeth Cady (1848). "Declaration of Sentiments: Women's Grievances Against Men." Delivered at Seneca Falls, July 19. www.standardsinstitutes.org/sites/default/files/material/a_declaration_of_sentiments_texTt.pdf.

Staples, Brent (2018). "How the Suffrage Movement Betrayed Black Women," *The New York Times*, July 28.

Stevens, Caleb (2014). "Securing Rights, Combating Climate Change: How Strengthening Community

Forest Rights Mitigates Climate Change." *World Resources Institute.* www.wri.org/events/2014/07/securing-rights-combating-climate-change.

Stoler, Ann (1989). "Making empire respectable: The politics of race and sexual morality in 20th-century colonial cultures." *American Ethnologist* 16(4), pp. 634–60.

Strausbaugh, John (2007). *Black Like You: Blackface, Whiteface, Insult & Imitation in American Popular Culture.* New York: Tarcher.

Strayer, R. W. (2012). *Ways of the World: A Brief Global History* (2nd ed.). Boston: Bedford/St. Martin's.

Summers, Anne (1975). *Damned Whores and God's Police: The Colonisation of Women in Australia.* Ringwood, Victoria: Penguin Books.

"Tony" (2019). "KSHB-TV Dumps Married Couple and Announces Newsies Christa Dubill and Kevin Holmes as Evening Lead Anchors." *Tony's Kansas City: Opinions, Jokes and Stories from KC*, April 10.

Wallace, Charity (2001). "Radio Address by Mrs. Laura W. Bush: Crawford TX, November 17, 2001." George W. Bush Presidential Center, February 1.

Watts, Jonathan (2018). "Almost Four Environmental Defenders a Week Killed in 2017." *The Guardian*, February 2.

Wekker, Gloria (2016). *White Innocence: Paradoxes of Colonialism and Race.* Durham, NC: Duke University Press.

Wells, Ida B. (1892). *Southern Horrors: Lynching in All Its Phases.* www.digitalhistory.uh.edu/disp_textbook.cfm?smtid=3&psid=3614

White, Deborah Gray (1985). *Ar'n't I a Woman? Female Slaves in the Plantation South.* New York: W. W. Norton.

White, Jenni (2019). "The Worst Racism My Children Have Experienced Came from Black Peers." *The Federalist*, January 10.

Winegard, Bo, and Noah Carl (2019). "Superior: The Return of Race Science—A Review." *Quillette*, June 5.

Wright, Clare (2018). *You Daughters of Freedom: The Australians Who Won the Vote and Inspired the World*. Melbourne: Text Publishing.

Yunkaporta, Tyson (2019). *Sand Talk: How Indigenous Thinking Can Save the World*. Melbourne: Text Publishing.

Zion Market Research (2019). *Skin Lightening Products Market by Type [. . .]: Global Industry Perspective, Comprehensive Analysis, and Forecast, 2017–2024*. www.zionmarketresearch.com/market-analysis/skin-lightening-products-market.

RUBY HAMAD is a journalist, author, and academic completing a PhD in media studies at the University of New South Wales. Her *Guardian* article "How White Women Use Strategic Tears to Silence Women of Colour" became a global flashpoint for discussions of white feminism and racism and inspired her debut book, *White Tears/Brown Scars*, which has received critical acclaim in her home country of Australia. Her writing has also been featured in *Prospect*, *The New Arab*, and other publications. She splits her time between Sydney and New York.